The Modern Child and the Flexible Labour Market

Studies in Childhood and Youth

Series Editors: **Allison James** and **Adrian L. James**

Titles include:

Kate Bacon
TWINS IN SOCIETY
Parents, Bodies, Space and Talk

David Buckingham and Vebjørg Tingstad (*editors*)
CHILDHOOD AND CONSUMER CULTURE

Allison James, Anne Trine Kjørholt and Vebjørg Tingstad (*editors*)
CHILDREN, FOOD AND IDENTITY IN EVERYDAY LIFE

Anne Trine Kjørholt and Jens Qvortrup (*editors*)
THE MODERN CHILD AND THE FLEXIBLE LABOUR MARKET
Early Childhood Education and Care

Helen Stapleton
SURVIVING TEENAGE MOTHERHOOD
Myths and Realities

Studies in Childhood and Youth
Series Standing Order ISBN 978–0–230–21686–0 hardback
(*outside North America only*)

You can receive future titles in this series as they are published by placing a standing order. Please contact your bookseller or, in case of difficulty, write to us at the address below with your name and address, the title of the series and the ISBN quoted above.

Customer Services Department, Macmillan Distribution Ltd, Houndmills, Basingstoke, Hampshire RG21 6XS, England

The Modern Child and the Flexible Labour Market

Early Childhood Education and Care

Edited by

Anne Trine Kjørholt and Jens Qvortrup
Norwegian University of Science and Technology, Norway

palgrave
macmillan

First published 2012 by
PALGRAVE MACMILLAN

Palgrave Macmillan in the UK is an imprint of Macmillan Publishers Limited,
registered in England, company number 785998, of Houndmills, Basingstoke,
Hampshire RG21 6XS.

Palgrave Macmillan in the US is a division of St Martin's Press LLC,
175 Fifth Avenue, New York, NY 10010.

Palgrave Macmillan is the global academic imprint of the above companies
and has companies and representatives throughout the world.

Palgrave® and Macmillan® are registered trademarks in the United States,
the United Kingdom, Europe and other countries.

ISBN 978–0–230–57932–3

This book is printed on paper suitable for recycling and made from fully
managed and sustained forest sources. Logging, pulping and manufacturing
processes are expected to conform to the environmental regulations of the
country of origin.

A catalogue record for this book is available from the British Library.

Library of Congress Cataloging-in-Publication Data
The modern child and the flexible labour market : early childhood
    education and care / edited by Anne Trine Kjørholt, Jens Qvortrup.
        p.   cm.
    Includes index.
    Summary: "This book sheds light on new research related to welfare state,
    childcare policies, and small children's everyday lives in instuitutions in
    a variety of countries. In uniting recent social childhood research, welfare
    perspectives and historical and comparative approaches, the book
    explores institutionalization as a feature of modern child life."—Provided
    by publisher.
    ISBN–13: 978–0–230–57932–3 (hardback)
    ISBN–10: 0–230–57932–9 (hardback)
    1. Childcare—Government policy—Europe.   2. Early childhood
    education—Government policy—Europe.   3. Family policy—
    Europe.   4. Labor market—Europe.   I. Kjørholt, Anne Trine.
    II. Qvortrup, Jens.
    HQ778.7.E85M63 2011
    362.71′2—dc22   2011013808

10   9   8   7   6   5   4   3   2   1
21   20   19   18   17   16   15   14   13   12

Printed and bound in Great Britain by
CPI Antony Rowe, Chippenham and Eastbourne

Contents

Tables

Preface

This book is the final result of an interdisciplinary project conducted at the Norwegian Centre for Child Research in Trondheim, Norway. We are grateful to the Norwegian Research Council for having funded our project, 'The Modern Child and the Flexible Labour Market. Institutionalization and individualization of children's lives in modern welfare societies'. The project commenced in 2004 and terminated in 2009 with a large international conference in Trondheim. As all the chapters in this book were written in 2008 and submitted for publication in 2009, information in some of them does not, understandably, take into consideration political and economic events that have taken place thereafter. On its way, the project has kindly been supported by an international group of renowned scholars in the field:

- Professor Guðný Björk Eydal, Faculty of Social Work, University of Iceland, Reykjavik, Iceland
- Associate Professor Eva Gulløv, Pedagogical University College, Copenhagen, Denmark
- Professor Gunilla Halldén, University of Linköping, Sweden
- Professor Michael-Sebastian Honig, University of Trier, Germany; now at the University of Luxembourg
- Professor Allison James, University of Sheffield, UK
- Professor Peter Moss, University of London, UK
- Associate Professor Harriet Strandell, University of Helsinki, Finland.

We appreciate the commitment and encouragement from the international group, whose have members have with enthusiasm taken part in annual meetings for exchange and promotion of insight, ideas, discussions and inspiration on the issue of early childhood education and care. We want to thank the group and are pleased, not least, that most of its members have been able and willing to join in this last undertaking of the project, namely, writing a chapter for this book.

Finally, we want to express our gratitude to Officer Manager Barbara Rogers and Senior Executive Officer Karin Ekberg for their experienced and qualified assistance in bringing the book safely over quite a few obstacles to, we hope, an interested readership.

The editors

Notes on Contributors

Berit Brandth is Professor of Sociology in the Department of Sociology and Political Science, Norwegian University of Science and Technology (NTNU), Trondheim, Norway. Her research focuses on gender, work/family and welfare state policies. One central area of study has been fathers' use of care policies to reconcile work and childcare. She is the author (with E. Kvande) of the book *Flexible Fathers*, and co-editor of *Gender, Bodies and Work* (2005) and *Valgfrihetens tid. Omsorgspolitikk for barn i et fleksible arbeidsliv*. Her research topics also include gender in agriculture- and forestry-based work, which she has studied through such inroads as technology, organization, family, body and the agricultural media.

Guðný Björk Eydal is Professor in the Faculty of Social Work, University of Iceland, Reykjavik, Iceland. Her main research topics include the welfare state and policies on families and children, in particular childcare policies. She participates in REASSESS, the centre of excellence in welfare research. Among her recent publications are articles on childcare policies in the Nordic countries, Icelandic family policy, and children and the Nordic welfare states (e.g. 'Equal rights to earn and care, the case of Iceland' (ed. with Gíslason); 'Social work and Nordic welfare policies for children – present challenges in the light of the past' 2008 with M. Satka, in *European Journal of Social Work*).

Eva Gulløv is Associate Professor in the School of Education, University of Aarhus, Denmark. Her research concerns children's social relations, formations of identity and meaning within educational institutions, and processes of inclusion and exclusion related to children of ethnic minorities. Her recent publications include 'Institutional Upbringing: A Discussion of the Politics of Childhood in Contemporary Denmark' 2008 (in James & James, *European Childhoods*); 'Targeting Immigrant Children' 2008 (with H. Bundgaard in N. Dyck, *Exploring Regimes of Discipline*); 'Children of Different Categories' 2006 (with H. Bundgaard in *Journal of Ethnic and Migration Studies*); and *Children's Places: Cross-Cultural Perspectives* 2003 (with K. F. Olwig).

Gunilla Halldén is Professor in Child Studies at Linköping University, Sweden. She has carried out research on children's ideas about family life and on the role of preschool in children's everyday life. Her work deals with the construction of childhood in relation to gender issues and modernity. Her recent publications include 'Children's Narratives as Ways of Exploring Caring and Control, Power and Relationships' in *International Journal of Critical Psychology* 2004 and 'Children's Strategies for Agency in Preschool' in *Children & Society* 2008; and in Swedish, *Den Moderna barndomen och barns vardagsliv* 2007.

Allison James is Professor of Sociology and Director of the Centre for the Study of Childhood & Youth at the University of Sheffield; Director of the Interdisciplinary Centre of the Social Sciences (ICOSS); and Professor II at the Norwegian Centre for Child Research, NTNU. As one of the pioneers of childhood studies she has carried out a wide range of empirical and theoretical research, most recently exploring children's perceptions of hospital space and children's perspectives on food. Author of numerous books and articles, her latest book is *European Childhoods* 2008 (with A. L. James).

Birgitte Johansen, PhD, is based at the Norwegian Centre for Child Research, NTNU. Her fields of interest are work–life studies, gender studies, family policy and welfare state studies as well as Foucauldian perspectives on government. She has published in Norwegian and international books and journals. Her recent publications include the article: 'Trick or Treat? Autonomy as Control' 2005 (edited by R. Barret, in *Management, Labour Process and Software Development*) and in Norwegian: 'Fleksibilitet som utfordrer til kvinners deltidsarbeid?' 2007 (edited by E. Kvande and B. Rasmussen, in *Arbeidslivets klemmer – paradokser i det nye arbeidslivet*).

Anne Trine Kjørholt is Director of and Associate Professor at the Norwegian Centre for Child Research, NTNU. Her research fields include discourses on childhood and everyday life, including in African countries, children's rights and perspectives, citizenship, and early childhood education and care in a global perspective. Her publications include *Global Childhoods: Globalization, Development and Young People* 2008 (with S. Aitken and R. Lund); *Flexible Childhood? Exploring Children's Welfare in Time and Space* 2007 (with H. Zeiher, D. Devine and H. Strandell); *Beyond Listening: Children's Perspectives in Early Childhood Services* 2005 (with A. Clark and P. Moss).

Tora Korsvold was Senior Research Fellow at the Norwegian Centre for Child Research, NTNU, at the time of writing this chapter and is currently Professor at Queen Maud University College of Early Childhood Education (QMUC). Her main research fields are the history of welfare states and children, childhood and childcare in a historical perspective. During the years 2004–2011 she was a co-editor of the Nordic journal *Barn*. In 1998 she published her dissertation *For alle barn. Barnehagen framvekst i velferdsstaten*, which was reprinted in 2005 and 2008. Recent publications are *Barns verdi* (2006), *Barn og barndom i velferdsstatens småbarnspolitikk* (2008) and editor of *Barndom. Barnehage. Inkludering* (2011).

Elin Kvande is Professor of Sociology in the Department of Sociology and Political Science, Norwegian Centre for Child Research, NTNU. Her research interests include work and organizations, gender studies, welfare state, and work and family. Her recent publications include *Doing Gender in Flexible Organizations* 2007; *Gender, Bodies and Work* 2005 (edited with D. Morgan and B. Brandth); *Valgfrihetens Tid, Omsorgspolitikk for barn i et fleksible arbeidsliv* 2005 (edited with B. Brandth and B. Bungum); and in 2009 'Work-Life Balance for Fathers in Globalized Knowledge Work. Some Insights from the Norwegian Context' in *Gender, Work and Organization*.

Peter Moss is Professor at the Thomas Coram Research Unit, Institute of Education, University of London. His research interests include services for children, the workforce in these services, gender issues in work with children and the relationship between employment, care and gender, with a special interest in leave policies. Much of his work has been cross-national, especially within Europe. He currently edits a multi-national and multi-lingual magazine *Children in Europe*; and co-ordinates an international network on leave policies and research. Recent books include *Beyond Quality in Early Childhood Education and Care: Postmodern Perspectives* 1999 (with G. Dahlberg and A. Pence); *From Children's Services to Children's Spaces* 2002 (with P. Petrie); *Ethics and Politics in Early Childhood Education* 2005 (by G. Dahlberg and P. Moss); *Beyond Listening: Children's Perspectives on Early Childhood Services* 2005 (with A. Clark and A.T. Kjørholt); and *Care Work in Europe* 2007 (with C. Cameron).

Randi Dyblie Nilsen is Professor at the Norwegian Centre for Child Research, NTNU. She has carried out ethnographic research and published on several issues: children as social actors, everyday life and space/place in family home and daycare centre settings, generational relations, constructions of child(hood), cultural (re)production, socialization, and methodological and theoretical issues. She currently leads the research project 'Day-care Centres in Transition. Inclusive Practices'. A recent publication in English is 'Children in Nature: Cultural Ideas and Social Practices in Norway' 2008 (in James & James, *European Childhoods*).

Jens Qvortrup is Professor of Sociology in the Department of Sociology and Political Science, NTNU; former Director of and, at the time of editing this work, Adjunct Professor at the Norwegian Centre for Child Research, NTNU. He directed the large international study 'Childhood as a Social Phenomenon' (1987–1992). He was founding president of the International Sociological Association's section on sociology of childhood (1988–1998) and a co-editor of the Sage journal *Childhood* (1999–2008). He has published extensively in the field of childhood, including *Childhood Matters* 1994 (with M. Bardy, G. Sgritta and H. Wintersberger); *Childhood and Children's Culture* 2002 (with F. Mouritsen); *Studies in Modern Childhood* 2005; and *Palgrave Handbook of Childhood Studies* 2009 (with W. Corsaro and M. S. Honig).

Minna Rantalaiho is Researcher at the Norwegian Centre for Child Research, NTNU, and the Nordic Gender Institute, Finland. Her research interests include Nordic welfare state and policy from different gender and/or childhood-related perspectives. Currently she is studying policy and practice of children's rights in the context of family change at NTNU, and the impact of gender-related organizing on women's social citizenship at the Nordic Gender Institute, Finland.

Monica Seland was a PhD student at the Norwegian Centre for Child Research, NTNU, at the time of writing this chapter. She has ten years' work experience in daycare centres, both as preschool teacher and manager. She is currently Associate Professor at Queen Maud University College of Early Childhood Education (QMUC), Faculty of Education. Her research interests include new discourses in Norwegian daycare policy and everyday life in daycare institutions. Her publications include her Master's thesis, *Barnesamtalen: Narrative gruppeintervju med barn som en vei til medbestemmelse og nye erkjennelser i barnehagen* (2004) and her PhD thesis, *Det moderne barn og den fleksible barnehagen. En etnografisk studie av barnehagens hverdagsliv i lys av nyere diskurser og kommunal virkelighet* (2009).

Harriet Strandell is Associate Professor in the Department of Social Research, University of Helsinki, Finland. Her research interests are in institutional childhood, childhood space, governance and child politics. Her recent publications include *Flexible Childhood? Exploring Children's Welfare in Time and Space* 2007 (with H. Zeiher, D. Devine and A.T. Kjørholt), 'After-School Hours and the Meaning of Home. Re-defining Finnish Childhood Space' 2007 in *Children's Geographies* (with H. Forsberg) and 'From Structure–Action to Politics of Childhood – Sociological Childhood Research in Finland' in *Current Sociology* 2010.

The Modern Child and the Flexible Labour Market: An Introduction

Anne Trine Kjørholt

The aim of the book

A growing institutionalization of children's lives is a characteristic feature of childhood in (post)modern societies. As discussed by Jens Qvortrup (Chapter 13), 'institutionalization, as it is used here, stands for a secular trend, which is characteristic of the historical development towards modernity, and which befalls or includes also persons who are not necessarily deviant, unruly or intractable' (Qvortrup, Chapter 13, p. 264). From an early age, children spend a major part of their everyday lives within institutional education and care. Various institutions, such as daycare centres, kindergartens, preschools, schools and after-school programme, are seen as a 'proper place' for children and childhood. Children are by this placed in an age-segregated social order, spending their time mostly together with children belonging to the same age group, which we may argue, is at the cost of being integrated into an intergenerational social order in society. Modern childhood is thus characterized by age and spatial segregation, locating children in particular places separated from the rest of society both physically and socially (Honig, 1999; Strandell, 2007). This institutionalization of childhood is closely connected to the need for a workforce in the labour market. At the same time, these institutions for children are seen to be in the best interests of the child, as a proper place for growing up, ensuring children a safe and qualitatively rich environment for learning and development in the early years, and for 'practising childhood'.

On the political agenda, there has been increased interest in expanding institutions for children below school age during recent decades in many European countries, and a move towards full coverage

1

of the three- to six-year-old age group in particular. In the summary of the report *Starting Strong*, the reasons for this growing interest are explained in the following way:

> Among the immediate factors turning governmental attention to [early childhood education and care] ECEC issues are: the wish to increase women's labour market participation; to reconcile work and family responsibilities on a basis more equitable for women; to confront the demographic challenges faced by OECD countries (in particular falling fertility rates and the general ageing of populations); and the need to address issues of child poverty and educational disadvantage. (OECD, 2006, p. 1)

This quotation clearly reveals how childhood and the place of children in society are closely intertwined with larger political issues, such as gender equality and the aim of increasing women's participation in the labour market. ECEC is, we can see, also perceived as a tool to increase the fertility rates and prevent further ageing of the population in Europe (for further analysis of ageing in Europe, see Jensen and Qvortrup, 2004).

The term 'early childhood education and care' (ECEC) used in this book includes all arrangements providing care and education for children under compulsory school age, regardless of setting, funding, opening hours or programme content (OECD, 2001). Covering a variety of institutions with different names, such as daycare nursery, kindergarten and preschool, to mention a few, it reflects an emphasis on a combination of care and education, also reflected in the term 'educare'. However, the unique ways in which care and education are combined and expressed in the curriculum of ECEC in the different countries, also to some degree reflected in different terms of the institutional care, are anchored in historical and contemporary notions of childhood as well as in national policies. The particular ECEC arrangements in a country, and not least how they are related to the policy for children below the age of three years, are closely linked with the nature of available parental leave arrangements. The term 'childcare', which is also used in several of the chapters in this book, covers all sorts of care arrangements: public or private as well as parental leave systems. The term 'childcare policies', as defined by Guðný Eydal in Chapter 2, refers to support provided to parents with young children, regardless of whether the support refers to paid parental leave or cash grants for care or services (Rostgaard and Fridberg, 1998).

This book aims to shed light on new research related to the welfare state and childcare policies, on the one hand, and, on the other, small children's everyday lives in institutions in different European countries. In uniting recent social childhood research, welfare perspectives, and historical and comparative approaches, it endeavours to contribute to knowledge about institutionalization as a feature of modern child life. There is a dynamic interconnectedness between everyday life and practice in various ECEC institutions, and the cultural and political contexts in which the institutions are located. In order to gain insight into modern childhood as this is practised by children and practitioners within institutional education and care settings, a broad analytical perspective is needed. As also underlined by the Organization for Economic Co-operation and Development (OECD) report *Starting Strong*, the different political and cultural contexts 'have shaped different views of early childhood, the roles of families, and the purposes of ECEC, and in turn, how these views have shaped policy and practice' (OECD, 2001, p. 2).

A new orientation in terms of sociological and constructionist approaches to childhood was specifically asked for in relation to policy on ECEC with the aim of coming to terms with children's perspective and experiences in daycare centres (OECD, 2001, p. 134). ECEC institutions are constituted as a space for children's identities through particular political and cultural understandings of the child and 'the good childhood'. While being regarded typically as 'natural', such understandings are part and parcel of childcare practices and policies in modern welfare societies, but not without inherent ambiguities and contradictions seldom problematized as ideological and culture-specific perceptions, which might also differ from one country to another.

This book takes as a point of departure a close connection between labour market and work life on one side and development of particular care arrangements for small children on another. Both the labour market and daycare institutions are influenced by partly similar concepts and phenomena, such as flexibility, neoliberal approaches and user orientation. Changes in time organization in the labour market and in society at large will be met with specific demands for time organization in a family with children. The labour market has eventually changed from standardized time as the main principle for work time in industrial society to increased flexibility and differentiation in a postmodern society. The implications of the changes in the labour market from standardized time and space in industrial society to neoliberal approaches in contemporary welfare societies, conceptualized in terms of flexibility, user orientation and individual choice, are a main approach in most of the chapters.

This book has the ambition to look at recent developments in childcare policies and practices in North Western Europe by combining perspectives of childcare policies with young children's experiences in childcare services. It consists of 14 chapters, written by an international and interdisciplinary group of experts in the field, and it presents analyses from seven countries: Iceland, Sweden, Denmark, Finland, England, Germany and Norway. It also focuses on the changes in childcare policies and practices with the alleged effect that childcare as a tendency is being brought in line with new demands of the labour market. Given the significance of an understanding of children's everyday lives within different ECEC institutions and of the quality of the different services, a broad analytical perspective is required that embraces the dynamics between welfare policies, notions of childhood, and everyday life and practices.

Childcare policies and labour market: Historical and comparative perspectives

European welfare states are diverse with respect to early childhood education and care policies, with different origins, priorities and developments. Comparative and historical perspectives, exploring the roots of childcare and childcare facilities, can help us to understand some of the differences in the conditions in which children grow up in different European welfare states today. In Chapter 1, Tora Korsvold compares ECEC arrangements in three different countries – Sweden, former West Germany and Norway – from a historical perspective, starting in 1945. Focusing on the transformation of the labour market that took place in the post-war period and the succeeding decades, she argues that the expansion of childcare, in particular daycare centres, depended greatly on the fluctuation in the need for a workforce in the labour market. Discourse from the Second World War and the following decades reveals slightly new ways of talking about children and the 'good' childhood. Institutional care, like daycare centres and kindergartens, are in the Nordic countries emphasized as proper places for children, offering possibilities for positive development, play and learning. Furthermore, children's need to spend time together with peers as well as be stimulated so as to develop cognitively, socially and emotionally within a supportive environment and to their potential is underlined.

In mainstream comparative welfare state research, Norway and Sweden, on the one hand, and Germany, on the other, are regarded as representing different welfare state models or regimes. Whereas Norway and Sweden have been classified as representative of the social demo-cratic and institutional principle of welfare state, Germany is seen as a conservative type, connected to the subsidiary principle of welfare state (Esping-Andersen, 1990). As Korsvold argues, connected to different welfare state regimes, different concepts of childcare and early child-hood education have been developed in the three countries. Whereas Norway, and especially Sweden, has a longer history of state interven-tion in and responsibility for childcare, the right to provide care for younger children in Germany is still seen as the responsibility of par-ents, in particular for children under the age of three years. Today, however, as her chapter reveals, the German is approaching the Scan-dinavian model, at least in some care arrangements, such as parental leave.

The parental leave system is part of contemporary childcare pol-icy in several European countries. The system to some degree affects the expansion and use of ECEC for infants and children under three years old. As Berit Brandth and Elin Kvande show in their chapter, parental leave in Norway is embedded in neoliberal policy discourses aimed at increased gender equality, flexibility and freedom of choice for parents regarding childcare arrangements. The father's quota is an individual part of the leave scheme given to fathers as employees and with hardly any possibility of choice, while parental leave is designed as gender neutral and optional. In recent decades, gender equality and fathers' rights to parental leave have been an important focus. In exploring this growing emphasis on the father's quota scheme, Brandth and Kvande formulate the provoking question: Free choice or gentle force? How can parental leave change gender practices? Empirical stud-ies on this reveal that the principle of free choice does not contribute to a change in traditional gender practices. Whereas fathers use the father's quota, they do not to the same extent use the optional part of the leave, which is a subject of freedom of choice. The reasons for this, they argue, is the dynamic interrelatedness between the different types of leave and special characteristics of the working life and labour market, still favouring men in various ways. Paradoxically, then, this reflects how discourses on free choice give less change regarding fathers' time with their children, whereas limited freedom of choice results in fathers spending more time with their children as part of their leave. Furthermore, as Brandth and Kvande argue, 'we see a continuation of the prevailing gender pattern where it is taken for granted that infant children are the mother's responsibility, which tells us that free choice impedes change. Parents slide into the same patterns when it comes to work division, even if they understand it as their individual choice' (Brandth and Kvande, Chapter 3, p. 69).

Although each Nordic country has developed extensive childcare policies, as argued by Guðný Björk Eydal in her comparison of childcare policies in Norway and Iceland from the 1970s until today, their approaches differ. Whereas the childcare policies had strong resemblances in the 1970s, the two countries diverged and chose different paths from the early 1980s. Iceland takes an active part in Nordic cooperation and shares a common framework of values on the role of the public sector in ensuring the children's best interest and promoting gender equality. As Eydal's analysis clearly reveals, there is a complex set of interrelated factors contributing to the differences, mirroring the dynamics between, on the one hand, notions of childhood and the degree to which children are seen as belonging to the private domain and, first and foremost, the family and, on the other hand, public welfare policies. In the discussion of the development of the Icelandic childcare policies during the past two decades, she reveals that in 2006, Iceland was second to Denmark regarding the percentage of children enrolled in daycare services, but the period of paid parental leave is shorter. The political aim of extending this leave, as stated by the government before the economic crisis, is at risk. Eydal argues: 'Thus Iceland seems to be at a crossroad: Will childcare policies be developed in line with the goals set prior to the economic crisis or will cutbacks lead to a change in policy'? (Eydal, Chapter 2, p. 51).

Compared with the rest of Western Europe, the care of young children in Denmark is distinct in several ways. This distinctiveness is described by Eva Gulløv as follows. 'Firstly, contrary to Norway, national, tax-financed day care, with only minor payment required of the parents, is offered to all families. Secondly, the level of public engagement and state intervention is comparatively high. Thirdly, as in other social democratic states, a principle of universalism prevails, meaning that every child is offered a seat irrespective of parental income, education or the child's gender, religion, social or ethnic background' (Gulløv, Chapter 5, p. 98). Daycare centres or kindergartens are thus meant to be integrative in order to overcome social boundaries and classes. From a historical perspective, Gulløv identifies and discusses lines of continuity and change regarding the position of ECEC in the contemporary Danish society.

In contrast these characteristics of ECEC in Danish society, as described by Gulløv, England represents a very different case, as described by Allison James (Chapter 6) and Peter Moss (Chapter 7). As in many English-speaking countries, it was not until the second half of the 1980s, together with an increase in the number of employed women with young children, that ECEC for children expanded. Unlike the Nordic countries, the various institutions in the UK have been traditionally, and still remain today, despite administrative responsibility for all ECEC services, integrated into education since the end of the 1990s. They are characterized by a split between 'early education' and 'childcare', and to a very low degree they have been on the political agenda as a public responsibility. The responsibilities for institutional care and education for children below school age are still, to a greater degree than in Nordic countries, left to the private and domestic sphere. As Moss argues in his chapter, 'Post-war governments, of Left and Right, viewed mothers' employment either with hostility or indifference; either way, "childcare" was deemed a purely private matter, except for basic regulation of all "day-care" services to ensure minimum standards' (Moss, Chapter 7, p. 132).

Neoliberalism, user sovereignty and freedom of choice

ECEC is, like other sectors of European welfare societies, affected in various ways by neoliberalism. Referring to David Harvey, who uses the concept of neoliberalism as a 'new economic orthodoxy', Moss describes how this thinking has affected ECEC in the UK, which he describes as being characterized by a 'strongly governed market'. He asserts that 'the rationality of neoliberalism placed even higher value on targeting, reducing social risks and markets as well as emphasizing other values, including individual choice, flexibility, competition and private provision of services. Markets gave expression to these values, facilitating choice, competition and flexibility through the diversity and responsiveness of private providers' (Moss, Chapter 7, p. 133).

The market as the organizing principle for the supply and delivery of early childhood services is striking. In the UK, Moss argues, it should be called a 'quasi-market', since the neoliberal English state – the most centralized and powerful in Europe – plays an active role in managing the market, including legislation and strong regulation of services. He explores the history, rationale, assumptions and form of this approach, and he assesses how the current 'quasi-market' approach works in practice, including whether parents and practitioners conform to the understandings of their identities and relationships assumed by the market model. Furthermore, his chapter clearly illuminates some of the contradictions in the current approach, in particular between a rhetoric of diversity and choice, on the one hand, and, on the other, a practice by government of centralization, standardization and regulation.

In Finland, as elaborated by Harriet Strandell, the emphasis on flexibility in daycare policy has been pertinent since the 1990s, representing a shift from a former centralized governance with national curricula and a prescriptive approach towards deregulation and a call for flexible solutions that take into consideration local needs and individual variations. How can we understand this shift? Referring to Sipilä, Strandell argues that 'Increased flexibility and the opening up to local and individual variations can be interpreted as an adaptation to major changes in the *operating environment* of ECEC: a globalized economy with open competition, an information-based society and a transformation of vital functions of the welfare state in a direction that, in Finland, has been called a *competitive state*' (Strandell, Chapter 12, p. 233).

User sovereignty and the notion of choice as key values have assumed great influence in developments and reforms of ECEC in many European countries. In Norway, the influence of neoliberalism in childcare policies was particularly strong from the mid-1990s. It is first and foremost parents who are defined as users and choosers, whereas children are hardly mentioned as users in political documents from the early 1990s. At that time, Norway was lagging far behind other Nordic countries in the development of daycare services, at the same time as maternal employment was high in the country. The pressure for more daycare institutions was therefore immense. By exploring political discourses of the 1990s and early 2000s, and by comparing these to corresponding policy in the 1980s, Minna Rantalaiho illuminates the emergence of a 'neoliberal' orientation in the Norwegian ECEC policy, which highlights 'flexibility' and 'user orientation' as key terms. In her analysis, she addresses the following question: 'What is the problem for which flexibility is introduced as a solution?' Her analyses reveal how the concept of flexibility 'was moved from being first a policy instrument (a means of reaching policy goals) to representing a quality (a goal in itself) of Norwegian kindergarten' (Rantalaiho, Chapter 4, p. 86). Her analyses also illustrate the ambiguities related to a user-oriented ECEC policy aimed at promoting the interests of parents (that is, working adults in the changing labour market) while at the same time encouraging children's wellbeing. Rantalaiho thereby raises a critical question regarding to what extent the emergence of flexibility has been a quality investment in children's wellbeing in kindergarten from their perspective.

The key terms flexibility and user orientation also relate to the shift from standardized time in the labour market to flexible time. The flexibilization of time with regard to working life entails the blurring of boundaries between 'working time' and 'family time'. This transition to more flexible and individualized working hours, so pertinent in many European countries, implies a new triangle between family, working life and childhood (Jurczyk and Lange, 2007). New questions and dilemmas related to the balance of the work–care dilemma appear. However, despite discussions of temporal consequences of contemporary working patterns in the field of work-life studies, questions of how parents experience dilemmas and challenges related to care and work, and how they use daycare centres, remains under-researched. Birgitte Johansen addresses these topics (Chapter 8) by focusing on experiences of parents working in a flexible working time regime in Norway. She argues that flexible work time is potentially both greedy and generous regarding the opportunities it may provide for combining care and work. Yet daycare opening hours in Norway remain standardized. Her discussion is based on a qualitative study of parents' use of daycare services in Norway, with fixed and standardized opening hours. Among the questions that she discusses are parents' solutions to potential conflicts between demands of productivity, creativity and individualized responsibility in a competitive labour market, on the one hand, and expectations of being a caring parent and spending time with their children, on the other. A significant question addressed in her chapter is how parents deal with the standardized and fixed opening hours of daycare centres while at the same time complying with the flexible working time regime.

Marketization of ECEC and childhood as an investment

Notions of the 'modern child' and the (good) childhood in contemporary societies are complex and are characterized by a diversity of different and competing public discourses. Generational relations have been characterized by blurring boundaries between children and adults

(Stephens, 1995). However, recent trends emphasizing childhood as an object of investment are pertinent in all the countries included in this book. In her analyses of the connection between the labour market and ECEC, Korsvold points to children representing an *indirect* investment. Institutional care for children below school age is seen as an economic investment because it ensures participation by the parents in the labour market, which stimulates a prosperous national future. The emphasis on children seen as an investment in the future is not something new. Allison James underlines this point by referring to Harry Hendrick:

> Hendrick argues with respect to the history of educational developments in the UK, educational policies have always built upon 'the value of children as investments in future parenthood, economic competitiveness and a stable democratic order'. (James, Chapter 6, p. 111)

By posing a set of critical questions, James addresses the issue of which ways the market-oriented and regulatory discourses contribute to shaping the everyday experiences of children.

The growing emphasis on children as an investment in the future is connected to the concept of human capital, seen as a vital resource for ensuring economic growth and national development. Embedded in this is the growing accent on children as learning subjects (Kryger, 2004). This construction of children as human capital from an early age is discussed in several chapters in this book. Strandell relates the discussion of children as human capital to *the social investment state* in a globalized economy, underlining Esping-Andersen's point that life chances and social inclusion are increasingly dependent on the social, cultural and cognitive capital. An issue raised in her chapter, as well as in others, is the increasing concern about the European Union's capacity to compete in a global market, linked to the growing emphasis on assessment of children and national tests from an early age.

These discourses, constructing children as investment and human capital, are linked to an emphasis on children as future citizens and workers, and on them as *becomings* rather than *beings* (Qvortrup, 1985). Of relevance to this is also critique of the social investment strategy, which has been raised by several experts (Lister, 2006; Olk and Wintersberger, 2007).

As discussed in several chapters, this trend of emphasizing children as human capital is followed by an increasing *academization* of the curriculum and content of ECEC services. Similar findings are documented in the report *Starting Strong*, pointing to a tendency for public childcare to become oriented towards the preparation of preschool children for their later role as citizens and labour market participants. This implies moving towards a more structured and school-oriented curriculum, with formal instruction, discipline orientation, and emphasizing subjects such as literacy and maths from an early age. However, as elaborated in *Starting Strong*, two main approaches regarding ECEC can be identified: a 'readiness for school' approach, as in France and the UK, emphasizing cognitive development and the acquisition of skills and knowledge; and a social pedagogy tradition (Nordic and Central European countries), seeing kindergarten in a perspective of lifelong learning development and a play-oriented curriculum (Moss, Chapter 7; OECD, 2006).

The change towards ECEC as a place, first and foremost, to learn is discussed in several of the chapters. Referring to similar trends presented by researchers from Australia, James argues that: 'As in England, the kind of child-centeredness characteristic of an earlier era, which encouraged children's development socially, emotionally, physically and cognitively through play, is being replaced by a new curriculum that is "reducing the distance between the preschool child and the school child" and centring on children's needs largely in terms of their future contribution to the state' (James, Chapter 6, p. 125).

As elaborated by Gulløv, the content of the kindergarten and the traditional social pedagogy approach in Denmark is particularly under pressure. Kindergartens today are forced to focus on outcome, that is, skills relating to the educational system rather than regarding social processes among children as a result in itself. She states that the play-oriented and social pedagogical tradition means stressing values such as inclusion, tolerance, social behaviour and forms of communication rather than more subject-oriented learning (Borchorst, 2000). However, recently there has been a change, putting this pedagogy under pressure: 'From a state primarily occupied with the frames of organization and economic guidelines, the new political attention concerns the priorities of the educational content and the role of institutions to prevent and solve politically predefined problems' (Gulløv, Chapter 5, p. 105).

In Norway a similar trend is also significant. The new National Curriculum (*Rammeplan*) reflects a shift towards a more school-oriented programme, including learning and subjects such as maths and literacy (Kunnskapsdepartementet, 2006). As in the UK, Finland and Denmark, the administration of ECEC services has been transferred to the Ministry of Education. As discussed by Anne Trine Kjørholt and

Monica Seland in Chapter 9, this shift may also be reflected in the architecture of the 'new kindergarten building', moving away from the home as an ideal for a 'good' kindergarten to a bazaar with special rooms designed for specific learning activities.

Flexible spaces, flexible children?

Alongside discourses constructing children as becomings and citizens of the future are discourses constructing children as rights claimers with competence, agency and rights as citizens from an early age. Children's rights to social participation, as stated in the United Nation Convention on the Rights of the Child, are increasingly accentuated. These rights discourses constructing children as competent subjects with rights to have a say, also in ECEC institutions, represent a focus of attention in the book. The following quote from the UN *Report of the Committee on the Rights of the Child* clearly illuminates the powerfulness of contemporary rights discourses, also with regard to children below school age:

> There has been a shift away from traditional beliefs that regard early childhood mainly as a period for the socialization of the immature human being towards the mature adult status. The Convention requires that children, including the very youngest children, be respected as persons in their own right. Young children should be recognized as active members of families, communities and societies, with their own concerns, interests and points of view. For the exercise of their rights, young children have particular requirements for physical nurturance, emotional care and sensitive guidance, as well as for time and space for social play, exploration and learning. (United Nation Children's Working Committee, 2006, p. 53)

As different chapters reveal, children are positioned as subjects within contemporary discourses, constituting ECEC as a space for different positions and framing their actions in particular ways. This opens up the need for new and critical questions to be addressed, such as what it means to be a 'child user' or a 'child citizen'.

In Chapter 9, Kjørholt and Seland discuss how children are positioned as social participants with rights to have a say in a kindergarten in Norway. Flexibility is a key word in discourses on 'the new kindergarten', also connected to the endorsement of flexible places, flexible groups and individual freedom of choice for children through their participation in a daily 'Children's meeting'. Flexible curricula are also underlined in *Starting Strong*, which sees this as a tool to adapt overall goals to 'local needs and circumstances'. Furthermore, it argues for curricula developed in cooperation with staff, parents and children, allowing practitioners to experiment with different methodological and pedagogical approaches (OECD, 2001).

In light of recent changes in ECEC policy and various adult constructions of (good) childhoods, one may ask how children are together working out identities like the 'active and participant child', 'the natural child', 'the flexible child' and 'the individual child'. Given neoliberal trends in the welfare state, it has been argued that citizenship does not seem to be connected to solidarity, security and welfare in a community but is turned into questions about the subject's individual 'free choice' and self-realization (Edwards, 2000). Since 2000 there has been growing emphasis on children as users and consumers in Nordic countries, also within ECEC institutions. This relatively new construction of young children with rights as users and consumers of daycare centres reflects the blurring between 'traditional' notions of a 'good' childhood and neoliberal approaches to its realization. In relation to this, Strandell points to an interesting ambivalence built into the concept 'the child's way of acting' in relation to the stress on children's individuality: by depicting a specific children's culture, differences between individual children are downplayed. On the other hand, a picture of separation and difference between children and adults is being generated (Kjørholt and Lidén, 2004), making children 'the Others' (Strandell, Chapter 12, pp. 237–238).

In Chapter 11, Randi Dyblie Nilsen discusses children's and adults' social practices in the so-called nature kindergartens or nature daycare centres (*naturbarnehager*). These are specific kindergartens in some of the Nordic countries, strongly emphasizing nature and outdoor play all year round. In Norway, such daycare centres have increased in number during the last decade. Nilsen argues that in contrast to ordinary kindergartens, the material borders at the nature kindergarten are flexible, with negotiable and multiple landmarks. The spatial aspects of the 'nomadic practice' contribute to a different version of an 'institutionalized' childhood. Her analyses illuminate the complexities of contemporary discourses on childhood and show that multiple meanings of child subjectivities and places are intertwined and shifting. She suggests that current social circumstances call for 'flexible' and 'fluid' ways of being, and, based on fieldwork in a 'nature kindergarten', she discusses tensions between such features of a modern childhood and 'traditional' constructions of a 'good' childhood outdoors connected to the spatial realm of home and neighbourhood, in which playing at non-fenced places and patches of nature environment is highly valued.

Gunilla Halldén in Chapter 10 also clearly reveals how children in everyday life in kindergarten are active participants by engaging themselves in social meaning-making processes with each other. Drawing on findings from three ethnographic studies, she shows how children defend a place, transform a space into a private place and use places in flexible ways as part of practising child culture. She argues for the importance of taking a child perspective in order to gain knowledge about how children experience everyday life in contemporary institutions. The fieldwork on which her chapter is based reveals that children create 'counter-cultures' to adult control, based on positions in contemporary discourses on the competent child that goes along with the individualization and institutionalization of childhood.

Qvortrup discusses in Chapter 13 the question of who are actually the users of daycare centres. On the face of it, children are the primary users, but there are other candidates as well: parents, staff, business, the state and/or society. Given the overall theme of the book, namely the influence of neoliberal thinking on daycare centres, Jens Qvortrup generalizes it to suggest that at any time the dominant economy and society determine where children are and what they do. The provocative thesis is therefore formulated that, had daycare merely aimed to serve children, they would hardly ever have been established on a massive scale. Thus, the real users of daycare centres are various interested adult parties – in terms of the labour market or, as suggested in many of the chapters, to give way for both parents to work for an income or to use their education. The suggestion that children in this sense are the second priority does not prevent them from enjoying and benefiting from their stay in the institutions.

References

Borchorst, A. (2000) 'Den danske børnepasningsmodel – kontinuitet og forandring' (The Danish model of childcare – continuity and change), *Arbejderhistorie*, vol. 4, pp. 55–70.
Edwards, T. (2000) *Contradictions of Consumption. Concepts, Practices and Politics in Consumer Society* (Buckingham: Open University Press).
Esping-Andersen, G. (1990) *The Three Worlds of Welfare Capitalism* (Cambridge: Polity Press).

Honig, M.-S. (1999) *Entwurf einer Theorie der Kindheit* (Proposition for a theory on childhood) (Frankfurt am Main: Suhrkamp).
Jensen, A. M. and Qvortrup, J. (2004) 'A Childhood Mosaic: What Did We Learn?' in A.-M. Jensen, A. Ben-Arieh, C. Conti, D. Kutsar, M. Phádraig and H. W. Nielsen (eds) *Children's Welfare in Ageing Europe Vol. II* (Trondheim: Norwegian Centre for Child Research, Norwegian University of Science and Technology).
Jurczyk, K. and Lange, A. (2007) 'Blurring Boundaries of Family and Work – Challenges for Children' in H. Zeiher, D. Devine, A. T. Kjørholt and H. Strandell (eds) *Flexible Childhood. Exploring Children's Welfare in Time and Space Vol. 2 of COST A19: Children's Welfare* (Odense: University Press of Southern Denmark).
Kjørholt, A. T. and Lidén, H. (2004) 'Symbolic Participants or Political Actors?' in H. Brembeck and B. Johansson (eds) *Beyond the Competent Child. Exploring Contemporary Childhoods in the Nordic Welfare States* (Roskilde: Roskilde University Press).
Kryger, N. (2004) 'Childhood and "New Learning" in a Nordic Context' in H. Brembeck, B. Johansson and J. Kampmann (eds) *Beyond the Competent Child. Exploring Contemporary Childhoods in the Nordic Welfare States* (Roskilde: Roskilde University Press).
Kunnskapsdepartementet (Ministry of Education and Research) (2006) *Rammeplan for barnehagens innhold og oppgaver* (Framework Plan for the Content and Tasks of Kindergartens) (Oslo: Kunnskapsdepartementet).
Lister, R. (2006) 'An Agenda for Children: Investing in the Future or Promoting Well-being in the Present?' in J. Lewis (ed.) *Children, Changing Families and Welfare States* (Cheltenham, UK: Edward Elgar).
OECD (2001) *Starting Strong. Early Childhood Education and Care* (Paris: OECD).
OECD (2006) *Starting Strong II. Early Childhood Education and Care* (Paris: OECD).
Olk, T. and Wintersberger, H. (2007) 'Welfare States and Generational Order' in H. Wintersberger, L. Alanen, T. Olk and J. Qvortrup (eds) *Childhood, Generational Order and the Welfare State: Exploring Children's Social and Economic Welfare, Vol. 1 of COST A19: Children's Welfare* (Odense: University Press of Southern Denmark).
Qvortrup, J. (1985) 'Placing Children in the Division of Labour' in P. Close and R. Collins (eds) *Family and Economy in Modern Society* (Basingstoke: Macmillan).
Rostgaard, T. and Fridberg, T. (1998) *Caring for Children and Older People. A Comparison of European Policies and Practices Social Security in Europe 6* (Copenhagen: The Danish National Institute of Social Research).
Stephens, S. (1995) *Children and the Politics of Culture. Rights, Risks and Reconstructions* (Princeton, NJ: Princeton University Press).
Strandell, H. (2007) 'New Childhood Space and the Question of Difference' in H. Zeiher, D. Devine, A. T. Kjørholt and H. Strandell (eds) *Flexible Childhood? Exploring Children's Welfare in Time and Space. Vol. 2 of COST A19: Children's Welfare* (Odense: University Press of Southern Denmark).
United Nation Children's Working Committee (2006) *Report of the Committee on the Rights of the Child* (A/61/41) (New York: United Nations).

Part I

The Labour Market and Institutionalization of Modern Childhood: Historical and Comparative Perspectives

1
Dilemmas over Childcare in Norway, Sweden and West Germany after 1945

Tora Korsvold

Introduction[1]

Childcare in Sweden in the period from the 1930s to the 1970s has been described as a kind of political battlefield. Scholars such as the historian K. G. Hammarlund state that the field developed into a complexity of different factors and social formations, characterized by sharp differences of opinion and conflicts. Children were placed in the crossfire, as Hammarlund says (1998, p. 17). A battle was fought over what was in 'the best interests of the child' or what 'a good childhood' ought to be. My challenge is, therefore, to search for the trend in some of those dilemmas over childcare, and to determine how they have been solved. Norway, Sweden and Germany are, on the one hand, quite similar regarding childcare arrangements for small children, which make them comparable. On the other hand, they are also different, for example, regarding the role of the state. The three welfare states belong to two different welfare regimes. Norway and Sweden have been classified as representatives of the social democratic type and Germany as the conservative type (Esping-Andersen, 1990). By using a historical perspective on source materials, my aim is to obtain a greater insight into how children, childcare and childhood have been discussed in the post-war period.

Norway and Sweden

In order to understand important aspects of childcare in Norway and Sweden, I will examine some of the origins of public childcare. In Sweden, as early as the 1930s, new ideas about the relationship between the state, the family and the balancing of work and care were seriously discussed. In Norway, on the other hand, there was some reluctance on the part of the state (Korsvold, 1997); for a long time, the family was a non-subject, and a specific family policy did not emerge until the 1950s (Haavet,1999).

Sweden, therefore, had a head start in this respect. The well-known radical and intellectual Social Democrat, and social pedagogue, Alva Myrdal worked for equal rights between men and women, especially for new opportunities for married mothers to combine motherhood with a job outside the home. She and her husband, Gunnar Myrdal, set a new tone in the ongoing discussion about the threatening decline of the Swedish population (Myrdal and Myrdal, 1934). It was argued that support for childcare institutions does not necessarily lead to more children, but children of better quality.

In Alva Myrdal's view, all children should have the opportunity to attend an 'expanded nursery' or nursery school (*storbarnkammar*) (Myrdal, 1935, p. 158). She worked for a pedagogical form of childcare that was to help children (or better, to control children, mostly those living in towns) to become good citizens for the sake of the public good (Hatje, 1999, 2003). In the 1930s, one system, the day nursery, was directed at the children of poor working mothers, while the other, the preschool, was directed at children in general (but very often the more privileged) and offered a few hours of attendance, justified by pedagogical and social goals. The latter category was predominant, but Myrdal wanted a new one, the 'expanded nursery', which would be a mixed category. She sought to integrate and eliminate class and ideological differences so that all children would benefit from one institutional form of pedagogical childcare, ranging from crèches (*barnkrybber*) to kindergartens (*barnträdgårder*). The society, by way of state subsidies, were to provide certain services for the public, such as 'expanded nurseries' for all children.

Modernity, with its characteristic complexity, was visible in Myrdal's approach. To have a child growing up in a modern industrial society was too difficult a process for parents to cope with on their own. This social pedagogue therefore situated the children as individuals in a direct relationship with the state, and did so as early as the 1930s.

Equally important, Myrdal regarded married women with small children as both mothers and workers. This position of the woman was to become very important for childcare policy in Scandinavia in the following decades. The notion that every citizen capable of working should have a paid job, including married mothers with small children, can be seen as an expression of the special weight and value that eventually was given to economic independence in all Nordic countries, in contrast with Germany. Historically, too, mothers were seen as both care persons and contributors to the family economy (Blom and Sogner, 1999; Florin and Nilsson, 1999). In the 1930s, however, Myrdal's arguments were too radical to gain wide support. Indeed, although the state had a say in social matters, family life and care for small children still belonged in the private sphere. However, in the long-term, Myrdal's ideas were implemented – by other actors.

An active state

The period after the Second World War in Norway was one of expansion. The first priority was to build new industries and invest in infrastructure such as roads, electrical provisions and so on. Small children still belonged to the private sphere. Myrdal's influence was not yet really felt. Sweden, on the other hand, was able to continue as before, including in the development of its childcare ideals from the 1930s. More importantly, it took a small but important step in connecting childcare nurseries to the labour market, specifically to the demand for female workers. In order to recruit sufficient labour for Swedish industry, mothers with small children were regarded as potential industrial workers. In anticipation, a government subsidy for childcare institutions was introduced in 1944.

Equality, the labour market and caring institutions

As early as 1951, the Swedish Committee for Child Care, established in 1946, presented the report *Day Nurseries and Preschools* (SOU, 1951), arguing that if women chose employment before their role as housewives, then society should support them by offering childcare services. The committee recognized that in the future there would be a huge demand for female labour.

In Sweden in the 1950s and 1960s, the childcare question was defined in terms of how to increase female labour participation, including mothers, in order to mobilize as many workers as possible to maintain and increase the country's economic growth. The problems that resulted from this policy were how to qualify mothers and integrate them into the labour market, and how to provide sufficient public childcare facilities (Florin and Nilsson, 1999).

Like Sweden, in the 1950s and 1960s, Norway was governed by the Social Democratic Party, but somewhat differently than Sweden. At this time the party made a shift to the Right in its gender policy as part of its attempt to modernize Norwegian society (Hagemann, 2005). After the war, women were again told to concentrate on family life and the household. This conservative turn became especially clear in the 1950s, the 'golden era of the family' and the 'era of happy childhood' (Rudberg, 1983, p. 217). Up to this time, as later in the 1960s, the national union of housewives built up the system of preschools ('housewives' preschools' or *Husmødrenes barnehager*) to make the day comfortable and manageable for both children and mothers: to make it possible for children to meet their peers, and for 'stay-at-home mums' to do their work at home 'more smoothly' without the presence of children (Korsvold, 1998). In the Norwegian welfare-state model, quite unlike in Sweden, we can identify a stronger policy of supporting housewives and traditional family values until the 1960s (Hagemann, 2005). The Norwegian Government was concerned about the contemporary society, which did not offer satisfying living conditions for children, especially those living in towns:

These days, society in an urban setting has a tendency to promote an overly exaggerated outward and, if not also, restless lifestyle which is poorly conducive for providing small children any serenity in their co-existence with adults, whether it be in or outside the home, which is necessary for the development of a firmly established personality and character. (Komitéen til å utrede visse spørsmål om daginstitusjoner m.v. for barn, 1959, p. 65)

By contrast, in Sweden at the beginning of the 1960s, the question of equality between men and women had a very important impact on both the labour market and society in general, as already shown in the 1951 report (SOU, 1951). The political meaning of equality in this period was first of all to have equal opportunities (social, economic and geographical) for all groups in society as part of an emphasis on social justice. Equality between different groups of children was important – that is, all should have equal opportunities – and daycare and pedagogical systems should contribute to the child's conditions while it was growing up, especially for less well-off children.

Eventually, therefore, the emerging debate over gender roles (*kjønnsrolledebatten*) in Sweden at the end of the 1950s and the beginning of the 1960s spread the idea that men and women should enjoy equal roles in society. In Sweden in the 1960s, and later in Norway, equal opportunities and economic independence among married women through paid work outside the home and family became more and more visible. In Sweden, and somewhat less so in Norway, women's rights gained greater acceptance in the post-war era.

A 'good childhood'

During the late 1950s and the beginning of the 1960s, we can identify new ways of talking about children in childcare centres and of determining what 'a good childhood' ought to comprise. In Sweden in the 1950s a longer stay in day nurseries was regarded as being harmful to children, according to parliamentary documents from the commission (SOU, 1951). Day nurseries might be a risk for the child's physical and mental health, especially for infants. That statement builds on psychological knowledge from experts participating in this commission.

A moral evaluation of the family space as the 'proper' world for children conformed to the creation of a specific gender model. Institutions such as kindergartens or nursery schools (*lekskolan*) should be supported for 'the sake of the children'. A four-hour nursery school was regarded by the experts as the best solution for children between the ages of three and six years; the all-day nursery, by contrast, could mean far too long a period of absence from the home, especially for the youngest children (SOU, 1951, p. 183). Children under the age of three years should not attend such institutions but should stay at home because their own mothers were the best people to care for them. The child belonged with its parents, especially during infancy, and it was claimed that up to the age of three years they were in a pre-social phase and could not benefit from being together with other children in a peer group. From the age of three a child could attend a childcare institution, but even then the stay should not last for too long since contact with their parents was put at risk. Children, and childhood as a life course, were packaged into a certain understanding, into certain 'regimes of truth' where psychological knowledge about children prevailed. The discourse about long periods of stay in care institutions was based on an understanding that the care of young children properly took place within the family.

Yet although day nurseries were considered to constitute a risk to the small child's mental health, there were far worse alternatives, such as single mothers having to give up their children to foster parents or for adoption. For some groups of children, day nurseries had to be accepted as the best solution. In certain instances, parental circumstances trumped children's welfare. In such cases, a class perception was important.

In Norway too in the 1960s, the government hesitated to support child daycare, especially the day nurseries or *daghjem*. In 1963, the Norwegian Government started to provide permanent subsidies for day nurseries and kindergartens (or *barnehager*).

In Sweden, a stay of three to four hours was said to be the maximum that was in the 'best interests of the child'. The labour market and the standard working hours meant that a whole day's stay could be expected for children. Again, connecting childcare to the labour market, specifically for female workers, was accompanied by a number of dilemmas.

The new demand for more employment

How were the dilemmas discussed? In Sweden at the end of the 1960s, the main purpose of childcare policies was to provide places in public facilities for all those who needed them, especially families in which the mother was working outside the home. Within both a welfare discourse and a gender egalitarian discourse, all resources should be concentrated on day nurseries. According to the historian Hammarlund (1998), up until then there was an understanding, implicitly or explicitly, that the nursery school was the type of childcare that should be given priority. In 1963 the parliament (*Riksdag*) decided to raise the yearly subsidy for all-day nurseries to a quarter of the standard level, and two years later it passed a bill that meant excluding the nursery schools (*lekskolan*) from further subsidies. From then on, all resources were to be concentrated on all-day nurseries. The main goal of this reform was to improve early childhood education and to meet parents' needs for the care of their children. As was the case in other European countries, a new understanding of education as an economic resource that could stimulate labour supply and thereby economic growth influenced this reform.

A fundamental shift took place. The new construction of childhood, with children staying partly at home and partly in day nurseries, better suited the new conditions in the labour market and the demand for more employment, as did the new gender contract. The latter developed towards an individual earner-carer model, supporting women's economic independence.

In this new situation, the formerly disliked system of day nurseries was discussed alongside a part-time system for more privileged children. The two traditions had to be combined into a modern preschool (*dagis*), which became viewed as having an integrating role involving both education and care, now seen as inseparable activities for all children aged between one and six years.

First in Sweden, and then in Norway, the government sought to meet the needs of industry – a new political strategy. Therefore the development of policies for small children was quite strongly influenced by national economic development, but the shift was hardly purely instrumental. The process of social integration demanded more paid jobs, education and care for the whole population (Sejersted, 2005). Now new ideas of childhood saw a stay in day nurseries as less harmful to children, as shown in the Norwegian Government's White Paper:

> In a situation when there is an extra ordinary demand for labour and thus an increased demand for the supervision of children, there may be some flexible solutions at hand. For example, provisional day-care homes may be located in community halls or other vacant buildings. In order to fulfil this extra ordinary demand, the qualifications of the personnel and the building standards and their content should be abated. (St. meld. nr. 89, 1961–1962, p. 10)

The needs of the labour market played a major role. A flexible alternative was the solution, although there were still some differences between the two welfare states in terms of solving childcare dilemmas. Again, in Norway the state played a more passive role. In 1965 about 3 per cent of all children aged three to six years attended a preschool or day nursery. By comparison, in Sweden the rate for children in the same year was about seven per cent. The flow of women into paid employment in Sweden increased, which enabled the government to invest more public funds in the development of public childcare facilities and services for young children. Between the 1960s and the 1980s the employment rate for mothers with young children increased from around 37 to 75 per cent in Sweden and from around 14 to 47 per cent in Norway. In Sweden, in 1980 the number of children from three to six years old attending public childcare had increased to the majority for this age group, while in Norway the corresponding number had increased to 21 per cent (Korsvold, 2011).

The flow of women into paid employment in Sweden increased the pressure to invest more public funds in the development of public childcare facilities and services, but there was still a considerable gap between mothers' employment rates and the number of places available in public childcare. Therefore, mothers in employment in both countries made their own arrangements through private childminders, relatives or neighbours.

The 'modern public childcare child'

The 1970s marked the start of a new policy of increase and accelera-tion in the development of full-time childcare, at least in Sweden. The former nursery schools with typical stays of three to four hours were adapted for longer stays. In this way, the former educational institu-tions were made compatible with the demands of the labour market, especially with regard to standard working hours. The new childcare nurseries or all-day childcare had to fit with the schedules of modern working life. Also, the possibility of childcare centres remaining open day and night was discussed. The parents' needs as well as the children's should, however, be met (Korsvold, 2008).

The dilemmas to be discussed in a broader context, therefore, were the needs of both the children and the parents. However, at this time, children's institutions shifted from the domain of social policy to that of labour policy or, rather, social policy was becoming inte-grated with the goals of labour market policy. Childcare now seemed to have become subordinated to the demands of industrial growth, com-bined with women's right to paid work and also households' purchasing power. Children's interests were also considered because children were in a certain position in the welfare state reforms, at least at certain levels (Therborn, 1993). Furthermore, in the welfare policies for chil-dren in the Nordic countries, the universal principle was clearly visible (Kristjansson, 2006; Satka and Eydal, 2005).

The best way to ensure good conditions for children was to give both parents the opportunity to enter paid employment. From the 1970s, a sophisticated and generous work-related family policy was developed in the Scandinavian countries, which clearly turned parents into both breadwinners and caregivers. After paid parental leave was introduced, first in Sweden in 1973, with the possibility of such leave being shared between the father and the mother, both parents were expected to return to their jobs, leaving the children to be taken care of outside the family. Moreover, such care was equivalent to care by parents at home. The focus was on women's labour market participation and hence the need for sharing childcare. Again, it would be wrong to say that the shift was only instrumental. More contributory factors played an important role here, but space does not allow me to go further into the issue. Nevertheless, the political agenda was focused more on gender equality than on children's rights and interests. The priorities and interest of adults thus still dominated public social welfare policies.

Also, fundamental economic structures in society were transformed. The tax system was changed in the 1970s, again first in Sweden (in 1971), to encourage gender equality. Since there was no longer any tax or other benefits for families with only male breadwinners, families actually depended on both incomes for their livelihoods – or at least, this was the trend.

A stay in the day nursery became a central aspect of childhood in modern society, which demanded of its citizens that they should cooperate with others in a changing environment, having in their possession a certain individual competence and uniform qualifications (SOU, 1972) – in Alva Myrdal's words, to become good citizens for the sake of the public good. A new construction of childhood had been created, namely 'the modern public childcare child', for all children in the society due to the universal principle. Childcare in the 1970s in both Norway and Sweden was linked to the state and the family in new ways. Despite the differences between these two countries, there are many striking similarities concerning the commitment of the welfare state to the formation of childhood and of the public childcare policy in the forming decades after the Second World War. Especially for Sweden, childcare was based on urgent demands for labour to recruit mothers with young children. The women wanted paid work to earn a good wage but still had to tackle the question of what a 'good childhood' ought to be. In addition, the demand for equality as a democratic right between men and women (e.g. a married woman's right to be economically independent of her husband) was met. As a result, this process implied that children were increasingly shifting from being defined within the framework of the family to being seen as individuals who were the responsibility of the state. The relationship between the welfare state, the labour market and families was thus (re)constructed.

Germany

According to Esping-Andersen (1990), the welfare state of the former West Germany represents a different model from that of Sweden and Norway, namely a conservative type. In this chapter, I use this welfare state as a contrast to the social democratic one.

After 1949, a conservative corporate welfare state was constructed within the framework of a federal state system. Following the principle of subsidiary (*Subsidaritätsprinzip*), the main service providers of childcare, apart from the family, were mainly church-affiliated welfare associations. The two most important ones were controlled by the churches, both Catholic and Protestant. As a result, the German welfare state was from the beginning to be subordinate to the private forms of welfare, such as families, extended family networks and unpaid female work. According to these principles, the state reservation was expressed in many ways, among others by regarding childcare as the task of the family and voluntary organizations.

Research has demonstrated that social and economic policies in Germany promoted a traditional gender division of labour. In the forming decades after the Second World War, West Germany was governed by a conservative political party. The underlying concept, which shaped education, the labour market, and social and welfare policy alike, was the 'breadwinner/housewife' family model. This model, even though weakened over time (Hagemann, 2011; Kolbe, 2002), was implemented far more coherently by the German welfare state than by many other Western European states, at least the two Scandinavian welfare states of Norway and Sweden.

Furthermore, a state reservation in West Germany took place in many ways, from supporting a strong male breadwinner model in the law relating to marriage, to regarding childcare as not falling under its responsibilities – yet it did support half-day nurseries for children over the age of three years (*Kindergarten*) (Korsvold, 2008).

An alarming development

What was different, especially compared with the Norwegian development, was the participation of married mothers in the labour force in the 1960s. However, this was regarded as an alarming development rather than a solution to the labour shortage. This shortage could to some extent be compensated for by using refugees from East Germany and Eastern Europe, but not completely. Therefore, the federal government encouraged the systematic recruiting of so-called guest workers from Southern Europe from the end of the 1950s and especially after 1961, when the Berlin Wall was built. In the 1960s when the labour shortage still existed, the number of part-time workers increased. Nearly all of them were female (Kolbe, 2002).

The attitude towards the employment of mothers was rather restrictive, however West Germany wanted to distinguish itself from former fascist politics. There was scepticism towards state interference, again due to the experience with the Nazi regime, but the political reluctance concerning state interference also corresponded well with a deeper cultural value with an attitude towards the state that was rather reserved compared with that in Sweden and Norway (Fure, 2001; Henningsen, 1986). Accordingly, the state was reluctant to support daycare facilities. The shadows from the East were also important. The East German Republic came to represent something that was harmful for a child and undesirable for a free and democratic society: a standardized, strictly organized and disciplined daily routine, ideological indoctrination and long 'working hours', even for the youngest children.

Day nurseries as a means of female participation in the labour market were therefore accompanied by new dilemmas over childcare and what 'a good childhood' ought to be. In West Germany the Cold War context was of special importance to a broad scepticism towards all-day childcare. Childcare nurseries were therefore presented as a counter-image to the East German state, with its 'working mothers' and 'collective all-day childcare'. Child nurseries served as important cultural markers of the fundamental difference between 'the East' and 'the West'. In this context, the Swedish system of childcare had several trends in common with the East German one. The Swedish system was not a point of departure for a broad scepticism towards all-day childcare or a heated debate.

Connecting childcare nurseries to the labour market, and specifically the demands for female workers, was accompanied by a number of struggles. Again, researchers' results played a certain role. Results concerning children in institutions were transferred in the public debate to a completely different territory – children with 'working mothers'. Their mothers left their children on their own, or rather had someone else look after them while they went out to work. This was the rising public representation of the child that can be found in government documents (see Korsvold, 2008). The normative understanding of institutional care was related to the understanding that working mothers were 'forced out' of full-time motherhood.

Thus, mothers' employment was rather seen as a social problem due to the undocumented assertion that children could develop properly only with unlimited maternal attention. This view's cultural dominance became stronger in the 1960s because the ideal became affordable and feasible for more families. The 1950s and 1960s in West Germany were the 'golden years' of the *Normalfamilie* too, not unlike in Norway. Actually, social and cultural traditions of care by the mother were stronger than in Sweden, especially regarding very young children. Properly, the origin of such care lie in an industrial bourgeois concept in the nineteenth century, with a close association of the female housekeeper model and of femininity related to motherhood (Jurczyk et al., 2004), but also influence from contemporary society (Korsvold, 2008). This gender model was more dominant than in the Scandinavian countries. According to the model, which was connected to industrial progress, care was privatized and made feminine. Care was turned into a responsibility of women and customized more or less to each individual mother. A moral valuation of the family's space as the 'proper' world for children was in line with the formation of this gender model, and the solutions in terms of balancing work and care and also child welfare continued as an individual problem or a problem for the individual family, rather than a problem for the state.

A conservative family policy

The nursery school system massively expanded its number of places. In 1950 nursery school places were only available for 34 per cent of the children in West Germany, but by 1975 places were available for 66 per cent of them. Only a few of the places were available for the whole day. In the 1960s and 1970s, therefore, it was argued that it was acceptable to support nursery schools, the *Kindergartens*, in order to help women who had children and a husband, but not to build up all-day childcare (*Krippen* or *Tagesstätten*) for the sake of care. Mothers in full-time employment were said to be harmful for family life and for the development and wellbeing of young children, although the resistance to this kind of childcare was weakening (Korsvold, 2008).

   In this respect, the taxation rules were important because they privileged a certain family structure and children in maternal care. In taxation law, joint tax assessment for married couples ensured a significant privileged status for single-earner marriages. The joint tax assessment of married couples had an effect of strongly pronounced negative disincentives for increased participation in paid work by mothers, but also for public childcare. The same was true for the non-contributory insurance of family members in the health insurance scheme. Again, the structural system did not encourage gender equality (Jurczyk et al., 2004). While in Norway and Sweden in the 1970s the tax system was changed to encourage gender equality in the family and working life, this was not the case in West Germany. As a result, family policy and dilemmas over childcare changed only to a limited extent.

Sweden, Norway and Germany in the 1990s: Neoliberal trends?

In the last section of this chapter I will briefly look at developments in the 1990s in order to identify some changes in the relationship between the labour market and particular care arrangements for small children. Important political, economic and social changes took place in all three welfare states. Childcare was formed in new ways, and for all three welfare states there were new dilemmas concerning childhood.

Developments in the most recent two decades have been characterized by increases in differentiation, individualization and the 'freedom to choose'. According to Nicolas Rose, neoliberal ideology implies techniques of governing the subjects while it seeks to shape individuality (Rose, 1999). The notion of the individual's 'free choice' as a key value also acquired great influence over reforms of childcare in the 1990s, at least rhetorically. In Sweden and Norway the notions of solidarity, security and public welfare were challenged by the current support for citizens' individual 'free choice' and 'self-realization' (Korsvold, 2008).

The weight on 'freedom of choice' in public policy confirms the increased individualization. As mentioned, a new trend can be identified towards neoliberalism, although flexible service-oriented institutions were seriously discussed in the 1960s, due to the demands of industry. Assuming a new type of link between the labour market and its new demands, the changed circumstances will have an impact on childcare, but in new ways that are still unknown.

Sweden and Norway

In the early 1990s Sweden went through deep economic crises that resulted in substantial cutbacks in social expenditure on families and children. The country faced severe economic problems followed by increased unemployment. The cutbacks challenged a continued increase in welfare spending. The cure was to retrench the welfare state and change the state–society relations through privatization, deregulation and decentralization. Although the universal social democratic welfare state model with its gender equality was not endangered, the result was less generous social benefits. During the 1990s the subjective right to a place in public-funded childcare was extended to cover all preschool children, including those under the age of three years. A new reform (*maxtaxa*) was introduced at the end of the 1990s: a fee limit for childcare or uniform fee categories that increased universalism. Compared with the 1970s and 1980s, the 1990s were indeed a period of retrenchment. However, the changes were quite small when we consider the whole picture. The cutbacks in social expenditure in Sweden did not result in a decline in universalism. The access to all-day childcare became even more important, with support of the universal principle (Hiilamo, 2002).

The development of support of families with small children continued, without deep structural changes and with a particular emphasis on universal social policies. Yet the notion of 'freedom of choice' meant in the Swedish context that the state should delegate more responsibility to parents for the care of children. However, this could be a risky undertaking, leading to more inequality among children. The neoliberal rhetoric focused on responsibility for every citizen, quite unlike the former rhetoric, with a focus on equality between different groups (Korsvold, 2008).

Unlike those of many advanced industrial societies, childcare provisions in Norway did not fall victim to the trend towards state retrenchment that had occurred in the wake of recent global economic restructuring. More importantly, since the 1980s Norway had become one of the wealthiest countries in the world, due primarily to its fortune in finding a large quantity of maritime oil in the late 1960s, and later also gas reserves. Childcare had increased modestly, but in Norway during the 1990s it became one of the most expansive fields of the welfare state. The new care regime kept social democratic attributes, but at the same time it pointed in the direction of neoliberalism, with an emphasis on 'free choice' (Korsvold, 2008).

The focus on individual responsibility for welfare may, however, lead to increasing inequality between different groups of children, at least with new challenges and dilemmas regarding childcare, particular care arrangement and what is in 'in the best interests of the child'.

Germany

During the 1990s childcare had fresh new input from important political influences: the fall of the Berlin Wall and the German reunification. The latter had an impact in terms of children's rights to childcare. During reunification the right to half a day of childcare for children between the ages of three and six years was pushed through. A high level of market integration of mothers with small children, and an extensive system of public childcare also for the youngest children, was not, however, achieved. The new policy served as a basis upon which the compromise for the abortion law could be taken; thus, the introduction of a right to a *Kindergarten* place in Germany should not be mistaken as a sign of a radical turn in the principles of German childcare policies. Rather, the politics were symbolic. They introduced, however, a new element into German childcare policy: the strengthening of the subject status of individual family members. The status of children moved from 'the private property of the family' to a closer position to the state, similar to the Scandinavian developments. Now the state was called upon to create more basic conditions for younger children, solving the deficit in childcare, and to update the gender contract (Korsvold, 2008).

At the end of the 1990s, in former West Germany the *Kindergarten* tradition, with three to four hours' stay daily, was still to be observed in this part of Germany where the half-day system continued to be dominant. The former West German facilities offered all-day places for 17 per cent of all children in the age group three to six years. The provision of childcare for very young children in terms of crèches (*Krippen*) increased marginally over time, from 1 per cent in 1965 to only 2.8 per cent in 1998 (Deutsches Jugendinstitut, Zahlenspiegel, 2002).

Social and family policy applied in the West German welfare state was oriented towards the subsidiary principle of the welfare state. Care for children was more or less the responsibility of the parents. However, the labour force patterns show that there have been some changes. The employment rate of mothers with young children increased in West Germany between the 1960s and 1980, from around 30 per cent to 33 per cent. The employment rate for mothers was about 50 per cent in 1999 (Hagemann, 2011). In 2006 the proposal of paid parental leave (*die Elternzeit*) was passed by Parliament (*der Bundestag*), and this parental leave system was quite similar to that of Scandinavia (Korsvold, 2008).

To summarize, the historical roots of the West German half-time politics of public childcare have had far-reaching economic, social and cultural consequences, which can still be observed. The lack of places especially for children under the age of three and the lack of all-day places makes it difficult for mothers to undertake paid work outside the home. On the other hand, all three welfare states are facing the same challenges with influences from more superior structures: to create a stronger relationship between early childhood, care arrangements for small children, and parents' participation in the labour market.

Concluding remarks

This chapter took as its theoretical starting point welfare regime theory. The provision of childcare and especially the dilemmas over childcare have often been neglected in the analysis of welfare states. Exploring the roots of childcare and childcare facilities can help us to understand some of the differences in the conditions in which children grow up in different European welfare states today. The concept of welfare regimes and dilemmas of balancing work and care can also be used to shed light on how childhood is embedded in different national identities.

In comparative welfare regime theory the importance of civil society – such as the influence of conservative parties and churches which has occurred in Germany – has been acknowledged. Here we find the roots to the residual principle. In the case of the social democratic welfare regime, including those in Sweden and Norway, the universal principle was a cornerstone. Norway and especially Sweden have a longer history of state intervention in and responsibility for childcare, while in (West) Germany the right to provide care for younger children is still understood as the responsibility of parents, at least for children under the age of three years. Today, however, in all three welfare states, the state has become an important factor in constructing the new welfare architecture in the matter of childcare. In this respect, the changes in the labour market play an important role. The German welfare state is approaching the Scandinavian welfare state model, at least in some care arrangements, such as parental leave.

Obviously, there are clear similarities in the growth of public childcare in the three welfare states, but they have also had different priorities in solving dilemmas regarding childcare. In Sweden, at the beginning of the 1970s, 'the modern public childcare child' was created: all-day care for all children in the age group one to six years. In West Germany in the mid-1970s the half-day model for children in the age group three to six years was extended to one-third of all children in this group. It is still the ideal, but this ideal is changing due to developments in the labour market and the new shift from standard to more flexible working hours. The same is true for new rights for children as citizens.

In addition, especially in Sweden, the demand for equality as a democratic right between men and women – that is, a married woman's right to be economically independent of her husband – was met.

In contrast, in (West) Germany, childcare policies were debated in the context of child development and, from the 1970s, also education, less so than labour market policies or gender equality. A strongly pronounced conservatism in German childcare and family policy made it difficult to promote new childcare arrangements.

Today, as in the 1960s, there are still dilemmas over care arrangements for small children and the development of the labour market. Global needs seem to be important as well as national needs. Developments in the two most recent decades have also been characterized by increases in differentiation and, again, individualization. In the 1960s and 1970s in Norway and Sweden, the notions of equality and social justice were clearly visible, including equality between different groups of children or all children. Today, the notion of 'freedom of choice' confirms the increase in individualization. Assuming a new type of link between the labour market and its new demands, the changed circumstances are again having an impact on childhood and children's lives. A more flexible labour market in the use of time and working hours is, however, changing the former standardized time as the main principle for work time. These changes in the labour market will affect children's and parents' lives differently within welfare state regimes or models, though in all cases in the direction of diversity and increasing inequality, and new dilemmas regarding childcare.

Note

1. 'Welfare State Policy Towards Small Children at a Cross Road: A Historical-Comparative Study of Norway, Sweden and Germany' is a subproject within the interdisciplinary project led by Jens Qvortrup and Anne Trine Kjørholt, The Modern Child and the Flexible Labour Market (Qvortup and Kjørholt 2004), funded by The Research Council of Norway. I really appreciate the contributions of all of them. (This chapter draws heavily on Korsvold in Hagemann et al. (2011).)

References

Blom, I. and Sogner, S. (1999) *Med kjønnsperspektiv på norsk historie* (A gender perspective on Norwegian history) (Oslo: Cappelen).

Deutsches Jugendinstitut, Zahlenspiegel (2002) (The German Youth Institute, Database) (Munich).

Esping-Andersen, G. (1990) *The Three Worlds of Welfare Capitalism* (Cambridge: Polity Press).

Florin, C. and Nilsson, K. (1999) 'Something in the Nature of a Bloodless Revolution. How New Gender Relations Became Gender Equality Policy in Sweden in the 1960s and 70s' in R. Torstendahl (ed.) *State Policy and Gender System in the Two German States and Sweden 1945–1989* (Lund: Opuscula Historica Upsaliensia vol. 22).

Fure, O.-B. (2001) 'Nationale Habitusentwicklung in Norwegen und Deutschland. Konstellationen und Grunderfahrungen' (National habitus development in Norway and Germany. Constellations and basic experiences) in H. Uecker (ed.) *Deutsch – Norwegische Kontraste. Spiegelungen europäischer Mentalitätsgeschichte* (German – Norwegian contrasts) (Baden-Baden: Nomos Verlagsgesellschaft).

Haavet, I. E. (1999) 'Framveksten av velferdsstatens familiepolitikk i Norge og Sverige' (The expansion of the welfare state's family policy in Norway and Sweden), *Tidsskrift for velferdsforskning* (Journal for Welfare Research), 2, 67–84.

Hagemann, G. (2005) 'Housewife and Citizen? Gender Politics in the Post-War Era' in G. Hagemann and H. Roll-Hansen (eds) *Twentieth-Century Housewives. Meanings and Implications of Unpaid Work* (Oslo: Unipub).

Hagemann, K., Jarausch, K. H. and Allemann-Ghionda, C. (2011) *Children, Families, and States. Time Policies of Childcare, Preschool, and Primary Education in Europe* (New York and Oxford: Berghahn Books).

Hagemann, K. 2011 'A West German "Sonderweg"? Family, Work and the Half-Day Time Policy of Public Education' in K. Hagemann, K. H. Jarausch and C. Allemann-Ghionda (eds) *Children, Families, and States. Time Policies of Childcare, Preschool, and Primary Education in Europe* (New York and Oxford: Berghahn Books).

Hammarlund, K. G. (1998) *Barnet och barnomsorgen: Bilden av barnet i ett socialpolitisk projekt* (The child and childcare: A picture of the child in a socio-political project) (Diss.) (Gothenburg: University of Gothenburg).

Hatje, A.-K. (1999) 'Political Meaning of Pedagogic Childcare in the 1930s and 1940s' Paper at the seminar 'Alva Myrdal's Question of Our Time', 6–8 March 2002, University of Umeaa.

Hatje, A.-K. (2003) 'Private and Public Welfare: Sweden's Child Day Care in Comparative Perspective' in N. Götz and J. Hackmann (eds) *Civil Society in the Baltic Sea Region* (Aldershot: Ashgate).

Henningsen, B. (1986) *Der Wohlfahrtsstaat Schweden in Nordeuropäische Studien. Bd. 2* (The welfare state Sweden. Studies of Northern Europe Vol. 2) (Baden-Baden: Nomos Verlagsgesellschaft).

Hiilamo, H. (2002) *The Rise and the Fall of Nordic Family Policy. Historical Development and Changes during the 1990s in Sweden and Finland* (Helsinki: Stakes Reports 125).

Jurczyk, K., Olk, T. and Zeiher, H. (2004) 'German Children's Welfare Between Economy and Ideology' in A.-M. Jensen, A. Ben-Arieh, C. Conti, D. Kutsar, M. N. G. Phádraig and H. W. Nielsen (eds) *Children's Welfare in Ageing Europe Vol. II* (Trondheim: The Norwegian Centre for Child Research).

Kolbe, W. (2002) *Elternschaft im Wohlfahrtsstaat. Schweden und die Bundesrepublik im Vergleich 1945–1995* (Parenthood in the welfare state. A comparison of Sweden and West Germany 1945–2000) (Frankfurt and New York: Campus).

Korsvold, T. (1997) *Profesjonalisert barndom: statlige intensjoner og kvinnelig praksis på barnehagens arena 1945–1990* (Professionalized childhood: State intentions and women's praxis in the day-care arena 1945–1990) (Diss.) (Trondheim: Norwegian University of Science and Technology).

Korsvold, T. (1998) *For alle barn. Barnehagens framvekst i velferdsstaten* (For all children. Day-care expansion in the welfare state) (Oslo: Abstrakt).

Korsvold, T. (2008) *Barn og barndom i velferdsstatens småbarnspolitikk. En sammen-lignende studie av Norge, Sverige og Tyskland 1945–2000* (Children and childhood in welfare states' child-policies. A comparative study of Norway, Sweden and Germany 1945–2000) (Oslo: Universitetsforlaget).

Korsvold, T (2011) 'The Best Interest of the Child: Early Childhood Education in Norway and Sweden Since 1945' in K. Hagemann, K. H. Jarausch and C. Allemann-Ghionda (eds) *Children, Families, and States. Time Policies of Childcare, Preschool, and Primary Education in Europe* (New York and Oxford: Berghan Books).

Komitéen til å urede visse spørsmål om daginstitusjoner m.v. for barn (The committee to unravel certain issues about day institutions etc. for children), oppnevnt ved kgl. res. av 6 mars 1959.

Kristjansson, B. (2006) 'The Making of Nordic Childhoods' in J. Einarsdottir and J. Wagner (eds) *Nordic Childhoods and Early Education. Philosophy, Research, Policy and Practice in Denmark, Finland, Iceland, Norway and Sweden* (Greenwich: IPA).

Myrdal, A. and Myrdal, G. (1934) *Kris i befolkningsfrågan* (Crises in the issue of the population) (Stockholm: Bonnier).

Myrdal, A. (1935) *Stadsbarn. En bok om deras fostran i storbarnkammare* (Town children. How to bring them up in 'expanded nurseries') (Stockholm: Bonnier).

Qvortrup, J. and Kjørholt, A. T. (2004) 'Det moderne barn og det fleksible arbeidsmarked' (The Modern Child and the Flexible Labour Market), *Barn*, 1.

Rose, N. (1999) *Powers of Freedom. Reframing Political Thought* (New York: Cambridge).

Rudberg, M. (1983) *Dydige, sterke, lykkelige barn. Ideer om oppdragelse i borgerlig tradisjon* (Virtuous, powerful and happy children. Ideas of upbringing in a bourgeois tradition) (Oslo: Universitetsforlaget).

Satka, M. and Eydal, G. B. (2005) 'The History of Nordic Welfare Policies for Children' in H. Brembeck, B. Johansson and J. Kampmann (eds) *Beyond the Competent Child. Exploring Contemporary Childhoods in the Nordic Welfare Societies* (Roskilde: Roskilde University Press).

Sejersted, F. (2005) *Sosialdemokratiets tidsalder. Norge og Sverige i det 20. århundre* (The social democratic era. Norway and Sweden in the 20th century) (Oslo: Pax).

SOU (1951) Daghem och förskolor (Day nurseries and preschools) (Stockholm).

SOU (1972) 27 Förskolan Del II (Preschool Vol. II) (Stockholm).

St. meld. nr. 89 (1961–62) Om retningslinjer for utbygging og drift av daginstitusjoner for barn (Government White Paper No. 89 Rules for building and running day-care institutions for children) (Oslo).

Therborn, G. (1993) 'The Politics of Childhood. The Rights of Children Since the Constitution of Modern Childhood: A Comparative Study of Western Nations' in I. F. Castles (ed.) *Families of Nations: Patterns of Public Policy in Western Democracy* (Dartmouth: Aldershot).

2
Childcare Policies at a Crossroads
The Case of Iceland

Guðný Björk Eydal

Introduction

Comprehensive childcare policies are one of the main characteristics of the Nordic welfare model (Hatland and Bradshaw, 2006; Kangas and Rostgaard, 2007). Although each Nordic country has developed extensive childcare policies, their approaches differ (Ellingsæter and Leira, 2006; Finch, 2006). The aim of this chapter is to analyse the childcare policies of the smallest Nordic state, Iceland.

Iceland has a population of just over 300,000. Earlier research has shown that the Icelandic welfare system deviates from the Nordic welfare model in some important aspects. During the 1990s, Iceland's proportion of GNP spent on social affairs hovered around 18 per cent, which is low by Nordic standards, not least when compared with the rest of Europe (Ólafsson, 1999). However, in the 2000s the gap between expenditure figures in Iceland and the other Nordic countries narrowed, both for total social expenditure and for expenditure for families and children (Eydal and Kröger, 2009). Despite less public support, Icelandic mothers were as active in the labour market as their Nordic counterparts and the fertility rate was higher than in any other Nordic country (Eydal and Gíslason, 2008). However, it was first in the 1990s that family policy and work–life balance gained wide attention from Icelandic policy makers. During the 1990s there was an increase in volume of preschooling, in terms of both placements and the number of hours each child spent in preschool (Eydal and Ólafsson, 2008). In 2000, Iceland enacted a law on paid parental leave that ensured both fathers and mothers with the same individual entitlements to three months' paid maternity and paternity leave.[1] The stated aim of the 2000 legislation was twofold: to ensure that children enjoy the care of both parents; and to enable both women and men to coordinate family life and work outside the home (Act on Maternity/Paternity and Parental Leave no. 95/2000). Thus, during the period from 1990 to 2000, the policies changed radically. The focal aim of this chapter is to analyse the development of the Icelandic care policies during the past two decades. In order to put the case in context, a comparison with the policies in the other Nordic countries is conducted.

The first section of this chapter provides insight into the Nordic context and policies. Thereafter, the development of the Icelandic policies on parental leave, cash-for-care and daycare services is discussed and compared with the policies in the other Nordic countries. In conclusion, the characteristics of the Icelandic childcare policies and the influences of the ongoing economic crisis are discussed. The data for the policy analysis were collected as part of the research project 'Combining Work and Care', which is supported by the Iceland Research Fund (*Rannís* – The Icelandic Centre for Research), the Icelandic Equality Fund and the University of Iceland Research and Assistantship Fund.

The Nordic context

The Nordic family of nations share both a historical and a cultural heritage. Formal cooperation of the Nordic countries in the field of family law began during the first decade of the twentieth century. In 1962, the Nordic countries signed the Helsinki Agreement, with a goal to synchronize Nordic family law as much as possible. In order to achieve this goal, the Nordic countries exchange information and cooperate in developing family law and policy (Bradley, 1996). While the duties of fathers and mothers to provide and care for their children has been clearly articulated for more than a century in Nordic family policy, a more recent phenomenon is the growing concern for the rights of children to be provided care by both parents, regardless of the parental relationship (Hatland and Mayhew, 2006). From the 1980s and onward, all of the Nordic countries have, through various polices, placed an emphasis on strengthening the active role of fathers in caring (Bergman and Hobson, 2002; Björnberg and Dahlgren, 2008; Skevik, 2008). Ellingsæter points out, in the case of Norway, that policy makers have put political fatherhood on the agenda, and 'the caring father and the domestication of men is the new issue of the 1990s' (Ellingsæter in Skevik, 2003, p. 3). In turn, this has influenced the approach that the Nordic countries have taken in their quest for gender equality, and the emphasis on the active participation of fathers in care can be claimed to be the latest addition to the policies that promote the dual worker/carer project.

Furthermore, care policies in the Nordic countries have also been influenced by the increase in children's legal rights, which has set a clear mark on childcare policies; for example, in the emphasis on children's voices and participation in decision making in daycare and their legal claim to rights to this care from a certain age (Eydal and Satka, 2006; Kjørholt and Lidén, 2005). Icelandic childcare policies have been created within this Nordic framework, and they aim to ensure children's best interests and, at the same time, promote gender equality (Eydal and Gíslason, 2008).

Parental leave

The Nordic countries developed schemes of paid maternity leave during the immediate post-war period (Gauthier, 1996). Furthermore, in the late 1970s and early 1980s, all Nordic countries extended their maternity leave schemes to include parental leave (Ellingsæter and Leira, 2006). Iceland was last among the Nordic countries to develop a universal scheme; first, in 1980, all Icelandic parents were entitled to three months of paid parental leave. The law gave the mother the opportunity to transfer her entitlements to the father, 30 days after parturition. In 1987, this leave entitlement was extended to six months. The law ensured all parents a fixed sum of benefits and, in addition, working mothers and students could get an extra monthly supplement in accordance with the hours that they had been working or studying in a 12-month period prior to their leave. Thus the scheme differed from the schemes in the other Nordic countries, which calculated payments as a percentage of previous wages. Some of the major unions negotiated that the workers should be entitled to full wage pay during their parental leave. This resulted in a twofold system that created large cleavages between those who were only entitled to the state benefits and those who had managed to negotiate full wage pay (Eydal and Gíslason, 2008).

Despite the fact that fathers had the option to take part of the paid parental leave, very few did (Gíslason, 2007). This was also the experience in the other Nordic countries. Hence, during the 1990s all the Nordic countries established an independent right of fathers to paternity leave in order to increase fathers' participation in parental leave (Lammi-Taskula, 2007).

In 1993, Norway became the first Nordic country to establish a 'use or lose' paid one-month paternity leave scheme, sometimes referred to as the 'daddy month' (Brandth and Kvande, 2003). Leira points out that the legal acknowledgement of the role of fathers as caregivers is a significant milestone in the development of care polices:

> Instituting a right of fathers to care for their children signals a new approach to fatherhood and gender equality: a state intervention in employment via the general work environment legislation to promote the care-giver role of fatherhood. Reserving part of the leave for the father represents an effort to influence the division of labour at home and to change the gender balance of caring responsibilities. (Leira, 1999, p. 275)

In the case of Iceland, such changes took place for the first time in 1998 when Icelandic fathers gained legal entitlement to two weeks' paid paternity leave that could be taken during the first eight weeks after birth (Gíslason, 2007). In 2000, Iceland, hitherto a laggard in comparison with the other Nordic countries, followed in the footsteps of Norway and enacted a new law on paid parental leave that ensured both parents the same individual entitlements to paid maternity and paternity leave.

The bill was presented in the Icelandic Parliament in spring 1999, and it stated that the traditional division of labour between mothers and fathers often did result in fathers being deprived of opportunities to be with their children. References were made to research showing that a majority of men claimed they wanted to be able to reconcile labour market participation and childcare to a greater extent. The bill stated that equal and independent rights to maternity/paternity leave plays an essential role in ensuring that both parents have the opportunity to reconcile work and family life (*Þingskjal* 1065, 1999–2000). The stated aim of the legislation was twofold: to ensure that children received care from both parents and to enable both women and men to coordinate family and work responsibilities (Act on Maternity/Paternity and Parental Leave no. 95/2000). In other words, the policy defines it as the state's role to support all parents in order to take care of their young children and actively encourage fathers to participate in the care by earmarking part of the parental leave for them.

In order to ensure that these goals are reached, each parent was given an independent right to maternity/paternity leave of up to three months, which could not be assigned to other persons. Additionally, a joint three-month period of leave could be used as the parents themselves chose. Under this law, the mother has to take maternity leave for no less than two weeks after the birth of her child, but otherwise the parents can exercise their rights during the child's first 18 months as they choose, including both parents taking leave at the same time, which is quite common during the child's first month (Eydal and Gíslason, 2008).

While on leave, parents are entitled to a monthly payment that equals 80 per cent of each parent's average income over the previous two years (Act on Maternity/Paternity and Parental Leave no. 95/2000). First, there was no ceiling on the amount that could be paid, but in 2004 changes were made to the policy, which placed a cap on the amount of money received during parental leave (Act on Maternity/Paternity and Parental Leave no. 90/2004) (Table 2.1). The scheme is financed by a specific fund, the Birth Leave Fund, which was financed by part of the employer's insurance levy.

The Icelandic Parliament passed the new act in record time. Discussions lasted for a total of less than four hours and when it came to the final vote no member of parliament objected, although one abstained (Eydal and Gíslason, 2008). Thus, the original bill was accepted without changes in record time (*Þingskjal* 1310, 1999–2000).

Gallup polls from 2003 show broad support for the act (Gallup Iceland, 2003). It enjoyed a broad base of support from all political parties, as well as from both employers and employees, along with wide acceptance in Icelandic society (Eydal and Gíslason, 2008). According

Table 2.1 Overview of entitlements to parental leave according to the Act on Maternity/Paternity and Parental Leave from 2000

Type of leave/period	Age of child	Payment
3 months maternity leave;	0–18 months*	For parents participating in the labour market 12 months before birth: 80% of total pay**
3 months paternity leave;		For other parents: flat rate payments
3 months divided as the parents choose		
13 weeks for mothers	18 months – 8 years	No payments
13 weeks for fathers		

Note: *Age of child changed to 3 years in June 2009; **ceiling of payment implemented in 2004.
Source: Eydal and Gíslason (2008).

to Eydal and Gíslason (2008), the fact that Iceland was a laggard when it came to developing extensive rights to paid parental leave for such a long period seems to be one of reasons why the laws have enjoyed such strong general support, since the entitlements of the fathers were an addition to the leave period and the mothers could continue to take six months' leave.

The ultimate test of the relevance of the legislation is the uptake by fathers and mothers. The statistics from the Parental Leave Fund Iceland show that the majority of fathers in Iceland have used their individual entitlements of three months' leave. In 2007, 88.5 per cent of the fathers applied for paid parental leave and used on average 101 days. Table 2.2

Table 2.2 Mothers' and fathers' uptake of maternity/paternity leave in Iceland, 2001–2007

	2001	2002	2003	2004	2005	2006	2007
Mothers (n)	4054	4070	4167	4291	4302	4444	–
Applications from fathers as % of mothers	82.4	83.6	86.6	89.8	88.2	88.6	88.5
Average number of days used by fathers	39	68	97	96	99	99	101
Average number of days used by mothers	186	187	183	182	184	185	181
% fathers using more than their basic rights	14.5	13.9	16.1	17.1	19.5	19.7	21.2
% mothers using more than their basic rights	94.2	93.4	90.9	90.5	89.7	90.3	93.1
% fathers using less than their basic rights	5.1	10.1	14.2	17.9	19.5	18.5	16.4
% mothers using less than their basic rights	0.9	0.8	1.0	1.1	0.1	0.3	1.5
% fathers taking all of the leave in one package	45.2	21.2	17.9	15.0	25.8	25.7	25.7

Source: Eydal and Gíslason (2008).

shows the development from 2001, when the act came into effect, until 2007.

The law came into force gradually, and Table 2.2 shows how the increase in uptake rates follows the increase in entitlements from 2001 to 2003. From 2003 and onward, most fathers are using their three-month entitlement. In the majority of cases the mother uses more of the joint period than the father. In 2006, 19.7 per cent of the fathers used more than their basic rights compared with 90.3 per cent of the mothers.

When compared with the Nordic countries, Icelandic fathers take a larger share of the total days available in paid parental leave than fathers in the other countries according to the annual calculations from the Nordic Social Statistical Committee (as Table 2.3 shows). The difference in the time allocated to fathers is reflected in the total number of benefit days used by fathers. Thus, the Icelandic scheme provides longer leave for fathers than do the other Nordic countries and, according to Moss and O'Brien (2006, p. 22), 'this scheme contains one of the most generous "father-targeted" leave entitlements so far developed in modern economies in terms of both time and economic compensation'. Furthermore, studies show that Icelandic parents are dividing paid work and the care of their young children more equally since the law came into effect. Thus, the overall development is towards the twofold goal of the law on paid parental leave from 2000 (Eydal and Gíslason, 2008).

Table 2.3   Parental leave in Nordic countries, entitlements and the percentage of total number of benefit days used by fathers in 2007

	Denmark	**Finland**	**Iceland**	**Norway**	**Sweden**
% of income	100	70	80	100/80	80
Total weeks	50–64	44	39	42–52*	69
– individual entitlements of the mother	18	18	13	9	8
– individual entitlements of the father	0	(2)	13	6*	8
– individual entitlements of the father but the mother has to be on leave at the same time	2	3	0	2	2
– % of total benefit days used by fathers	6	5	33	9	20

Note: *56 weeks in total and 10 weeks for fathers from 2009.
Source: Nordic Social-Statistical Committee (2008), p. 30.

However, Table 2.3 also shows that the total leave period allocated to parents is shortest in Iceland 39 weeks compared 69 weeks in Sweden.

Before the parliamentary elections in Iceland in spring 2007, all political parties expressed their will to extend the length of paid parental leave. A coalition of the Social Democratic Alliance and the Independence Party (right of centre), which came into power in 2007, stated in its policy declaration that the aim was to gradually extend the maternity/paternity leave in phases and the discussions prior to the election centred on a total period of 12 months (Eydal and Gíslason, 2008). In October 2008 the Icelandic bank system collapsed, the national currency (*krona*) fell sharply in value and a severe economic recession hit the country (Jónsson, 2009). In December 2008 the government proposed reductions in social expenditure, including the amounts paid to parents in parental leave, and the ceiling of payments was reduced from 480,000 ISK to 400,000 (*Þingskjal* 357, 2008–2009).

After a period of protesting from the general public, elections were held and a new coalition government left of centre came into power in spring 2009. In June the new government proposed further reductions to the ceiling, from 400,000 to 350,000 ISK. The report attached to the bill emphasized that this change was made in light of the serious situation of the government deficit and that this would be changed back as soon as possible. Furthermore, the length of the period that parents could take out their entitlements was extended from one-and-a-half to three years (*Þingskjal* 155, 2009). In December 2009 the government proposed a new bill that suggested that one month of the paid parental leave would be delayed until the child had reached the age of three years and should be used before the child reached the age of five (*Þingskjal* 315, 2009–2010). There was powerful opposition from the labour unions to the ideas of cutting the period and the result was that the parliament proposed instead further cuts to the amount (*Þingskjal* 442, 2009–2010). Hence, the ceiling was reduced to 300,000 and parents with more than 200,000 would receive 75 per cent instead of 80 per cent of their previous income. These changes came into force on 1 January 2010 (*Þingskjal* 496, 2009–2010).

Thus, neither government changed the character of the scheme, but experts from the Birth Leave Fund have pointed out that the cuts to the amount of benefit will influence negatively the uptake rates, in particular among fathers, and such worries were also discussed in the parliament in December 2009 (*Þingskjal* 496, 2009–2010). Furthermore, it is not impossible that the government might suggest further cuts in the near future since the agreement that the government made with the International Monetary Fund on how to restore the country's economy requires further cuts in public expenditures. The comparison above revealed that the total period of paid parental leave is shorter in Iceland than in the other Nordic countries and this fact, combined with possible further cuts to the benefit amount, might leave Icelandic parents with considerably less public support than is the case in the other Nordic countries.

Cash-for-care

Finland (1985) and Norway (1998) have implemented cash-for-care schemes on a national level for parents of children until they reach the age of three. In Finland the parents have to choose between daycare services and cash-for-care, but in Norway they can use part-time care and get proportions of the benefit in accordance with the time used in daycare (see Rantalaiho, Chapter 4). Sweden enacted laws on a home care allowance scheme in 2008, and the scheme is optional for the municipalities, which can decide to pay cash-for-care to parents until their children reach the age of three (*Lag om kommunalt vårdnadsbidrag*, 2008, p. 307).

One of the characteristics of Icelandic childcare polices is that, besides parental leave, there have been no other state-funded schemes on cash grants for care. Thus, when the relatively short period of parental leave ends, parents have to make private arrangements to bridge the gap between paid parental leave and daycare since children are usually not enrolled into the latter until the age of two years (Eydal, 2008).

In autumn 2006, three Icelandic municipalities started to pay cash grants for childcare in those instances where the children were not enrolled in daycare. These schemes were quite different in character. One of the arguments for implementing such schemes on a local level was that the municipality in question was forced to make such arrangements while waiting for the state to extend the parental leave to one year (Einarsdóttir and Ólafsdóttir, 2007). Furthermore, many municipalities have not been able to hire qualified staff and this has hindered them from reaching their goals regarding services for children, in particular the youngest children from one to two years old. Thus, the municipal schemes have been introduced as an answer to the care gap rather than as a way to increase the choices for the parents, as has been the case in the other Nordic countries (Eydal, 2008; Salmi, 2006).

In 2008, Reykjavik, by far the largest municipality in Iceland, started paying so-called service insurances (i. *þjónustutrygging*) to parents waiting for daycare, but the payment is only available until the children are two years old and are offered placement in daycare centres (Eydal, 2008). By the end of 2009, 12 out of 77 municipalities in Iceland had enacted schemes of cash-for-care.

There has been a lack of comparable statistics on the uptake ratios for the cash-for-care schemes in the Nordic countries and their influences on parents' labour market participation, thus comparison of the influences of the Icelandic schemes with the other countries is not possible at this point in time. The schemes have been debated, in particular in Norway and Sweden (Hiilamo and Kangas, 2006). They are claimed to result in long absences of mothers from the labour market and thus work against the gender equality policies. Furthermore, in some cases they have also been criticized for working against the children's best interests since the children would benefit from preschool rather than staying at home (Leira, 2006; Salmi, 2006; Stefansen and Farstad, 2008). The Icelandic schemes have not been an issue in public debate, but when Reykjavik enacted the scheme of service insurances in 2008, the politicians wrote articles about their different views on the issue.

The economic crisis has already influenced the schemes for cash-for-care, and in Reykjavik, for example, the monthly payment that was 35,000 ISK in 2009 will be reduced to 20,000 ISK during 2010 (*Reglur um þjónustutryggingu 1. janúar 2010*). The future of the municipal cash-for-care schemes will be influenced both by the economy of the municipalities and by the development of other care options. Thus, if both paid parental leave and daycare provision were extended, the lifetimes of the schemes would immediately be affected. However, increases in volumes of paid parental leave and daycare are unlikely to take place during the aftermath of the crisis, which might in turn lengthen the lifetime of the cash-for-care schemes. Experience from the Finnish crisis in the 1990s shows that the uptake of the cash-for-care scheme increased during the period of high unemployment. This could also happen in Iceland (Salmi, 2006). The short historical tradition of the Icelandic local schemes and the fact that they are enacted and financed by the local authorities might contribute to different results than was the case in Finland. In 2010 already, two municipalities have abolished their cash-for-care schemes due to the lack of resources and, as pointed out above in the case of Reykjavik, the amount of payment has been cut and will be cut again later in the year.

Daycare

During the 1960s and the 1970s, public daycare became an important issue in the social discourse within the Nordic countries. The main reasons were labour shortages and an increased emphasis on women's rights to waged employment on a par with men (Sipilä, 1997). However, the policies developed in the Nordic countries emphasized that children should be *entitled* to public daycare in order to *ensure their best interest* (Rauhala et al., 1997). The underlying constantly debated question has been how to ensure the best interests of the child, that is, whether through care in the home or in institutions (see Korsvold, Chapter 1). Despite these debates, the perspective that children should be entitled to public daycare in order to ensure their best interests has dominated policy making in the Nordic countries (Rauhala et al., 1997).

During the 1960s and 1970s all the Nordic countries increased subsidized daycare services and enacted a new law on daycare. According to the law, the municipalities played a major role in developing the services, which were subsidized and based on universal rights, and public regulations were developed concerning the administration (Broddadóttir et al., 1997; Sipilä, 1997). Iceland developed daycare in accordance with the Nordic daycare model, and in 1973 the Act on the Creation and Administration of Daycare Institutes (no. 29/1973) came into force, stating that the 'aim of daycare institutes is to give the children access to the guidance of pedagogy professionals and provide an environment that cultivates their personal and social development'. Daycare was, according to the law, under the jurisdiction of the Ministry of Education, which indicates that daycare in Iceland was regarded as an educational rather than a social issue (Broddadóttir et al., 1997). Family daycare was quite usual in Iceland, in particular for the younger children was regulated by the municipalities, in accordance with the Act on Local Social Services (no. 40/1991), and under the administration of the Ministry of Social Affairs.

Despite the similar characteristics, the volumes of daycare in the Nordic countries were quite different during the 1980s, as Table 2.4 shows.

Sweden and Denmark provided a larger number of children with daycare. Iceland and Norway provided relatively low volumes of daycare for children under the age of three years. The volume of daycare for children aged three to six was greater, but the majority of placements were part time. Thus, daycare provision in both countries was characterized by a modest provision of public daycare, where pedagogical goals and part-time care were emphasized (Broddadóttir et al., 1997; Finch, 2006; Leira, 1992; Rauhala et al., 1997).

The volume of daycare increased gradually in Iceland during the 1980s, but despite this the services did not match the growing need

Table 2.4 Children aged 0–2 years and 3–6 years enrolled in daycare institutions and family daycare in the Nordic countries in 1984, shown as a percentage of all children in the age groups

	0–2 years		3–6 years		
	Daycare	Family care	Daycare Full time	Daycare Part time	Family care
Denmark	18	23	43	8	7
Finland	7	12	17	10	4
Iceland	5	14	9	34	12
Norway	6	1	16	25	1
Sweden	17	13	33	21	19

Source: Hanssen and Elvehoj (1997), pp. 181–183.

among working parents. Iceland enacted a Pre Schools (Nursery Schools) Act no. 48 in 1991. This emphasized the educational and peda-gogical aspects of care for young children. This was, among other things, reflected in new terminology: all institutions would be called 'preschools' (the exact translation play school, Icl. *leikskóli*) and the nannies would be called preschool teachers. A new curriculum was also established in which children's play was defined as an educational tool (Eydal, 2008; Pre Schools (Nursery Schools) Act no. 48/1991). Fur-thermore, this act emphasized the independence and the role of the municipalities, which were considered to be responsible for the vol-ume and organization of daycare. It states: 'The local authorities shall supervise the building and running of pre-schools and bear the expenses involved, each in its own local government area; they shall be obliged to take the initiative to ensure places for the children in good pre-schools' (Pre-Schools (Nursery Schools) no. 78/1994). Thus, Icelandic parents do not have a legal guarantee for their child at a certain age as in the other Nordic countries. Furthermore, the Icelandic local authorities make their own policies within the framework of the Pre-school Act (Eydal and Satka, 2006).

Gradually the volume of daycare increased. In 1994 an electoral alliance of parties, left of centre, with the centre party came into power in Reykjavik. One of their main issues was to increase both with regard to the number of children enrolled and the hours attended. The alliance did increase the volume of daycare and similar development took place in other municipalities during the 1990s (Eydal and Ólafsson, 2008). Table 2.5 shows clearly a change in 2007 in comparison with 1984 (Table 2.4).

Table 2.5   Children aged 1–2 years and 3–5 years enrolled in daycare in the Nordic countries in 2006–2007, shown as a percentage of all children in the age groups

	0–1 years	1–2 years	3–5 years	0–5 years
Denmark	17	90	96	81
Finland	1	40	72	49
Iceland	7	80	95	75
Norway	4	69	94	71
Sweden	–	70	97	73

Source: Nordic Social-Statistical Committee (2008), p. 47.

Table 2.5 shows that the Icelandic volume of daycare is among the highest in the Nordic countries and only Denmark provides more care for children. The main explanations for the differences in daycare volumes are, on the one hand, the length of paid parental leave, as is the case in Sweden, and, on the other hand, cash-for-care schemes. Examples of the latter are of importance for the volume of daycare for children under three years in Finland (Salmi, 2006). Thus, the Nordic countries have chosen different paths to enable parents to work and care.

As already discussed in the section above on cash-for-care, most Icelandic municipalities are forced to make cuts in their budgets. Care and education for young children is financed by the municipalities and users' fees from parents, which covers only a small portion of the expenditure. For example, the figures from Reykjavik for 2008 show that the city pays 85 per cent of full-time care for children of two parents and 95 per cent of the costs for children of single parents (Viðskiptablaðið, 2009). This means that the financial circumstances of the municipalities can influence the level and quality of the services. There exist no comparable data on how the municipalities have met the need for cuts, but all have reduced their costs to some extent by reorganizing, and there are examples of increased user fees. The income of most municipalities is expected to decrease in the coming years due to the economic crisis; hence they will probably be forced to take further steps towards lower expenditure. How this will affect the quality and volume of is difficult to predict at this point in time.

Conclusion and discussion: Care policies at a crossroads?

Historically, the care of young children seems to have been defined as a private matter in the case of Iceland. Public care support for parents of young children developed at a slower rate in the 1970s and 1980s than was the case in the other Nordic countries, and the first laws on universal rights to paid parental leave were enacted relatively late in 1980 (Eydal, 2008). Gradually the volume of daycare services increased and in 2006 Iceland was second to Denmark when the number of children in daycare in the Nordic countries was compared. In 2000 Iceland enacted laws on equal entitlements of both parents to paid parental leave for three months for each parent, plus an additional joint three months. Thus, in a relatively short period of time, Iceland has moved from being the Nordic country with the least public care support given to parents of young children to being a country in which care policies clearly support the dual-earner model and where high daycare volumes and increased rights to paid parental leave have resulted in a large number of fathers utilizing their benefits (Finch, 2006). However, at the same time, Iceland offers less total support than the other Nordic countries. The period of paid parental leave is shorter, which, in the absence of cash-for-care or higher volumes of daycare for children under two years, creates what Ellingsæter (2006) has coined a 'childcare gap', describing the period from the end of parental leave until the enrolment in preschool is available. It was the stated aim of the government that came into power before the crisis to extend the period of paid parental leave, but the economic crisis created different results and instead several cuts have been made to the payments. Thus, Iceland seems to be at a crossroads: Will childcare policies be developed in line with the goals set prior to the economic crisis or will cutbacks lead to a change in policy?

So far there have been no changes in the character of the paid parental leave scheme and cutbacks have been aimed at the amounts paid to parents; the maximum amount paid has been reduced three times as well as the percentage for parents with an income over a certain amount. The municipalities have also been forced to make cuts in their budgets and there are already examples of higher user fees and lower cash-for-care benefits. The municipalities have also rearranged the services in order to cut costs. The services have not been changed in character nor have the policy goals been questioned. An important characteristic of the daycare services in Iceland is that the enrolment of children into preschool has never been considered in relation to the labour market status of the parents, thus children of unemployed parents have the same rights to preschool as children of parents with paid work. But will the public sector be forced to make further cuts and might these lead to changes in childcare policy?

The government that came into power after the crisis has emphasized that families with children should be protected against the influences of the crisis and it declared its will to create a Nordic welfare state in Iceland. A special welfare watchdog has been established. Its task is to observe the social and economical consequences of the crisis for families and individuals, and to report and make policy suggestions that will meet their needs (Velferðarvaktin, n.d.). The possibilities of the government following these goals will be defined by the recovery of the country's economy, but not even the specialists are in agreement about the severity and the length of the crisis. In light of heavy debts in both the public and the private sector, it is unavoidable that welfare expenditure will have to be reduced heavily during the next few years. It remains to be seen if or how these reductions will affect the benefits and services provided for children and their families.

Note

1. The Icelandic legislator uses the concept in the following way. Parental leave is used as an umbrella term that includes all paid leave in connection with childbirth (i. *Fæðingarorlof*), and the terms maternity and paternity leave refer to the individual entitlements of each parent to three months' paid parental leave.

References

Act on Local Social Services no. 40/1991.
Act on Maternity/Paternity and Parental Leave no. 95/2000.
Act on Maternity/Paternity and Parental Leave no. 90/2004.
Act on the Creation and Administration of Day-Care Institutes no. 29/1973.
Bergman, H. and Hobson, B. (2002) 'Compulsory Fatherhood: The Coding of Fatherhood in the Swedish Welfare State' in B. Hobson (ed.) *Making Men into Fathers. Men Masculinities and the Social Politics of Fatherhood* (Cambridge: Cambridge University Press).
Björnberg, U. and Dahlgren, L. (2008) 'Policy – The Case of Sweden' in I. Ostner and C. Schmitt (eds) *Family Policies in the Context of Family Change. The Nordic Countries in Comparative Perspective* (Wisbaden: Verlag fur Sozialwissenschaften).
Bradley, D. (1996) *Family Law and Political Culture – Scandinavian Laws in Comparative Perspective* (London: Sweet and Maxwell).
Brandth, B. and Kvande, E. (2003) *Fleksible fedre. Maskulinitet, arbeid, velferdsstat* (Flexible fathers. Masculinities, work and welfare state) (Oslo: Universitetsforlaget).
Broddadóttir, I., Eydal, G., Hrafnsdóttir, B. and Sigurðardóttir, S. H. (1997) 'The Development of Local Authority Social Services in Iceland' in J. Sipilä (ed.) *Social Care Services the Key to the Scandinavian Model* (Aldershot: Avebury).

Einarsdóttir, H. R. and Ólafsdóttir, I. B. (2007) Greiðslur til foreldra ungra barna í Kópavogi og Reykjanesbæ (Payments to parents of young children in Kópavogur and Reykjanesbaer) Unpublished BA thesis (Reykjavik: Faculty of Social Sciences, University of Iceland).

Ellingsæter, A. L. (2006) 'The Norwegian Childcare Regime and Its Paradoxes' in A. L. Ellingsæter and A. Leira (eds) *Politicising Parenthood in Scandinavia. Gender Relations in Welfare States* (Bristol: Policy Press).

Ellingsæter, A. L. and Leira, A. (eds) (2006) *Politicising Parenthood in Scandinavia. Gender Relations in Welfare States* (Bristol: Policy Press).

Eydal, G. B. (2008) 'Policies Promoting Care from Both Parents – the Case of Iceland' in G. B. Eydal and I. V. Gíslason (eds) *Equal Rights to Earn and Care – Parental Leave in Iceland* (Reykjavík: Félagsvísindastofnun Háskóla Íslands).

Eydal, G. B. and Gíslason, I. V. (2008) 'Paid Parental Leave in Iceland – History and Context' in G. B. Eydal and I. V. Gíslason (eds) *Equal Rights to Earn and Care – Parental Leave in Iceland* (Reykjavík: Félagsvísindastofnun Háskóla Íslands).

Eydal, G. B. and Kröger, T. (2009) 'Nordic Family Policies: Constructing Contexts for Social Work' in H. Forsberg and T. Kröger (eds) *Social Work and Child Welfare Politics through Nordic Lenses* (Bristol: Policy Press).

Eydal, G. B. and Ólafsson, S. (2008) 'Family Policies in Iceland: An Overveiw' in I. Ostner and C. Schmitt (eds) *Family Policies in the Context of Family Change – The Nordic Countries in Comparative Perspective* (Weisbaden: Verlag fur Socialwissenschaften).

Eydal, G. B. and Satka, M. (2006) 'Social Work and Nordic Welfare Policies for Children. Present Challenges in the Light of the Past', *European Journal of Social Work*, 9, 305–322.

Finch, N. (2006) 'Childcare and Parental Leave' in J. Bradshaw and A. Hatland (eds) *Social Policy, Employment and Family Change in Comparative Perspective* (Cheltenham: Edward Elgar).

Gallup Iceland (2003) *Viðhorfskannanir Gallup nr. 93 og 109*, http://www.hgj.is, accessed 11 November 2007.

Gauthier, H. A. (1996) *The State and the Family: A Comparative Analysis of Family Policies in Industrialized Countries* (Oxford: Clarendon Press).

Gíslason, I. (2007) *Parental Leave in Iceland. Bringing the Fathers In* (Akureyri: Centre for Gender Equality).

Hanssen, J-I. and Elvehoj, O-M. (1997) 'A Statistical Summary of the Development of Social Services' in J. Sipilä (ed.) *Social Care Services the Key to the Scandinavian Model* (Aldershot: Avebury).

Hatland, A. and Bradshaw, J. (eds) (2006) *Social Policy, Employment and Family Change in Comparative Perspective* (Cheltenham: Edward Elgar).

Hatland, A. and Mayhew, E. (2006) 'Parental Rights and Obligations' in A. Hatland and J. Bradshaw (eds) *Social Policy, Employment and Family Change in Comparative Perspective* (Cheltenham: Edward Elgar).

Hiilamo, H. and Kangas, O. (2006) *Trap for Women of Freedom to Choose? Political Frames in the Making of Child Home Care Allowance in Finland and Sweden*, Publications of the Department of Social Policy, University of Turku A18/2006.

Jónsson, Á. (2009) *Why Iceland? How One of the World's Smallest Countries Became the Meltdowns Biggest Casualty* (Columbus: McGraw-Hill).

54   *Modern Childhood: Historical and Comparative Perspectives*

Kangas, O. and Rostgaard, T. (2007) 'Preferences or Institutions? Work-Family Life Opportunities in Seven European Countries', *Journal of European Social Policy*, 17, 240–256.
Kjørholt, A. T. and Lidén, H. (2005) 'Children and Youth as Citizens: Symbolic Participants or Political Actors?' in H. Brembeck, B. Johansson and J. Kampmann (eds) *Beyond the Competent Child. Exploring Contemporary Childhoods in the Nordic Welfare Societies* (Roskilde: Roskilde University Press).
Lag om kommunalt vårdnadsbidrag, 2008:307 (Laws on cash-for-care from local authorities).
Lammi-Taskula, J. (2007) *Parental Leave for Fathers? Gendered Conceptions and Practices in Families with Young Children in Finland* (Helsinki: STAKES).
Leira, A. (1992) *Welfare States and Working Mothers: The Scandinavian Experience* (Cambridge: Cambridge University Press).
Leira, A. (1999) 'Cash-for-Child Care and Daddy Leave' in P. Moss and F. Deven (eds) *Parental Leave: Progress or Pitfall? Research and Policy Issues in Europe* (The Hague and Brussels: NIDI CBGS Publications).
Leira, A. (2006) 'Parenthood Change and Policy Reform in Scandinavia, 1970s–2000s' in A. L. Ellingsæter and A. Leira (eds) *Politicising Parenthood in Scandinavia. Gender Relations in Welfare States* (Bristol: Policy Press).
Moss, P. and O'Brien, M. (eds) (2006) *Employment Relation Research Series no. 57 International Review of Leave Policies and Related Research* (London: Department of Trade and Industry).
Nordic Social-Statistical Committee (2008) *Social Protection in the Nordic Countries 2006–2007. Scope, Expenditure and Financing* ((Copenhagen: Nordic Social-Statistical Committee (NOSOSCO)).
Ólafsson, S. (1999) *Íslenska leiðin* (The Icelandic Way) (Reykjavík: Tryggingastofnun Ríkisins).
Pre-Schools (Nursery Schools) Act no. 48/1991.
Pre-Schools (Nursery Schools) Act no. 78/1994.
Rauhala, P.-L., Andersson, M., Eydal, G. B., Ketola, O. and Warming, H. (1997) 'Why are Social Care Services a Gender Issue?' in J. Sipilä (ed.) *Social Care Services the Key to the Scandinavian Model* (Aldershot: Avebury).
Salmi, M. (2006) 'Parental Choice and the Passion for Equality in Finland' in A. Leira and A. L. Ellingsæter (eds) *Politicising Parenthood in Scandinavia Gender Relations in Welfare States* (Bristol: Policy Press).
Sipilä, J. (ed.) (1997) *Social Care Services – The Key to the Scandinavian Welfare Model* (Aldershot: Avebury).
Skevik, A. (2003) 'Children of the Welfare State: Individuals with Entitlements, or Hidden in the Family?' *Journal of Social Policy*, 32, 423–440.
Skevik, A. (2008) 'Family Policies in Norway' in I. Ostner and C. Schmitt (eds) *Family Policies in the Context of Family Change – The Nordic Countries in Comparative Perspective* (Weisbaden: Verlag fur Socialwissenschaften).
Stefansen, K. and Farstad, G. (2008) Småbarnsforeldres Omsorgsprosjekter (Parents of young children projects of care), *Tidsskrift for samfunnsforskning*, 49, 3, 343–374.
Velferðarvaktin (n.d.) (The Welfare Watch), http://www.felagsmalaraduneyti.is/velferdarvaktin/, accessed 15 December 2009.
Viðskiptablaðið (2009) Skattfé: Raunkostnaður leikskólanna um 8 milljarðar. Hvert bern kostar um 125 þúsund krónur á mánuði (Tax Money: Real Costs

of the Play Schools is 8 Billion: Each Child Costs 125 Thousand Kronas pr. Month) 21 January 2009, 3, 17.

Þingskjal 1065 (Parliamentary document 1065) (1999–2000) Frumvarp til laga um fæðingar- og foreldraorlof (Bill of laws on birth and parental leave). *Alþingistíðindi A-deild*, 125.

Þingskjal 357 (Parliamentary document 357) (2008–2009) Frumvarp til laga um ráðstafanir í ríkisfjármálum (Bill of laws on changes in the state finance). *Alþingistíðindi A deild*, 136.

Þingskjal 1310 (Parliamentary document 1310) (1999–2000) Lög um fæðingar- og foreldraorlof (Bill of laws on birth and parental leave). *Alþingistíðindi A deild*, 125.

Þingskjal 155 (Parliamentary document 155) (2009) Frumvarp til laga um ráðstafanir í ríkisfjármálum (Bill of laws on changes in the state finance). *Alþingistíðindi A-deild*, 137.

Þingskjal 315 (Parliamentary document 315) (2009–2010) Frumvarp til laga um breytingu á lögum um almannatryggingar, lögum um félagslega aðstoð, lögum um Ábyrgðasjóð launa, lögum um fæðingar- og foreldraorlof, lögum um málefni aldraðra og lögum umhúsnæðismál, með síðari breytingum (Bill of law on changes in various laws). *Alþingistíðindi A-deild*, 138.

Þingskjal 442 (Parliamentary document 442) (2009–2010) Breytingartillögurvið frv. til l. um breyt. á l. um almannatryggingar, lögum um félagslega aðstoð, lögum um Ábyrgðasjóð launa, lögum um fæðingar- og foreldraorlof, lögum um málefni aldraðra og lögum um húsnæðismál, með síðari breytingum (Proposals of changes to the bill of law on changes in various laws). *Alþingistíðindi A-deild*, 138.

Þingskjal 496 (Parliamentary document 496) (2009–2010) Lög um breytingu á lögum um almannatryggingar, lögum um félagslega aðstoð, lögum um Ábyrgðasjóð launa, lögum um fæðingar- og foreldraorlof, lögum um málefni aldraðra og lögum um húsnæðismál, með síðari breytingum (Law on changes in Acts on Social Security, Social Assistance, Parental leave, Affairs of Elderly and Housing). *Alþingistíðindi A-deild, 138*.

3
Free Choice or Gentle Force?
How Can Parental Leave Change Gender Practices?

Berit Brandth and Elin Kvande

Introduction

The question of how to get fathers to take more leave during a child's first year is a recurrent theme in the public debate, and a key point of view is that fathers 'get' or 'take' too little leave. The use of leave has been a hotly debated topic where participants have eagerly pointed to a number of scapegoats. The focus has in part been on 'fathers wanting to take some of the mothers' leave' and in part on how 'mothers do not want to give up leave'. The theme in this chapter is fathers' use of leave.

In 1993, Norway introduced the father's quota, which was a special quota of four weeks reserved for fathers.[1] At the same time the total period of parental leave was extended to one year (with 80 per cent parental money), most of which was optional. The father's quota has been a resounding success as around 85 per cent of entitled fathers have been registered to use it. However, one must not lose sight of the fact that the father's quota only amounts to a small share of the total leave time, and this has generally amounted to the average time taken for leave by fathers. The fact that fathers use only a small share of the leave time is the background for the debate on fathers and the extension of the quota.

The bulk of Norwegian parental leave is designed so that the mother and the father can share it, making it optional for fathers. On the introduction of the father's quota, it was hoped that it would encourage fathers to take more leave beyond the compulsory weeks. But this has not developed as expected, and only about 15 per cent of fathers take more leave than four weeks; for example, by sharing the optional leave period with the mother. In this chapter we are concerned with the question of why mothers and fathers do not share the leave more.

The freedom to choose is a key topic in today's debate on care policies. As pointed out in a number of studies (Brandth and Kvande, 2005; Ellingsæter, 2003), freedom to choose was also a prominent issue in the debate on the childcare allowance paid to parents who chose to stay home with a baby after the first year, and was one of the principal rationales behind this reform. On the introduction of the father's quota, the main objection was that the parents were given too little freedom to choose. Using a positive turn of phrase the then Minister of Children and Family Affairs called this phenomenon 'gentle coercion'. When we focus on freedom to choose in this chapter, we will be focusing on the freedom to choose whether the mother or the father should be home on leave.

The discussion on how fathers should have more (leave) time with children revolves around two solutions. One is to give fathers a longer leave quota; for example, a solution that does not promote the freedom to share. The other is to encourage the father to share more of the leave time, which means the freedom to share is still the focus. As we see, the rights to leave have been formulated both with special rights (which mean little freedom to choose) and common rights that can be shared (and are thus optional). What is it that leads fathers to use their quota to the extent they do, and what is it that makes them choose to not share the parental leave more? Should one focus on 'father's leave' or 'parental leave' in order for fathers to have more time for their children? Comparing the use of the father's quota and parental leave allows us to shed light on the importance of optional sharing if the intention is that fathers should take more of the leave time.

To bring these issues more into focus, we first describe the leave schemes and their objectives. Then we discuss how the father's quota and parental leave function when they interact with, respectively, working life and the prevailing gender pattern. We pay special attention to the processes that promote change and thus lead to fathers having more time for their children.

From motherhood, equal rights and fatherhood to free choice

Parental leave has had a changing focus over the years. During the early days of leave schemes, motherhood was in focus. Typically the leave schemes were called maternity leave or post-natal leave. The idea was to protect the woman from the demands of work, this being in her interest as well as the child's. Thus the nature of the earliest leave schemes was to provide special protection for women. It is interesting to draw parallels between today's debate and that at the start of the 1900s when maternal leave for women was under discussion. Here special protection for women was considered 'an infringement on the female right to self-determination' (Bull, 1953, p. 122), and the point was to protect the rights of the woman to decide for herself. Thus we can claim that we see two contrasting principles: on the one hand, women's freedom to choose and the unrestricted right to paid work, and, on the other hand, the emphasis on motherhood and the principal duty and responsibility of the woman.

In the 1970s *the idea of equal rights* was behind the extensions of leave. Mothers were to be ensured the opportunity to combine participation in the labour market with giving birth and providing care. Totally new with the leave reform of the 1970s was that some of the leave time could be shared between the parents; thus moving away from the idea of parental leave being an individual special right for women. By granting fathers the right to share leave, the legislation on leave in the 1970s signalled a new political view of men's responsibilities and participation in childcare. Both the parents had then been given rights and obligations in relation to the household and workplace.

In the 1980s and 1990s, leave schemes were developed gradually, mostly by extending the period. The idea of equal rights continued to be a strong rationale for extending parental leave. However, the parental leave that could be shared did not noticeably influence the fathers' use of leave, and thus the vision of equal parenthood did not get a boost. To further stimulate fathers to take leave, the father's quota was introduced in 1993. As mentioned above, this is an individual right given to fathers and not to the family as a caregiving entity. If the father does not use it, it is forfeited. With the father's quota, an additional rationale emerged – the child's need for a father. 'To strengthen the father's place in the child's life, it is important that he should take part in care-giving already during the child's first year. Some of the parental leave should therefore be reserved for the father' (Report to Parliament no.4, 1988–1989, p. 32). The purpose of a special father's quota was that the child would have better contact with the father. Thus the aim was to bolster not only equal rights but also fatherhood. As Håland (2005) has pointed out, the debate on the father's quota also contained a conflict between a liberal ideology propounding freedom from state control and legislation that one might describe as more 'paternalistic'.

Right from its inception, paternity leave has been a *gendered* scheme, as first the mother and then also the father was granted special rights. The point of departure for introducing the father's quota was an explicit political aim to strengthen the father–child relationship, but also, as a consequence of this, to change the gendered work division with respect to caring for small children. To accomplish this, the principle of *special rights* for fathers was adopted. Hence the decision about who would take leave was moved out of the family and up to the structural level to apply to 'all' fathers. It is a right that has been negotiated for men as fathers and employees. It is thus not up to each individual father or parental couple to choose who stays at home with the baby. Much more clearly than the other elements of parental leave, the debate on the father's quota has concerned the relationship between the state and individuals and not only the relationship between the genders.

For its part, parental leave is a family-based right. Therefore the principle of gender neutrality and freedom to choose comes strongly into play. The freedom to choose has always been a factor in the debate on leave schemes, but it has increasingly grown into an aim in itself in care policies since the late 1990s. This is linked, for example, to the political consideration of increased flexibility and freedom to choose for families, relegating equal rights and father–child contact more into the background. Something to bear in mind for further discussion is that when it comes to optional parental leave, the freedom to choose has been linked to those elements of the leave that are most clearly aimed at equality.

Fathers do not choose in a vacuum

Fathers' choice of leave is influenced by the context in which the choice is made. The context enables some actions and also places restrictions on others. Context here means both the structural influences that impact the choice of action (labour market, family structure, welfare state) and cultural influences (values, norms, discourses). Leave research has attached most importance to such structural influences as mother's and father's education and professional situation, while norms and discourses relating to male and female aspects have been the main focus when it comes to cultural influences (see Brandth and Kvande, 2003). Our point here is that we cannot only deal with fathers as such when studying their choice of actions, but also with fathers who are different because they have different social positions and identities. New father practices, such as leave, are thus not chosen with complete freedom. They are always chosen within the possibilities and limitations inherent in the individual placement in and understanding of working life, marital relationship and children.

The context may also be understood as a process; for example, something created continuously in social interaction. Thus, not only does the context impact choices but the choices made also influence the structural and cultural context.

A key *structural influence* for mothers' and fathers' use of welfare state schemes is the manner in which society is organized according to gender. In spite of significant changes in the last decade, the traditional gendered work division is a familiar pattern where most women have the primary responsibility for childcare and spend the most time with their children (Kitterød, 2002). One of the consequences is that a large proportion of today's Norwegian women work part time. Even though the two-provider family is the most common, men spend most time in working life, which also results in working overtime while the children are young (Kitterød and Kjelstad, 2003). In our study, around 40 per cent of fathers of young children worked overtime and 40 per cent of mothers worked part time (Brandth and Kvande, 2003). Even if the majority of today's Norwegian mothers of young children are in paid employment, part time is a relatively heavy structural influence affecting how leave schemes are understood and used by fathers.

Another important influence in this connection is the organization of working life. The leave scheme has been expanded during a time of major transformations in working life. A key factor here is the transition to the 'new working life' or 'flexible time regime', which in many enterprises means work intensification, where working hours have become more flexible and the work more limitless. The flexible time regime also means a greater degree of employee responsibility and more interesting jobs for many workers. This duality in parts of working life means that work encroaches on family life and leisure, and that the intentions of the schemes – for example, having more time for children – clash with developments in working life. Working life exists as an important structural context for the use of these schemes, and it is important to understand the fathers' use of the schemes in view of their work. The question is thus how the use of the leave schemes interacts with working life.

When it comes to *cultural influence*, we focus on the norms governing femininity and masculinity. A cultural ideal for men is to be successful in working life. Research has pointed out how important work is for men's construction of their masculine identities (Morgan, 1992) and thus for their time priorities. Connell (1987) uses the construct 'hegemonic masculinity' to describe the dominant cultural ideals for men. There is competition between the dominant and subordinate practices of masculinity. They are in conflict with one another, where one will come to dominate. As hegemonic masculinity identity is constructed in relation to participation in working life, it may conflict with being a participating father (Brandth and Kvande, 2003). Even if childcare generally has become part of masculinity for Norwegian men, in some environments this is still a field where masculinity is put to the test because looking after children is gendered as feminine. Thus part of the foundation for men's motivation is the question of whether they are at risk of losing their masculine reputation if they take this leave. How well do the schemes challenge the dominant gender norms?

When it comes to women, there are also strong norms as to what makes a good mother. In society's central schema, female identity and motherhood are intertwined. For example, there are many signs to suggest that taking a long period of leave is an expression of good motherhood, and breaking with this (for example, returning to work earlier) threatens such an understanding (Holter and Brandth, 2005).

The leave schemes are based on paid work and have been used to promote the political goal of increasing women's participation in the labour market. The design of the leave scheme has complied with the prevailing gender system when the intention has been to change it in a particular direction. One of the questions in this chapter is how the design of various care schemes influences fathers' use of them. As pointed out in the introduction, the debate has been on how fathers should receive a larger proportion of the leave. If this is what is desired, the question is whether special allocation (earmarking) or freedom to choose is the adequate measure to influence more fathers to take more leave, thus challenging gender as an important framing condition in society.

In this chapter we use data from a project dealing with parental leave. As a stage in this project, questionnaire material was collected and interviews were conducted with parents of young children. The sample for the questionnaire study included all men who had a child in two municipalities during a 12-month period in the mid-1990s. A questionnaire was sent to a sample of 2194 fathers. Of these, 1377 responded, giving a response rate of 62.8 per cent. We interviewed 30 fathers from this sample and their partners. The fathers worked in several types of job. The analysis in this chapter is mainly based on the interview data.

From gender neutrality to special right

As mentioned above, the introduction of the father's quota may be designated as a success story in Norwegian care policy when it comes to getting more fathers to spend more time with their children. We are interested in how to explain this. Our point of departure is the development of fathers' use of the quota. A study from the end of the 1980s found that less than 1 per cent of fathers shared the parental leave with the mother (Brandth and Kvande, 1989). As long as the leave was relatively short and based on the mother and father being free to share the leave between them, the proportion of fathers using it increased modestly from 1 to 4 per cent. The father's quota was introduced in April 1993, after which there was a dramatic increase in the proportion of fathers who took leave the following years, from 4 per cent in 1993 to 85 per cent in 2000. During the first four years after its introduction, taking leave changed from a minority practice to a majority practice among the fathers. After the extension of the quota to five and then six weeks in 2005 and 2006, the use of it has continued to stay high with 75 per cent of eligible fathers taking five weeks and more in 2007.

When we thus compare the use before and after the father's quota, we see that the *special quota* for fathers must have had a great effect. Today almost 90 per cent of the fathers entitled to leave take it. We believe that this may illustrate the importance of a right that is *earmarked* for them. During the period of time when it was up to the parents to negotiate whether and how a relatively short leave would be shared, it was the mother who used the leave in the vast majority of cases. The use of the gender-neutral scheme, which in principle was and is *optional* with respect to who takes the leave, is influenced by the encounter with the gendered society and reflects the prevailing gender patterns. Particularly in a field such as care for young children, which is so strongly divided along gender lines, gender-neutral and optional schemes will lead the majority of parents to choose the traditional models.

After the expansion of the leave time, it has been commonly assumed that this would lead more fathers to share the leave with the mothers. However, this has only occurred to a very small degree, and we may therefore assume that giving fathers a quota (a special right) is the way to go if the aim is a comprehensive and rapid change in this field.

A special right for fathers as employees

An important point with the father's quota is that it is a right men are granted as employees and fathers. For many fathers, the father's quota has functioned as that extra nudge necessary to get them to take leave at all. One of the fathers we interviewed, who was a warehouse employee and took leave under the father's quota when his second son was born, says the following about using the father's quota:

> Nor was there anything at my place of work that made it difficult. If they are notified in advance it is quite simple to take leave. I thought perhaps it would be more difficult to obtain the leave than it turned out. They were very accommodating, then.

His was one of the workplaces where having the right to leave was considered a natural part of the employment contract that the employer had to provide. The right to leave may be compared to cutting down on working hours, which one should make use of. Complying with the rules and norms of working life is part of the cultural context. The main principle in this workplace was normal working hours, and the reward and career structure was tied to a standardized working-hour culture where the formal work contract regulated working hours. Standardized working hours means working regular hours with a clear line drawn between work and leisure.

How this 'gentle force' that characterizes the father's quota functions is seen when those who do not see the point of a father's quota take leave, albeit reluctantly. A printing press employee we interviewed actually found it unnecessary that he take the father's quota. He would rather have worked, also because the mother wanted to be home after the leave period was over. He tried to have the quota transferred to her, but when this was impossible he took the leave himself. He says: 'There was a lot to do at work [...but] I'm stubborn enough to take what is mine.'

We also find this motivation in the questionnaire study, where 67 per cent of the fathers said that a special right was important and that it should be used accordingly (Brandth and Kvande, 2003). They see the father's quota as a right the state has given them, virtually as a gift they cannot decline. Most fathers would not have taken leave if the father's quota scheme had not been in place. Therefore many of these accept the offer from the state with surprise or even some reluctance. Nevertheless, the father's quota is a right they have been given that they therefore think they must use.

When it is an earmarked right for fathers as employees, the leave also contributes to setting a boundary in relation to the working-life requirements placed on fathers. This is particularly important for fathers working in so-called 'limitless jobs'. Such jobs are found in, for example, the knowledge professions. A typical representative of those who use the father's quota to set limits against their job requirements might be a researcher in technology. In the type of company where this professional group is working, employees have a large degree of independence and responsibility in their work. It is possible to work at home and juggle working hours. Many of the employees work beyond normal working hours and unregistered overtime is common. They become deeply involved in their work, feeling obligations to their work tasks and their colleagues. The fact that their efforts mean something ensures that the job is seen as demanding and fun at the same time. Thus it can be difficult to avoid getting carried away by the interesting work tasks and to control one's use of time. If an employee is unable to do so, the result is that she or he has to work long hours without compensation.

To summarize up to this point, we have seen that in many work situations the father's quota functions as an already negotiated 'boundary' in relation to the demands of work. Male employees who have become fathers are thus not forced to undertake individual negotiations with their employers to be allowed to use the right to parental leave. When it is a right that potentially applies to 'all' male workers, this means that it is easier to avoid the strain of being one among a minority who must take steps alone to get their leave. Precisely because the father's quota functions as an employee right, it appears to fit with men's and fathers' norms for what is acceptable grounds for being absent from work. This has probably also contributed to the development of a majority practice in the course of only a few years when it comes to the use of leave.

Parental leave – when free choice is a gendered choice

As mentioned in the introduction, parental leave stems from care policy thinking that builds on the idea that both mother and father must have the same rights and obligations in family and working life. When this has not functioned fully as originally envisaged, some of the explanation might be that the shareable and, in principle, gender-neutral parental leave in practice is gendered traditionally. Thus it does not function the same way as the father's quota does in relation to work.

For many fathers, sharing with the mother is simply not an option at all. Shareable parental leave is defined as a mother's right, and it would be very difficult to give it status as an employee right for fathers. Both the prevailing discourse and practice indicate that this is a mother's leave. In the words of one of the fathers: 'We never considered that we could share the paid leave. We never gave it a thought, like, thinking that this was possible.' It is taken for granted that the mother must be home after giving birth. The fathers tend to understand this leave as reward for the mother – something that is only right and proper considering pregnancy, birth and breast feeding. One of the mothers says:

> I think it was always like this, that it's the mother who is most connected to the kids, seeing as she breast feeds and stuff, you know. So then it's like she should be home, I think. . . . Everybody I know, at least, who has had kids, then it's like the mother stays home. So that's how it was with us, too. We didn't talk about him being home and me going to work and stuff, no we never did.

This thinking supports the complementary work division and thus makes it appear completely natural and obvious. There is a strong perception in the social debate that suggests that the mother excludes the father. However, it is overwhelmingly taken for granted that the mother should be home. There is no contestation about this. The father leaves it to the mother. When the public debate presents this mother's practice as the mother wanting to have the leave to herself, it is referring to the traditional cultural practice rather than a negotiation conflict between mother and father.

Among the couples sharing the parental leave, the mothers have higher professional positions with higher education and good salaries in full-time work than other couples. Also the fathers have relatively high positions in working life with good education and medium wages. These are relatively speaking high-status couples, and how the mother and father choose to make priorities in working life therefore has a considerable impact on their choice of leave. When the mother has a job that is important to her, we more often find that the leave is shared. However, this is not a sufficient reason, and must be combined with a father who wants to be with his child on parental leave. For such couples, equal rights is an important argument, perhaps precisely because they already have relatively equal positions in their working lives. One mother states:

> We found out that a 50–50 division is quite fair really, and bearing in mind that our incomes are fairly equal, it really doesn't matter that much. I wanted to go back to work and not stay away too long, and he wanted to be at home.

As the above quote illustrates, the father's wish to be at home on longer leave than the quota is important. When the motivation grounds and the structural influence are present, the chances of the leave being shared increase substantially.

Mothers who share the leave earn just as much, or more than, the fathers do. If the mother's income is substantially lower, the financial situation has a negative impact on sharing the leave as there is a ceiling of how much wage compensation is paid by the state, and not all private employers compensate for a possible income gap. One good example of this is a couple where the mother was a teacher in a primary school and the father was a corporate consultant with a private consultancy firm. He earned approximately twice what she did, and would have had his gross salary halved if he were to take leave because the employer did not pay the difference between the parental money compensation and his wages. For them, not sharing the leave was so self-evident that they did not even bother discussing it: 'The solution was given based on our situation'. Thus the skewed relation between what men and women earn in society becomes yet another gender-structural barrier that free choice must overcome.

The fact that parental leave is not a special right, rather it is given to the parents, means that it becomes negotiable in relation to working life. Other perceptions and rules apply then to the father's quota. Not only does it mean that fathers must be away from work longer, it is simply considered unnecessary for fathers since the baby has a mother. Our material indicates that primarily it is men in knowledge professions who initiate such negotiations with their employers. One representative of this is a computer engineer we interviewed. When his daughter was born, he used the father's quota while his wife was back working full time. They shared the parental leave so that they would each have six months leave. He found that taking a long leave was not so easy for fathers, stating:

> When a woman is pregnant, it is entirely natural that she must be home for a year, and everybody finds that quite reasonable. But when a man comes and says that he wants to be home for six months, the reaction is more like, 'oh, yeah' and 'why?', and then we are talking about grounds for negotiation. You need to ask your employer whether you can do this, but for the women this is not an issue. It's more like a formality, just sign this paper!

His employer was not overjoyed that he chose to take such a long leave, and he was forced to explain the grounds for his choice. The negative attitude nevertheless made him even more determined to take leave, he says. At the time he was employed by a small computer company with ten employees. He was in charge of developing software products. As the head of a project organization, he was responsible for customer contact and development of a product that was very important for the company. The company therefore felt that it would lose an important player if the engineer were to stay away for an extended period of time. He says:

> They tried to propose solutions, everything from paying for a place in a day-care centre to ... whether I could work a little bit, not every day, only a few days, 50 per cent or something similar.... I fully understand them, I really do. But I never heard, 'Sure, we really would like you to do this. I really think you should do this!' I received no support from my boss. I was supported by my colleagues, but not by my boss.

Even if fathers have the right to share the parental leave, many of them encounter resistance from the company where they work. This is a type of resistance mothers rarely encounter. Such resistance is also less of a stated problem when it comes to the father's quota, which is shorter and which over time has become accepted as something fathers should use. This father is working for a knowledge company where his work capacity is in demand, and the company easily becomes a greedy organization where employee knowledge is a resource that must be exploited continuously. It is also interesting to observe how he not only negotiates with his employer, who offers resistance, but also with his colleagues, who support him.

The father's quota – leave for building the father–child relationship

More than 90 per cent of the fathers who had used the father's quota responded that they had taken it because they wanted to be with their child. Also, almost 90 per cent believed that the child needed the presence of the father. Thus the relationship with child was a great motivational factor for the fathers. It is the child that draws the father home. In the words of one of the fathers, an industrial worker: 'That the dad gets a month's leave, I really think that is great so that the father also has contact with the baby and not just the mother. We both thought this was a great idea.'

We also see how important the child is in the fathers' ideas of what the leave is when we consider how they assign priorities when they are on leave. They take care of the child, change diapers, play with it and feed it. They focus on child upbringing, giving the child challenges and protection. Housework and its division between the mother and father is something else. This is the field where disagreements and conflicts between mother and father are played out to a much larger degree (Brandth and Kvande, 2003).

Many of the fathers can see it as a benefit for equal rights that they have also received rights that increase their contact with the child, but it is the relationship with the child, not the mother, that is important. One of the fathers says the following when asked what the father's quota meant to him:

> What was most positive was that I had contact with my son – I could be together with him and he also got to know me, you know. I really think so. Even if he saw me on a daily basis at other times too, I think it was special then. . . . and if you spend a lot of time with your child and care for it, and all that, then I think the child gets more familiar with the father and feels more safe and trusting.

We can therefore state that the father's quota is a reform for the father and child. When the fathers take the quota, this is primarily to bolster their relationship to and orientation towards their child. The fathers do not take leave to achieve equal rights with the mother. Bekkengen (2002) made similar findings in a study in Sweden, pointing out that such a focus on the child is particular to the Nordic countries. Child-oriented masculinity is a different matter than equal rights orientation. For the 'new man', the child is in the centre (Brandth and Kvande, 1998). This is also a masculinity that appears to be appreciated by the mothers.

Limited free choice gives fathers more time for their child

In this chapter we have focused on free choice in the sense that it is up to the parents to choose which of them takes the leave. We have compared the parental leave, which is optional when considered this way, with the father's quota, which is not. The optional scheme does not impact the fathers' use of leave the way the father's quota does, and we have attempted to understand some of the processes that might explain this.

There is much to suggest that two of the qualities of the father's quota, the fact that it is, in principle, a special right for fathers and that it thus offers limited free choice, positively impacts fathers' use of leave. It has liberated fathers from individual negotiations with their employers, and helped determine the borders of work obligations. It is also important that this type of right should focus on the obligations of male workers as fathers.

Parental leave does not have these same qualities. This leave is designed as a gender-neutral right in that both the mother and the father may use it, which also renders it relatively optional for the father. What we have seen is that this gender neutrality in design leads to a traditional gendered choice. Thus we see a continuation of the prevailing gender pattern where it is taken for granted that infant children are the mother's responsibility, which tells us that free choice impedes change. Parents slide into the same patterns when it comes to work division, even if they understand it as their individual choice. When the leave is optional, sharing it becomes the object of negotiations between the mother and father. It turns out that mothers with good education working full time are the motivating power when fathers take more leave than the father's quota.

The father's quota is based on fatherhood and focuses on male employees' obligations as fathers. It has thus helped normalize and legitimize the fact that employees of both genders have care obligations for their children. Traditionally, these obligations have been considered 'liabilities' with female employees.

The father's quota has made the care potential of fathers visible. It has made fathers in general accustomed both to the idea and to take it for granted that they must take the leave. Even if it has been claimed in the debate that fathers take too little leave, and that the move towards greater equality is too slow, we would point out the major changes that have taken place in ideals and norms. The fact that, and in spite of everything, around 15 per cent of fathers take leave that is longer than the father's quota may be connected to the normative qualities of the father's quota more than to free choice.

If parental leave is to function as equalizing for more couples, or, to put it another way, if free choice is to lead to the desired result that more fathers take parental leave, the contextual influence must be changed. This means that the perceptions of gender work division must be changed. When it comes to pay, gender differences must be reduced and greediness of work must be counteracted. Thus, some structures direct choices in a particular direction and these are not easily changed by the principle of free choice.

Note

1. Our study was carried out while the father's quota was four weeks. The quota has gradually been extended since its introduction. From 1 July 2011 the father's quota will be 12 weeks, and the total length of the leave period (which includes maternity leave, father's quota and parental leave) will be 57 weeks with 80 per cent pay.

References

Bekkengen, L. (2002) *Man får välja – om föräldraskap och föräldraledighet i arbetsliv och familjeliv* (A choice must be made – on parenthood and parental unemployment in working life and family life) (Stockholm: Liber).

Brandth, B. and Kvande, E. (1989) 'Like barn deler best' (Birds of a feather share together), *Nytt om kvinneforskning*, 13, 3, 8–17.

Brandth, B. and Kvande, E. (1998) 'Masculinity and Child Care – The Reconstruction of Fathering', *The Sociological Review*, 46, 2, 293–314.

Brandth, B. and Kvande, E. (2003) *Fleksible fedre* (Flexible fathers) (Oslo: Universitetsforlaget).

Brandth, B. and Kvande, E. (2005) 'Fedres valgfrihet og arbeidslivets tidskulturer' (Fathers' free choice and working-life's time cultures), *Tidsskrift for samfunnsforskning*, 46, 1, 35–54.

Bull, E. (1953) *Arbeidervern gjennom 60 år* (Worker protection through 60 years) (Oslo: Tiden norsk forlag A/S).

Connell, R. (1987) *Gender and Power* (Cambridge: Polity Press).

Ellingsæter, A. L. (2003) 'The Complexity of Family Policy Reform. The Case of Norway', *European Societies*, 5, 4, 419–443.

Holter, T. and Brandth, B. (2005) 'Tidskonto: Valgfrihet for elitemødre?' (The time account scheme: Free choice for elite mothers) in B. Brandth, B. Bungum and E. Kvande (eds) *Valgfrihetens tid* (Oslo: Gyldendal).

Håland, K. (2005) 'Fra enighet til strid i familiepolitikken' (From agreement to disagreement in family politics) in B. Brandth, B. Bungum and E. Kvande (eds) *Valgfrihetens tid* (Oslo: Gyldendal).

Kitterød, R. H. (2002) 'Store endringer i småbarnsforeldres dagligliv' (Major changes in the day-to-day lives of parents with small children), *Samfunnsspeilet*, 16, 4/5, 14–22.

Kitterød, R. H. and Kjeldstad, R. (2003) 'A New Father's Role? Employment Patterns among Norwegian Fathers 1991–2001', *Economic Survey*, 1, 39–51.

Morgan, D. H. J. (1992) *Discovering Men* (London: Routledge).

Report to Parliament no. 4 (1988–1989) Langtidsprogrammet 1990–1993 (The Long-term Programme 1990–1993) (Oslo).

4
'Flexible Flexibility'
Norwegian Politics of Daycare
Minna Rantalaiho

Introduction

During the last two or three decades, both demographic changes and changes in family and working life have challenged existing welfare policy rationales. Standard models of adult and family life have lost accuracy as starting points for welfare policy making. Wage work outside the context of the family has become a normal part of women's life course and, especially in the Nordic countries, women engage in paid work also when they have small children. Adults' attachment to the labour market is also introduced as the key to sustaining countries' levels of welfare, and many European welfare states are in a new situation as childcare has become an increasingly more central social question and a matter of active welfare policy making (Esping-Andersen, 2002; Taylor-Gooby, 2004). In the family policy sector, the focus has turned to the reconciliation of work and family life, and childcare policies are being reformed to support adults when they have to cope simultaneously with their responsibilities as parents and employees. A common trait for different welfare states and policy regimes seems to be the emergence of *flexibility and free choice* as a rhetoric device and policy rationale that frames childcare policy making (Lewis et al., 2008; Morel, 2007; Morgan and Zippel, 2003).

Considering that flexibility and choice represent a new strategy for welfare states in responding to social change, it is important to approach the strategy in different contexts and from different perspectives. In this chapter I will elaborate on the emergence of *flexibility* in the context of Norwegian politics relating to daycare. During the last two decades, several childcare policy reforms have been carried out in Norway that are framed by a rationale that perceives flexibility and choice as a generating means in advancing the reconciliation of work and family life (Brandth et al., 2005; Ellingsæter, 2007). My focus is on how the emerging flexibility transforms the frame of perceiving and understanding daycare as a meaningful social institution and as a social space *for children* (cf. Kjørholt and Tingstad, 2007).

This chapter is based on a discourse analysis of central policy documents and texts relating to the reform of Norwegian daycare policy.[1] I pay attention especially to discursive constructions of policy problems that frame the emerging flexibility in the context of daycare policy (cf. Bacchi, 1999), and the permeating question in the chapter is: What is the problem that flexibility is introduced as a solution to? Accordingly, daycare policy is approached here as a *practice of articulation* that aims to connect, mobilize and activate both meanings and the people who may be attached to them (cf. Clarke, 2004, pp. 52–71).

Comparing practices of articulation in policy making over time helps to distinguish transformations in what daycare is about and whom it is intended for and why, and also to elaborate what is *new* in the rationale of daycare. For that reason I will start from the late 1980s, when flexibility had not yet emerged in Norwegian daycare policy.

Daycare policies prior to the 1990s: A platform for new policy

In 1987, the Norwegian Ministry of Consumer Affairs and Government Administration[2] released the report to the Storting (Norwegian parliament) *Day Care Towards Year 2000* (St. meld. nr. 8, 1987–1988), which argued for a new and more offensive daycare policy. At that time, one-third of children under school age attended daycare, although 70 per cent of the mothers of preschool children were actually in work (Leira, 1992, pp. 58, 93). A huge gap between the demand for and provision of public daycare services clearly existed.

In the report, the government outlined three goals. The first concerned meeting the actual demand for daycare services, articulated as attaining *full coverage* in the provision of daycare. By full coverage the government referred to a situation in which 70 per cent of all preschool children (children under the age of seven years) attended daycare. The deadline for achieving this goal was set to 2000 and to succeed in that aim a national programme was deemed necessary to speed up the development of daycare services. The two other goals concerned the quality of daycare services and responsibility for control over services. The government saw it as necessary to train more qualified daycare personnel and wanted to assign the responsibility for approving new daycare centres to the municipalities. During the years to come, increases in service supply and the development of professional quality in daycare became a policy focus that proved challenging to reach (cf. Ellingsæter and Gulbrandsen, 2007).

In the aforementioned report (St. meld. nr. 8, 1987–1988) daycare is introduced as a field of activity with several different functions that take place in different spheres of Norwegian society, including the everyday lives of children. A premise of the argument for the new daycare policy is that daycare is a positive institution, both for an individual child and for children in general. The premise, however, implies considerable efforts in explaining and reasoning, and the report gives several examples of why attending daycare is beneficial for children and, in certain circumstances, even a recommendable alternative to parental care. Daycare is argued as having broad social and equalizing functions in society:

> The point of departure is the importance of day care for children so that they receive a good and equal foundation at the start. Day care shall give children care and possibilities to develop and qualify themselves to meet a society which is rapidly changing and continuously imposes new demands on those growing up. Day care is necessary to give families with small children support and relieve them from the burdens of daily childcare. (St. meld. nr. 8, 1987–1988, p. 5)

It was left without further specification as to what the possible inequalities between children are, but the rationale behind daycare was elaborated upon in more detail. The report emphasizes the function that daycare has as a mediator of common social values in society and constructs daycare as a childhood environment for learning critical evaluation and social skills. It is argued that learning takes place through peer activities. Daycare is introduced as an environment within which children can practise solidarity and community, within which the meanings of peer groups are constructed as central. Such articulation is characteristic of the report as a whole:

> The informal interplay between children is an important source for learning how to cooperate with others, the development of the ability to work together, and the ability to resolve conflicts. It opens for the developing of unity, companionship and personal friendship. These are qualities that will, as much as formal knowledge, have an impact

on the possibilities [for a child] to succeed as an adult. (St. meld. nr. 8, 1987–1988, p. 7)

In a report to the Storting from the late 1990s, *Day Care for the Best of the Children and Parents* (St. meld. nr. 27, 1999–2000), a corresponding discussion on the meaning of daycare can be found, but although the report points out that for children daycare centres are a place to make friends, the importance of peer groups as an arena for learning is no more emphasized than it was in the late 1980s. Furthermore, as in other more recent policy documents, children's solidarity and community are given much less space in the argument than in the late 1980s.

In the report to the Storting dating from the late 1980s (St. meld. nr. 8, 1987–1988), daycare services were also framed as a solution to the rapid and extensive social change ongoing in work and family life and were presented as a necessary precondition for gender equality. Moreover, daycare was considered as an indirect contribution to staff recruitment, to both public sector jobs and corporate sector production. Daycare services were explained as solving societal problems on a macro level and daycare policy was framed by a discourse in which *common need* had a central role, and arguments concerning it were expressed as imperatives:

We have to take into account that society has made itself dependent on that in the families with small children both parents are working. . . . Children, families, enterprises and society need day care now. (St. meld. nr. 8, 1987–1988, pp. 9, 14)

Needs related to daycare were perceived and constructed as collective social or societal needs. Later, the functions of daycare as an institution that mediates solidarity and other collective values as contributions to the common good were replaced by a discourse on *individual needs* determined by time and place. The common need argument for daycare was also present in the 1990s daycare policy discourse, but it had been moved to the background, whereas the needs that were emphasized were individual and private. Compared with the late 1980s, the emphasis on children's *common* needs was replaced in the 1990s with an emphasis on every child's *individual* needs. Also, children acquired a new status as *users* of daycare, and at the beginning of the 2000s it was argued that optimally the need for daycare services is defined by the user (St. meld. 24, 2002–2003). At that time, however, it had become clear that in this context 'user' does not necessarily refer to children. The *new* way of presenting daycare abstracted the functions that daycare has in society. Increased attention to individual needs focused discussions on diversity, resulting in the descriptions of daycare as an institution for mediating common norms and social values being, if not 'inappropriate', less important. I will return to this interesting transformation by way of introducing and defining the meaning of daycare as a social institution for children later in the chapter.

The 1990s: Flexibility breakthrough

In the early 1990s, parental leave was extended to nearly one year, and a decision was made to lower the age for starting school from seven to six years. These reforms reduced the number of daycare age children, but the gap between the demand for and supply of daycare services continued to increase (Ellingsæter and Gulbrandsen, 2007). If, in the 1980s, there had been a need to exert great efforts to legitimize daycare in Norwegian society, in the 1990s that was replaced by statements that referred to a consensus on reaching full coverage. Questions and issues that required reflection and elaboration concerned the *way of organizing* the services. The question that came into focus in policy in the 1990s was thus not whether but how the welfare state should organize public services.

In the early 1990s the government proposed reforming the daycare act that had been in use since 1975. The aim of the reform was to adjust the law to a new situation and future challenges. Reforming the school age was meant to change the age structure within daycare and provide more places for new groups of children. In this context, flexibility started to emerge in Norwegian daycare policy discourse:

[The] majority of children in the country have a place in day care, and more day-care centres are built so that they can be a provision for *all* children where families wish that. This requires a day-care provision that is flexible, taking into consideration both the systems of organization and opening hours and hours spent in day care. Day care should satisfy the needs of all groups of users. (Ot. prp. nr. 68, 1993–1994, p. 5)

In 1995, one year before the new law on daycare was to come into force, the Ministry of Children and Family Affairs introduced the 'Developmental Programme for the Day-Care Sector' (hereafter referred to as the DP). The DP was conducted in order to produce information and good models for the organization of daycare services. It was directed towards municipalities with the idea of encouraging them in the development of means to enable them to attain two explicit goals: first, to find out how more children under three years could be offered a daycare place, and secondly, to organize daycare in such a way that it was more adjusted to the needs of the users (Q-0861, 1995, p. 3). Flexibility played a central role in attaining these goals. Three problems emerged in the DP, each of which framed the introduction of *flexibility* as an element of organizing Norwegian daycare.

Effective use of daycare provision

The first problem concerned the need to reorganize services according to the school reform. A considerable number of daycare places were 'suddenly' available in a sector where the demand for services was increasing and exceeding what municipalities and private service producers could offer. The demand was greatest among families with small children and the vacant places were planned to be channelled to children under the age of three years. The increased percentage of the younger children in daycare was, however, considered an economic, practical and pedagogical challenge. A crucial aspect of the problem was that the care of children under three years was more expensive than the care of older daycare children, yet the reorganizing of the daycare sector was not supposed to cost more. Hence, a new model for carrying out the services was needed.

A solution was found in reorganization, and flexibility was introduced as *an instrument* that could make the transformation of services feasible in an effective way. In a leaflet prepared for municipalities (Q-0861, 1995), the Ministry of Children and Family Affairs made it clear that the economic issue was central, and that the DP should lead to organizational changes that increased flexibility and contributed to effective utilization of the capacity in daycare. The combination of children with different hours of care, flexible group organization and corresponding arrangements were mentioned and introduced also as contributions to cost savings. Municipalities were encouraged to 'work out/further develop plans and implement measures which contribute to breaking down the traditional focus on age and unit division in daycare centres' (Q-0861, 1995, p. 9).

In the final report (Q-0962, 1998) of the DP, the experiences from participating municipalities were elaborated upon and examples were given showing how *permanent* structures in daycare were defined as belonging to the *past* when flexibility was implemented in daycare. The new rationale extended even to the age group of children, which was also to be made flexible:

> [The] tendency for change is that the (age) limit for small children (who count double) is lowered. . . . day-care centres are no longer formed by an established number of children with a fixed variation in provision. Number of children and variation in provision are changing continuously. . . . One can . . . reckon that the most part of increase of productivity hitherto has taken place through changed organization of day-care centres and day-care groups and the 'rejuvenated' age group for the big children. (Q-0962, 1998, p. 36)

The quotation above refers to the practice of redefining the age group of children eligible for daycare. Under the new practice, a child who was not yet three years could be counted as that. In Norwegian daycare centres, children were normally dealt with in two age groups: those under three years of age and those over three years. When an 'almost-three-year-old' child was moved into a group of older children, a new 'under-three-year-old' child – now a child 'under two-and-half years' – could be offered a daycare place. Treating children's ages as flexible thus enabled effective use of daycare capacity. The new rationale, and the practice of it, was mainly legitimaized by economic arguments. Corresponding arguments for the effective use of both place and personnel can also be found in more recent government reports. At the end of 1999, in the report to the Storting Day Care for the Best of the Children and Parents (St. meld. nr. 27, 1999–2000), the government argued for flexibility in the pedagogic quality requirements of daycare services:

> It is important to underscore that the rules we have about the pedagogic manning are not rules about the size of each group of children. The pedagogic norms apply to the day-care centre as an entity. . . . It should be allowed to exceed the norms at certain times in a day or a week if at other times there are fewer children present than the norm permits. (St. meld. nr. 27, 1999–2000, p. 57)

While the above quotation includes the statement that flexibility should not lead to undermining the formal norms, it also reveals how the practising of the new daycare policy goals was perceived as requiring 'flexible children' as well (cf. Kjørholt and Tingstad, 2007). Anne Ma Sandve (2000) has characterized this new rationale for daycare by comparing it with the 'material administration of enterprise economy'

(Sandve, 2000, p. 75). From the DP documents and government reports to the Storting, it is easy to expose a discourse that constructed daycare centres as enterprises filled with a maximum number of children and where every opportunity to increase the input was to be utilized.

Diversity in demand

An additional problem with introducing flexibility as a solution to the provision of daycare related to the demand for the service. It was argued that the organization of daycare should take place 'in such a way that it becomes more adjusted to user's needs' (Q-0861, 1995, p. 3). This was not a completely novel goal as already in the late 1980s it had been argued that the opening hours of daycare should correspond more closely to families' needs (St. meld. nr. 8, 1987–1988). In the mid-1990s, user adjustment was, however, framed in a different discourse. The user no longer referred to a social group with clearly defined congruent needs, as it had done in the late 1980s. In the discourse that emerged in the mid-1990s, users were constructed as active participants and co-constructors in the formation of Norwegian daycare. Their needs were no longer constructed as the fixed needs of a 'passive' group of service recipients, but as the needs of individuals whose wishes were recognized as important to take into consideration in the organization and running of daycare. Paradoxically, a problem was achieving full-coverage, which, since the late 1980s it had continuously been the main focus of daycare policy, yet it now seemed unrealistic unless the provision of daycare corresponded to the needs and wishes of the users:

> Improved day-care coverage will change the relation between the day care and the users.... In such a situation day care will have to be, more than now, open to users' wishes and users' needs.... When a more user-adjusted and flexible day-care provision is realized, it is also reasonable to assume that parents who were previously not inter-ested in having a day-care place will start demanding the provision of day care that is in accordance with their own needs. (Q-0861, 1995, pp. 7–8)

It was no longer sufficient to produce plenty of new daycare services. The services produced also had to be in line with the quality of the demands. Moreover, the DP argued that when a group of users were extended, it would become more powerful in making demands in terms of both the structure and the content of daycare provision. Full cov-erage and user adjustment became a *paradoxical circle*: the more user adjustment and flexibility there was in services, the greater the demand for new adjustments and increased flexibility.

In one of the final reports of the DP (Q-0963, 1998, pp. 54–64), flexibility was defined in more detail by dividing it into 'structural flexibility' and 'spontaneous flexibility'. While structural flexibility referred to the supply side in daycare and variation in different part-time and full-time services, spontaneous flexibility concerned everyday activities in the context of daycare centres, such as the solving of and responding to various everyday situations that were scarcely discussed in detail in any of the policy documents. In contrast with structural flexibility, which was explained as concerning the parents of small children in general, spontaneous flexibility also referred to children.

The problem that structural flexibility was introduced to solve is relatively easy to identify. Flexible organization of daycare services was considered as both contributing to the productivity of the service sector and ensuring that daycare centres were used effectively. As the existing provision of daycare was not seen to correspond with the needs of parents with small children, increasing structural flexibility would enable parents to make individually adjusted childcare arrangements. Inflexibility in daycare (for example, rigid opening hours) did not correspond with other childcare policy where policy measures had been reformed to better support the way in which parents combined part-time care and part-time work. The reason why spontaneous flexibility was needed was more complex:

> It is also important to be aware that the users, here the parents, are not a homogeneous group. Adjustment and how it is implemented by individual users can vary greatly. They may desire different solutions, which are not always easy to combine in one and the same day-care centre. ... Ability of personnel in spontaneous flexibility comes out in the actions both together with children and parents. Do they succeed in creating good secure relations for their users? Do they [personnel] succeed in acting together with them, in such a way that they [parents] feel that they themselves are respected, and taken seriously in relation to their own children and their own everyday tasks? (Q-0962, 1998, pp. 54–55)

It seems that spontaneous flexibility, which concerns everyday activities in the context of daycare centres, and hence also children's experiences, was a *precondition* for structural flexibility. Thus, the problem was that as there were no definite structures for running daycare services, and given the demand to adjust to the different needs of different users, the provision of daycare had become a complex action that required practising spontaneous flexibility.

It is important to mention here that both in the early DP documents and in the final report the demand for increased user adjustment had been approached also from a more critical perspective. It was pointed out that when 'increased user-adjustment poses extensive demands for flexibility and readjusting capacity on the daycare sector', the measures should 'create an understanding that user-adjustment must be balanced towards the role of daycare as a pedagogic supply for children' (Q-0861, 1995, pp. 3–4).

The early DP documents and the final report also referred to the dynamic relationship between individual and collective needs. It was argued that for daycare services to function well, both individual and collective needs had to be in balance:

> It is extremely important to make clear what the target group is that the user-adjustment is directed to. Success for one target group does not necessarily mean success for another.... Parents will not, in reality, gain from solutions that fulfil their individual needs if this is at the expense of the care that their children receive.... There is a certain risk that until now, in many places user-adjustment has been defined only as increasing the possibilities for making individual choices amongst all kinds of places offered in day care.... A challenge will be to find a level of user-adjustment and flexibility in day care with which all parties can be satisfied. (Q-0962, 1998, pp. 61–63)

These comments are important, as they channelled concerns based on the experiences of everyday life in daycare centres. Equally important is the mention that these concerns remained marginal compared with the strong ethos of flexibility and choice in daycare policy argumentation. Moreover, even the more concerned statements 'accepted' the rationale that as long as some potential users still lacked access to services it was difficult to give a more distinct definition of the appropriate level of user adjustment and flexibility in daycare.

In-synchrony of time regimes

The dominance of time discourse uncovers another function of flexibility. A mismatch between the time regimes of daycare users and daycare centres was identified as a problem and flexibility was constructed as the solution. User adjustment was constructed as 'complying with parents' need for increased flexibility by offering places with different hours of stay' (Q-0962, 1998, p. 46). The centrality of the time dimension in the implementation of new policy and reorganization of the Norwegian daycare system is clear in the DP's final report. Based on the municipalities' experiences, the report (ibid.) introduced 12 example operations that could increase flexibility in daycare of which nine concerned time:

- Divided full-time places.
- Extended opening hours.
- Selling of separate hours and days.
- Variation between full-time provision and shorter days.
- Different opening hours during different seasons.
- Changing the arrangement when the need changes. For example, parents keep their arrangement with the daycare centre when on parental leave, but as a part-time arrangement.
- Introducing open daycare centres for children in a neighbourhood for shorter periods; for example, a few hours per week.
- Removing core-time.
- Parents themselves choosing when they use the hours they have paid for.

Three examples that did not refer to time concerned developing different solutions based on the needs of the parents, adjusting services for immigrant parents and children, and developing and improving the play environment for children. The latter was the only example that explicitly focused on children.

Towards the 2000s: Flexibility becomes institutionalized

In the late 1990s, flexibility started to emerge in various different contexts and often without any clear specifications. There was no longer a solution to one, two or three fairly distinguishable problems in Norwegian daycare. Furthermore, I would argue that following the DP, flexibility started to represent an institutionalized element in the model of practising daycare at policy level as much as in daycare centres (cf. Kjørholt and Tingstad, 2007). As in other spheres of childcare policy (Brandth et al., 2005), also in the context of daycare the rationale of flexibility had started to grow into an aim in itself. Flexibility started to move from being a policy instrument to representing a *quality* of Norwegian daycare.

In 1999, the government released the report to the Storting Day Care for the Best of the Children and Parents (St. meld. nr. 27, 1999–2000), which introduced a two-fold goal for future daycare policy. Accordingly, daycare policy aimed for '*varied, flexible and user-friendly*' daycare services that were '*for all children*'. At first sight, the practice offered nothing very new. At the same time a new programme, 'The Good Day Care: Quality Development 2001–2003', was introduced. This paid attention to professional work, arguing that the existence of competent personnel was a condition for success in developing quality in daycare. Professional work was also related to managing user-adjusted daycare centres that ensured good conditions for children to grow up in and, at the same time, provided a service for parents, and thereby the programme continued with the previous emphasis on user adjustment. The quality development was introduced as a holistic approach to good daycare:

> The day-care service is a means of securing the conditions in which children are growing up, but is also a service provided for the families. The day-care sector must thus be both user and service-oriented. The *good day-care centre* shall cover the different needs of families with children. Simultaneously, day-care centres shall take care of children's needs for security, care and learning. In order to meet these ends, it is desirable that day-care centres are developed in cooperation with parents and children. (Q-1029, 2001, p. 3)

In the early stages of the new programme the daycare gap had still not been closed. The government's focus could not be solely on quality but also needed to reflect quantity. The full coverage goal had turned out to be a 'moving target' (cf. Ellingsæter and Gulbrandsen, 2007). Achieving full coverage was challenging as it had become increasingly interdependent on user adjustment:

> A right dimensioning of day-care sector depends … on how we succeed in catching up with the wishes parents have concerning the places for their children. The full-coverage goal includes also that families have the type of place they believe they need and wish for. (St. meld. nr. 27, 1999–2000, p. 31)

In the late 1990s and early 2000s, the daycare policy discourse 'daycare for all' was put forward as a quality investment, yet the policy texts were ambiguous as to the concrete meaning. Flexible and user-adjusted daycare centres that correspond to the needs of both children and parents were mentioned as representing quality, but, on the other hand, it was also argued that these goals must not affect quality:

> Day-care centres must have a pedagogic content, a view of life, organization types and opening hours that cover the needs parents have for flexible and user-adjusted provision.... Flexibility and user-adjustment in the provision of day care must not affect the quality of services that day-care centres provide for children. (St. meld. nr. 27, 1999–2000, pp. 76–77).

A more detailed analysis of the statements about quality, on the one hand, and flexibility and user adjustment, on the other hand, reveals that the two goals were also anchored in distinct rationales. Flexibility and user adjustment are mainly discussed in the context of parents' and families' individual needs, but quality is elaborated also in the context of abstract references to 'daycare for all children':

> [D]ay-care supply shall reach all children when families wish for that, regardless of place of residence, social, cultural, and economic background. (St. meld. nr. 27, 1999–2000, p. 73)

Referring to 'all children' did not indicate an assumption that each and every child should attend daycare but was rather meant to argue that no group of children should be excluded from daycare. At this point in time the rationale of life-long learning had started to play a more central role also in Norwegian daycare policy discourse. It was argued that daycare has an important role for special groups of children (for example, children with a non-Norwegian background and in need of cultural integration) as it can help to prevent social problems (St. meld. nr. 27, 1999–2000). Life-long learning had also been mentioned in some earlier documents (NOU, 1992, p. 16; St. meld. nr. 8, 1987–1988, p. 7), but learning then was articulated as a normal part of any childhood and as an integrated part of children's everyday activities in daycare. In comparison, in the late 1990s the social value of children's learning seemed to be moving 'outside' children's everyday activities and experiences in daycare.

Constructions of children and childhood

Before presenting the final discussion, I will return to the mid-1990s and reflect on how the 'new' policy rationale of daycare positioned children and constructed childhood. Two shorter extracts from policy texts serve to illustrate how the position of children was regarded in the reorganization of Norwegian daycare. The first extract concerns the needs of children and flexibility. In the DP it was pointed out that one of the challenges facing the daycare sector was serving the interests of both children and parents:

> It has proven that the flexibility that personnel are capable and will-ing to apply, to a great extent, affects how much children enjoy their stay at a day-care centre. (Q-0963, 1998, p. 12)

Flexibility was understood as a quality of daycare personnel that could have a positive impact on children's wellbeing in the daycare context, and was articulated as a means of fulfilling the goals of daycare. The premise was that personnel had the necessary resources and were willing to make flexibility work.[3] It was also acknowledged that such flexibility could have negative effects on children's wellbeing. The question was raised as to whether it was plausible that flexibility in group size, in the opening hours of daycare and in new interpretations concerning the age of children had negative impacts on children's wellbeing (Q-0962, 1998, pp. 60–61). Interestingly, perhaps also revealingly, no positive outcomes from the new policy model for children were mentioned. Flex-ibility in group formation was perceived as a response to the demand for increased user adjustment in daycare. In this context, children were constructed not as active users but as (passive) recipients of services. Neither inventive group forming nor higher spontaneity when reflect-ing on changing situations in particular daycare centres were considered as particular adjustments to children's wishes or needs.

The fact that adjustments to the needs of groups other than children could have a negative impact on children's wellbeing in daycare centres was acknowledged also reveals that flexibility was not considered as any guarantee of quality services for children – flexibility was, however, a legitimate strategy for daycare policy as long as it did not cause *any harm* to them.

My other reflection relates to the rhetoric of *choice*. In the policy texts that I have studied, there are frequent statements referring to parents' *wishes*, yet children are mostly presented as having *needs*:

> There has been established knowledge and experience on how far it is defensible to go, and about the role of daycare, in undertaking con-tinuous adjustment between parents' wishes and what are considered

to be children's needs, together with that which is considered a rational organization. (St. meld. nr. 27, 1999–2000, p. 38)

One may consider how these statements on wishes and needs positioned parents and children in the context of daycare. Pointing out that parents have wishes, and that these should be respected, constructs parents as subjects with the agency and power to define what 'good' daycare is. Pointing out that children have needs has a contrary effect. Although children can, through expressing their needs, also use agency, such *needs* are not open to variation in similar ways as *wishes* are. Moreover, if needs are referred to as natural 'givens' and self-evident, as they often are, children are perceived as recipients of that which meets those needs. In the daycare policy texts dating from the 1990s, the *dominant* discourse on flexibility did not perceive children in an actor position, their wishes were not mentioned, and they were clearly not considered as users of services *on a par* with adults (cf. Kjørholt and Tingstad, 2007; Sandve, 2000, pp. 80–81). In my view, this relates to a critical way of articulating the concerns that increased flexibility can cause some negative outcomes with regard to children. When the everyday lives of children are indirectly referred to in these more critical statements, children are mostly perceived as a group. The negative impacts of flexibility are identified where these become a threat to children as a 'collective'. Interestingly, the question of whether increased flexibility can cause harm to an individual child was not raised as a matter of concern.

Simultaneously, with increased focus on user adjustment, children's participatory rights were raised in the context of daycare policy (cf. Kjørholt and Tingstad, 2007). In the 1999 report to the Storting, the government argued that 'children must be allowed to be children on their own terms, based on their own interests, and they must be protected from "adult control"' (St. meld. nr. 27, 1999–2000, p. 73). Moreover, it mentioned that children could be given user status. It argued that children should be listened to and that based on their statements, the regulations and routines in daycare centres should be made flexible for individual adjustment (ibid., p. 77). It is important to note that in the report, children's status as users was constructed on an individual level and in a situational context. As users, children's democratic participation and power to influence daycare services was placed in the context of 'spontaneous flexibility' (see above) – in other words, the everyday activities of a daycare centre. Children's user status did not extend to larger structural questions, such as models for organizing age groups or appropriate ratios of competent personnel to children in daycare. Rather, children were attributed partial and incomplete user status and accordingly their statements and knowledge on daycare remained under-utilized. When more extensive structural changes were to be made, these would not be approached from a user perspective that emphasized children's experiences as a collective. This can be further illustrated with an example from a document in the early 2000s.

The report to the Storting, *Day Care Services for All – Economy, Manifoldness and Freedom of Choice* (St. meld. nr. 24, 2002–2003), argued strongly for freedom of choice in the provision of daycare for children and for the parents as well as for local actors. The background to the report was a daycare agreement that all political parties had signed and that defined major lines for daycare policy (for example, maximum rates for service fees). The main focus in the report was not on the activities in daycare centres but on larger structural questions. Upon initial reading it seemed to have less value for my analytical interest. However, after closer reading it reveals an interesting construction of the daycare user in the context of introducing a new model for financing ambitious daycare reform:

> There will always be limits as to how much of the resources can be used on the public sector. Municipalities have, based on their closeness to users, better possibilities than the state to prioritize these scarce resources in connection with variations in local needs and conditions. Meanwhile, effective service production requires engaged citizens and users who can 'control' the municipalities. (St. meld. nr. 24, 2002–2003, p. 7)

The ultimate responsibility for daycare services was thus 'decentralized' to users. High levels of state regulation were constructed as a threat to diversity in services, and critiques of an authoritarian public policy were given a central position in the report to the Storting. Although children were also given presence in many (often ambiguous) statements in the report, in the extract above the term 'user' can hardly be replaced by the term 'child'.

Discussion

According to Monique Kremer (2007), in order to understand childcare policy it is not sufficient to trust in a political or cultural explanation, but rather one needs to approach the *ideals* of childcare in a given society. In this chapter I have described how the concept of flexibility was moved from being first a policy instrument (a means of reaching policy goals) to representing a quality (a goal in itself) of Norwegian daycare. In the 1980s, the point in time where I started my analysis, flexibility did not belong to the ideals of Norwegian childcare. Ten years later, however, it was more or less an institutionalized dimension of the Norwegian daycare policy rationale. Representations of daycare as a particular social and cultural space were simultaneously changed and the images of childhood and what it means to be a child were transformed (cf. Kjørholt and Tingstad, 2007, p. 169).

Comparing articulations of daycare policy over time has revealed ambiguities in the user-oriented rationales that first started to emerge in the mid-1990s, and which soon became institutionalized as a dominant strategy in developing the sector. Although the interests of adults and children were not necessarily constructed as contradictory, it is important to bear in mind that most often it was the interests of adults that dominated as the point of departure while the interests of children, if mentioned, were articulated in more ambiguous ways. This ambiguity is embodied in the two-fold goal of Norwegian daycare; it should secure children's wellbeing but at the same time satisfy the needs and wishes of parents – who, in daycare discourse, configure as working adults in the changing labour market.

Contrast between the 'new' daycare discourse and that dating from the late 1980s came forth also in the way of constructing images of the 'good childhood'. In the 1980s, the daycare discourse emphasis was still on *children's* common needs and mutual solidarity as well as on the role of daycare in providing these. From the mid-1990s, the 'good childhood' was more often articulated in a discourse that concerns the *individual child*. The meeting of individual needs, whether of a child, a family or a parent, is explained by requiring user adjustment and flexibility in the organization of daycare. Another important reflection on flexibility here is that, as in the late 1980s policy texts when quality was articulated as a concrete goal of increasing the level of pedagogic investment in daycare, in the late 1990s the content of quality in daycare was 'opened' up to various interpretations. In addition, while in the late 1980s quality in daycare referred to competent personnel, by the late 1990s it also referred to competence in meeting the various needs and wishes of users – in other words, flexibility and user adjustment. From a child's perspective, a critical question this chapter raises is to what extent the emergence of flexibility has been a quality investment in their wellbeing in daycare.

Notes

1. Namely, government proposals relating to the reforming of daycare policy and other central written documents and reports that relate to daycare policy programmes on a national level.
2. Later the Ministry of Children and Family, and currently the Ministry of Children and Equality.
3. Whether this was the situation in daycare centres was not evaluated to the same extent as the models of user-adjusted and flexible organization of daycare and effective use of resources.

References

Bacchi, C. L. (1999) *Women, Policy and Politics. The Construction of Policy Problems* (London: Sage).

Brandth, B., Bungum, B. and Kvande, E. (eds) (2005) *Valgfrihetens tid* (Time for freedom of choice) (Oslo: Gyldendal).

Clarke, J. (2004) *Changing Welfare, Changing States: New Directions in Social Policy* (London: Sage).

Ellingsæter, A. L. (2007) '"Old" and "New" Politics of Time to Care: Three Norwegian Reforms', *Journal of European Social Policy*, 17, 1, 49–60.

Ellingsæter, A. L. and Gulbrandsen, L. (2007) 'Closing the Childcare Gap: The Interaction of Childcare Provision and Mothers' Agency in Norway', *Journal of Social Policy*, 36, 4, 649–669.

Esping-Andersen, G. (2002) 'A Child-Centred Social Investment Strategy' in G. Esping-Andersen, D. Gallie, A. Hemerijck and J. Myles (eds) *Why We Need a New Welfare State* (New York: Oxford University Press).

Kjørholt, A. T. and Tingstad, V. (2007) 'Flexible Places for Flexible Children? Discourses on New Kindergarten Architecture' in H. Zeiher, D. Devine, A. T. Kjørholt and H. Strandell (eds) *Flexible Childhood? Exploring Children's Welfare in Time and Space, Vol. 2 of COST A19: Children's Welfare* (Odense: University Press of Southern Denmark).

Kremer, M. (2007) *How Welfare States Care: Culture, Gender and Parenting in Europe* (Amsterdam: Amsterdam University Press).

Leira, A. (1992) *Welfare States and Working Mothers* (Cambridge: Cambridge University Press).

Lewis, J., Knijn, T., Martin, C. and Ostner, I. (2008) 'Patterns of Development in Work/Family Reconciliation Policies for Parents in France, Germany, the Netherlands, and the UK in the 2000s', *Social Politics: International Studies in Gender, State & Society*, 15, 3, 261–296.

Morel, N. (2007) 'From Subsidiarity to "Free Choice": Child- and Elder-Care Policy Reforms in France, Belgium, Germany and the Netherlands', *Social Policy & Administration*, 41, 6, 618–637.

Morgan, K. J. and Zippel, K. (2003) 'Paid to Care: The Origins and Effects of Care Leave Policies in Western Europe', *Social Politics*, 10, 49–85.

NOU (1992) Rammeplan for barnehagen (Framework plan for day care). Norges offentlige utredninger 1992:17 (Oslo: Statens forvaltningstjeneste).

Ot. prp. nr. 68 (1993–1994) Om lov om barnehager (About the day-care Act) (Oslo: Barne- og familiedepartementet).

Q-0861 (1995) Utviklingsprogrammet for barnehagesektoren. Informasjon til kommunane (Development programme for day-care sector. Information to municipalities) (Oslo: Barne- og familiedepartementet).

Q-0962 (1998) Utviklingsprogrammet for barnehagesektoren 1995–1997: sluttrapport (Development programme for day-care sector 1995–1997: final report) (Oslo: Barne- og familiedepartementet).

Q-0963 (1998) Barnehager til alle som ønsker det! Resultater og erfaringer fra Utviklingsprogrammet for barnehagesektoren 1995–97 (Day care for all who wish it! Results and experiences from the Development programme for day-care sector 1995–97) (Oslo: Barne- og familiedepartementet.)

Q-1029 (2001) Den gode barnehagen: Kvalitetsutvikling 2001–2003 (The good day care: Quality development 2001–2003) (http://odin.dep.no/bfd/norsk/publ/veiledninger/004071-120015/dok-bn.html, accessed 5 April 2004).

Sandve, A. M. (2000) Kvalitet i barnehagen – for hvem? (Quality in day care – for whom?) Hovedoppgave i barnehagepedagogikk (Oslo: Høgskolen i Oslo).

St. meld. nr. 8 (1987–1988) Barnehager mot år 2000 (Day care towards year 2000) (Oslo: Forbruker- og administrasjonsdepartementet).

St. meld. nr. 27 (1999–2000) Barnehage til beste for barn og foreldre (Day care for the best of the children and parents) (Oslo: Barne- og familiedepartementet).

St. meld. nr. 24 (2002–2003) Barnehagetilbud til alle – økonomi, mangfold og valgfrihet (Day care services for all – economy, manifoldness and freedom of choice) (Oslo: Barne- og familiedepartementet).

Taylor-Gooby, P. (ed.) (2004) *New Risks, New Welfare: The Transformation of the European Welfare State* (Oxford: Oxford University Press).

5

Kindergartens in Denmark – Reflections on Continuity and Change

Eva Gulløv

Introduction

The Danish model of childcare differs from that of most other European countries, as the market, the educational system and the family play less influential roles in the care of preschool children. Consistent with other welfare regimes based on a strong public sector and a high level of taxation, early childcare institutions in Denmark are characterized by a pronounced public engagement and funding, and a strong principle of universalism and social education. Daycare institutions are meant to be integrative with the aim of overcoming social boundaries and classes, and this purpose defines the curriculum. Rather than more subject-oriented learning or school preparation, the educational content stresses inclusion, social behaviour and forms of communication.

These features are, however, changing. In recent years, childcare has received much more political attention, resulting in new demands on institutional efforts. Institutions are now considered part of the educational system. Until recently, it was up to the institutions themselves to define and organize the educational visions within the broad mandate of the state. Now, the state defines aims and objectives, leaving it to the institutions to comply.

These changes are the topic of this chapter. In the first section, I will briefly describe the distinctive features of the Danish kindergarten in a historical perspective; in the second, I will present some reflections on the position of the kindergarten in contemporary society. Glancing over the long history of out-of-family care, it is possible to identify lines of continuity as well as change caused by changing political visions. The latter seem most evident in more recent years, where political attention to early childcare has been more pronounced. As I will argue, new ideological ideas are about to alter the kindergarten, since children have become objects of intense political interest and investment. The traditional virtue of social education is particularly under pressure. Kindergartens today are forced to focus on outcome, that is, skills relating to the educational system rather than regarding social processes among children as a result in itself.

Asylums and kindergartens in the nineteenth and early twentieth centuries

In many respects, the early history of daycare runs along the same lines in several Western countries. The process reflects the rise and consolidation of what researchers have labelled 'the social state' (Bloch et al., 2003, p. 14), a notion that refers to the discourses, policies and strategies for caring for citizens that developed in the nineteenth and early twentieth centuries. Though the means and timing differed across Western nations, the politics of childcare reflected new understandings of the normal child, the parent, education and care as well as individual and national wellbeing (ibid., p. 15; Rose, 1999, Part 3). New ways of reasoning combined with processes of industrialization and urbanization resulted in social welfare policies redefining the responsibilities of the state as well as the individual.

Though Denmark came relatively late to the process of industrialization, the process had the same kind of turbulent effects on demography, the labour market, work forms, social relations and family structure, as in other countries. The vast number of people who moved to the cities from the countryside in the last half of the nineteenth century in particular experienced a break-up of work forms and family patterns. Children were, to a large extent, left to guard each other as parents worked all day, and the number of children left home alone or loitering in the streets became a matter of public debate (Sigsgaard, 1978). As the dominant view on society held economic liberalism as its catechism, social responsibility, care and charity were, however, seen as a personal rather than a public concern. From the 1830s onwards, philanthropic associations and benevolent institutions were established on private initiative, targeting the growing number of people, particularly children, in need (Skovgaard-Petersen, 1985, pp. 130–131). In 1828, the first day nursery, *asyl* (asylum), opened and several other asylums and orphanages followed. By the end of the century, about 100 of these institutions existed, each accommodating 130–250 children, with very few adults and severe disciplinary practices (Coninck-Smith, 1995, pp. 10–11). The target group was children from the lower classes, as the aim of the institutions was to keep children away from the streets and bad company while their parents worked, and to instil basic manners through harsh discipline. Though charity was the outset, the treatment was not romantic.

As in other Western European countries, this protectionist project was, however, only one part of the story. Another form of childcare was inspired by the theories of Friederich Fröbel (1782–1852), who argued the significance of early education outside home where children, through play, should be intellectually stimulated. Inspired by ideas from the Enlightenment and progressive thinkers in contemporary society, he held the view that children have unique needs and capabilities, which ought to be nourished by specific educational programmes and artefacts. Activities such as playing, dancing, singing and gardening would influence the development of the child positively, as would carefully designed materials and toys. Fröbel invented the term 'kindergarten' as the name of the playing and activity institute he established in 1840 (Fröbel, 1980, first edition probably published in 1844).

Fröbel's ideas came at a time when children had become a subject of general interest, at least in better-off circles, and romantic ideas of the nature of children and the uniqueness of childhood were popular. His educational ideas and programme became widely known and influential, especially after his death. Also in Denmark, his ideas had an influence on discussions of upbringing, at least in certain social circles (Sigsgaard, 1978, p. 38). The first kindergarten, *børnehave*, in Denmark opened in 1871 and was soon followed by several others, all of which offered educational instruction for a few hours a day for well-off children. Based on his ideas, the world's first training college for kindergarten teachers in the world was established in 1885, which in 1904 were named *Frøbelseminariet* (Fröbel's Training College) (Tønsberg, 1980, p. 30). Just like the asylums and orphanages, these institutions had a philanthropic intent; they were privately funded and based on voluntary engagement.

Thus, from the outset, daycare institutions had a dual character as a pedagogical project for the bourgeoisie and a supportive project for the poor. This duality is recognizable in several Western European countries, as are the social forces leading to institutional care. Nevertheless, from the very beginning both the function and aims of the institutions, the view on teaching and learning, the means and methods of education, the modes of public and private financing, and the ways of organizing upbringing varied throughout Europe. In Denmark, the division between the two types of institution slowly began to dissolve by the turn of the century since the contrast between them became a matter of public concern. Particularly pronounced was the criticism of conditions in the asylums, but the limited educational offering in the asylums was also cause for concern. Influential people began to secure resources to transform the asylums into educational institutions because, it was argued, the poor were in particular need of proper education (Sigsgaard, 1978, pp. 50–52). In 1901, the first *folkebørnehave* (folk-kindergarten), aimed at children from the working classes and based on Fröbel's ideas, opened. With no public support initially, it was financed by private means and, to a minor extent, parental pay. However, this prevented the most needy children from benefitting (ibid., p. 72). Nevertheless, the number of folk-kindergartens slowly increased and they gradually replaced the asylums.

In 1919, the Danish state passed, as one of the first in the world, a resolution on economical support to early childcare institutions (Borchorst, 2005). This marked a change, as the state thereby became involved in care for children, though in economical terms it was a minor commitment initially. Child education had already been an obligation of the state for a long period. A publicly financed school system with compulsory attendance for all children in Denmark from the age of seven had been in operation since the milestone law of 29 July 1814. With the resolution of 1919, the care of preschool children also became a matter of public concern – at least in principle.

It seems to have been the case in all the Nordic countries that concern for children played a central role in the rise of the social state. In the late nineteenth century, children's needs and conditions were used as an argument for the necessity of some kind of political regulation of market forces (Christiansen and Markkola, 2006, p. 15). Restrictions on child labour and more comprehensive acts on the protection of children, as well as maternity leave for women working in factories, are some of the early regulations that indicate how the balance between state and market gradually changed in favour of employers' rights. The state slowly became a co-provider of social security for the individual, as well as the provider of what later became a universal system of upbringing and care. It is therefore possible to identify some premonitory symptoms of what was later termed the 'Nordic model' of the welfare state, and concern, for children seems to have paved the way. Thus, political interests and investments in children are not a new phenomenon. Neither are the delicate balances between state intervention and market forces, between central parliamentary legislation and local administration, individual and public concern, or between the private and the public sphere. Rather, the history of childcare institutions points out how intervention and support by the state have gradually increased, leading to new ways of conceptualizing children, families and obligations of care. This process is identifiable in all Western European countries, though the balance between state, market, family and institution differs, as do the aim and form of the caregiving programmes.

The expansion of childcare institutions

At the outset, childcare institutions were regarded as complementary provision for families in need, but they gradually evolved into a universal pedagogical offering aimed at helping parents and to imprint the basic social skills of society on children. As the social state evolved, one essential aim became to teach children and families to govern themselves with reason; that is, to solve problems and to be personally responsible in accordance with the norms of society. Institutions offered guidelines for social conduct as well as sound and stimulating environments.

During the first half of the twentieth century, kindergartens became more widespread, but they generally had severe economic problems as they were not yet tax-financed. Throughout this period, the obligations of both institutions and state were unsettled. After the Second World War, several new laws increased public responsibility. In this period the welfare state became labelled as such, and the role of the state as supportive and corrective was formed with a hugely expanding public sector addressing and preventing all kinds of social problems. In 1949, it was decided that even institutions for well-off children should be supported economically. Childcare institutions became a common upbringing, and despite different opinions about women's labour, it seems to have been the general perception that these institutions were a phenomenon that had come to stay (Borchorst, 2000, p. 60).

With an epoch-marking law about child welfare from 1964, the universality of childcare became a reality. The law specified institutional obligations, specified the state funding and repealed the estimation of parental income as a criterion for admission. By the same law, the juridical terminology changed from child welfare institutions to *daginstitutioner* (daycare institutions), indicating the status as a general educational offering to all children. This law was carried unanimously by all political parties, which argued either for the necessity of women's labour or for the need of children's education (Borchorst, 2005). It is worth noting that the law did not specify the educational content. Rather, latitude for local interpretations was upheld. Compared with early childcare programmes in other countries (for example, 'école maternelles' in France or 'preschools' in the UK), Danish childcare, from its beginning, lacked central specifications of purpose and curricula. The aim of the institutions has not, until recently, been linked to school entry and the programmes have not been regarded as part of the educational system. Instead, a strong emphasis on social education has marked the institutional profile.

Until the mid-1960s, childcare institutions had only been a relatively marginal phenomenon in the organization of society, but this changed from the early 1960s. Thus, the institutional expansion in Denmark began as early as the 1960s, which coincided with a period of full employment. Unlike most other countries, the increasing demand for manpower was met by married women rather than large-scale immigration, and by 1970 about half of all married women had entered the labour market (Borchorst, 2000, pp. 60–61). One of the means to achieve this was the establishment of childcare institutions, the number of which expanded enormously during the 1960s and 1970s. In this period, the status of the daycare sector changed, as childcare became a fundamental part of the organization of the expanding welfare society alongside hospitals, educational institutions and residential homes.

As in other welfare areas, the expenses of daycare institutions far exceeded expectations. The number of employees in the public sector exploded from the mid-1950s, most of them women engaged in the education, care, social work and health sectors (Christiansen and Markkola, 2006, p. 23). This expansion put pressure on the system of tax-funded welfare services, and by the end of the 1960s public debates criticized the enlargement of the public sector. From the beginning of the 1970s, the public funding of early childcare was reduced (with some consequences for parental payment, though not for low-income groups), and a maximum level of expenditures was introduced, which altered the child: teacher ratio. But as the expansion continued, so, too, did public expenditure.

From the mid-1970s and about 15 years beyond, economic problems with unemployment, stagnation and inflation resulted in very tight public finances that challenged the welfare solutions (Christiansen and Markkola, 2006, p. 26). However, unemployment and cutbacks in the sector of daycare institutions did not lead to a reduction in the number of seats of the number of children enrolled. On the contrary, the latter continued to increase, indicating that childcare institutions had become a routine part of children's lives whether or not their parents were active in the labour market. During the relatively short period of institutional expansion in the 1960s, daycare centres apparently had become a profound and integrated part of ordinary childhood as well as of the organization of the labour market, housing market, and family life and gender relations. Thus, institutional childcare was not a mere reflection of the needs of the labour market; it had become a significant component in the structure of society.

With the conservative government in the 1980s, privatization of welfare institutions became key with a wide ambition of contracting out public services. For childcare, this remained a theoretical plan, though the issue is not completely off the agenda. So far, the limited interest from private companies to engage in childcare can be considered a result of strong ideological opposition among the population. There seems to be a general confidence in the state as a regulating authority in matters of institutional care, and a widely held agreement on the principles of universalism and tax funding as the basic principles of the welfare state.

Contemporary daycare institutions

Nowadays, daycare institutions are an integrated part of the construction of society administered by the Ministry of Social Affairs. The system includes *vuggestuer*, nurseries that serve children from six months to age three years, and *børnehaver*, kindergartens for children between the age of three and six. Daycare centres are non-obligatory, but public authorities are obliged to offer a seat to every child from 12 months and older. All centres are run by certified *pædagoger* (preschool teachers), assisted by *medhjælpere* (assistants). All pre-primary teachers are trained in non-university training colleges for three-and-a-half years, including 15 months of practical training.

The municipalities regulate and fund institutions, most of which are public. Private non-profit institutions (run by churches or charity organizations) do exist, but they are not private in the market sense and, as long as they comply with regulations and standards set by the local authorities, they receive the same amount of public funding (local taxes and central governmental grants) (OECD, 2001, p. 161). This covers approximately 75 per cent of their expenses, while parental fees cover the rest. Each municipality decides the exact fees and ratios within the broad mandates of the Danish Government, to which they are accountable for providing care for all children irrespective of their families' economic and social status. Thus, the structure of early childcare consists of three parts: the central parliamentary legislation that sets the guidelines for childcare; local authorities that implement the guidelines as principles regarding institutional structure, resources, staff employment, fees, aims and visions; and local institutions that define and practice the pedagogical programmes within the structural and organizational framework defined by the municipality and the state. The decentralized structure leads to some local variations in parents' payment, opening hours, resources and activities, though the guidelines set by the state ensure some uniformity of aims and organization.

Over the last 30 years, the number of preschool children enrolled in the Danish daycare system has greatly expanded: 63.2 per cent of all children aged one to three, and 96 per cent of all children between three and five years (compared with 34 per cent in 1975) (Statistisk Årbog, 2007, p. 162, table 156). With the parental leave policies that give parents one year of leave, infants generally do not enter daycare before the end of the first year, though some begin at the age of six months. Since compulsory schooling begins at age six, most Danish children are in daycare for five to six years. Almost all children are enrolled full time although, in practice, attendance varies between five and eleven hours a day. As a result, daycare institutions are a fundamental part of the lives of almost all preschool children in Denmark today and an integral part of the organization of family life and the labour market.

Politically, public childcare is highly prioritized and regarded as an important means of preventing negative socialization patterns and social problems caused by poor upbringing. The families who are potentially most vulnerable – low-income single parents and children, families experiencing domestic violence or other kinds of social problems, immigrants and refugees – are given priority placement since public daycare is seen as both an equalizer and a potent force for the successful integration of the young into Danish society. In fact, many efforts are undertaken in order to have children from these groups enrolled in public daycare (Gulløv, 2008).

As argued by Anette Borchorst (2000), public daycare in Denmark is characterized by four features. First is the degree of state intervention. As described, the state engaged in supporting early childcare institutions quite early, and the investment in public daycare institutions is generally much higher than in most other countries in Europe (Bennett, 2005). Second is the principle of universalism. Every child is offered a seat independent of the means of the parents. Daycare is not part of the educational system as such but is meant as a pedagogical offering to support the development of the child, regardless of the social, ethnic and religious background of the family. Thirdly, the model is based on the idea of social education. The content of daycare is intended to increase children's social awareness rather than to prepare them for school. Thus, they are trained to respect others' views, to engage in dialogue, to take turns and to show consideration. The specific activities are, thus, of lesser importance than the ways of behaving with social inclusiveness as a keyword in the pedagogical ideology. Lastly, the model is based on a strong belief in gender equality. Boys and girls are treated as equal; they are enrolled in the same groups and participate in the same activities.

Though several of these principles are recognizable in other countries, the combination of the four seems quite rare and, despite some changes, they still characterize early childcare in Denmark. The inclusion of all children within a social educational frame is still highly prioritized, with local authorities standing as a guarantee for quality and equal treatment. State intervention continues to be exceptionally high; actually in recent years the state has expanded its influence to matters of content, which were formerly defined by the institutions themselves. Gender equality is highly prioritized and social education is still emphasized, though the latter in particular has come under pressure as critics, who refer to low scores in international ratings, stress the need for more subject-oriented learning.

Despite a widespread political consensus on these principles, the aims of the care system have, until recently, only been articulated in very vague terms in official documents. The texts stating the aims and ambitions for these institutions have been remarkably unspecific, especially compared with the neighbouring country, Sweden, where the purpose of kindergarten was centrally defined as early as 1972. Quality and aims of the local pedagogical practice have traditionally been an area of internal institutional concern more than matters of state or municipality intervention. Though a historical continuity can be identified in the overall ideology of daycare institutions have also been characterized by distinct local variations in practices and objectives. This, however, is one of the areas where changes in the childcare system are most evident. With a humble beginning with the *Lov om Social Service* (Law on Social Services) of 1997, common goals have been even more specific. Despite political rhetoric emphasizing decentralization, public intervention has increased dramatically during the 2000s, with explicit demands with regard to outputs and the introduction of technologies of control.

Neoliberal tendencies

The restructuring of the welfare society hit the public agenda as early as the beginning of the 1970s due to economic and political turbulence. Since then, the welfare state has been restructured through different reforms. From an attempt to standardize the social services to citizens, the aim is now a more flexible public sector offering more differentiated and individualized services within a centrally defined economical and political framework. This liberalization of the public sector has been intensified over the last ten years in order to give the individual citizen more choices, and more possibilities of negotiating. At the same time, the state's regulation of the public sector has increased significantly with detailed demands for transparency, measurement and explicit objectives. By such means, the state aims to control the institutional procedures and practices and to define the purpose and outcome of the institutional services.

These new tendencies can be considered an expression of a more global process of neoliberal economic and political transformation, where new terms and technologies of governance alter the ways in which public institutions are administered (Rose, 1996). The information technology revolution totally altered the expectations of information, data collection and communication, not least within structures of management. Although the new management ideas and forms look alike, their impact varies each time these technologies enter a new context, often in unpredictable ways (Shore and Wright, 2000, p. 58). In early childcare in Denmark, the process implies a rather instrumental way of conceptualizing the role of institutions. Daycare institutions are regarded as prime agents in effecting governmental decisions. They are seen as a means to prevent and solve the problems that politicians single out as the most pressing, such as children's misbehaviour, negative social heritage, non-integration of immigrant children, inadequate preparation for school, youth gangs and crimerates among youngsters. These areas serve as focal points 'for the rationalization of individual destinies' (Gordon, 1991, p. 44), and the institutions become the administrative means of identifying potential problematic individuals. The daycare settings are made responsible for targeting and finding solutions, and the purpose of the institutions has thereby changed from caregiving as a goal in itself to areas of broader societal concern. Positioned in the front rank of the welfare state, daycare institutions are expected to address the social problems of families and to guide individuals so that their aspirations and ambitions correlate with the aims of the state. Thus, the political focus has changed in the last ten years. From a perception of daycare as autonomous institutions with internally defined pedagogical aims, daycare institutions today are regarded as administrative agencies working in accordance with centrally defined educational objectives. From being a place where small children could stay while their parents were at work, they are now viewed as a societal investment in human resources and an outpost combating, and hopefully preventing, social problems. The responsibility of preventing societal problems is now delegated to the institutions, but this delegation entails increased control and processes of evaluation in order to ensure satisfactory administration.

The content of the kindergarten has also become an area of dispute, a pivotal point being the kind and amount of curriculum that should be part of the programmes. The traditional focus on universalism and social inclusion in early childcare, as well as in schools and education in general, was perceived as an important precondition for the social cohesion of society. By bringing up children in accordance with the democratic norms of society, teaching them social and political responsibility, the aim was to prevent unrest or anti-democratic forces in society and to create enlightened and socially engaged citizens. Slogans like 'never more Auschwitz', 'upbringing to democracy' and 'education for everybody' were all common in the public debate in the 1950s and 1960s, with an impressive impact on the educational reforms of the following decade (Skovgaard-Petersen, 2005, Øland 2010). The neoliberal policies do not oppose the traditional social democratic view that it is essential to educate the individual in order to keep a coherent society; neither do they deny the need of institutions to attend to this process. But the viewpoints differ with regard to the content and form of education and the role of the state in relation to welfare institutions.

The dominant concept in the 'golden age of welfare' (Christiansen and Markkola, 2006, p. 21), from the 1950s until the 1980s, was a broad approach to education that emphasized the social development of the child. For the early childhood institutions, this meant flexible and play-based programmes with a strong focus on social skills and child-initiated activities rather than a specified curriculum. This way of organizing early childcare has, however, been criticized severely in recent years. Demands have been made for a specification of the aim and content of daycare and for an upgrading of the amount of 'real' knowledge in order to make the educational component more efficient. Instead of a focus on democratic skills, the ideological viewpoint in the neoliberal and neoconservative ideology stresses subject-oriented learning and children's mastering of specific tasks (Apple, 2006). From this perspective, kindergartens are the first step in the educational career, and the programmes should therefore prepare the child for the cognitive demands of school as well as the demands of the labour market.

The focus is shifting from social and democratic mastery to educational success measured by a range of evaluating technologies in order to control the output. The ideal of the institutional enterprise seems to be an endeavour to enable every child to manage itself in accordance with the guidelines and demands of the educational system (Weber et al., 2005, p. 33). Thus, the child-initiated practice and ideology is under pressure. Also, the institutional autonomy concerning aims and educational priorities is challenged, as nationally defined goals and tests are being introduced in order to control, standardize, regulate and evaluate the institutional outcome. However, compared with other countries (for example, the UK and France), the specifications of content are still rather vague, as are the processes of evaluation. In the everyday practice of the institutions, the child-centred pedagogy is still prevalent, as is the ideological view that connects the preschool child to playing rather than scholarly learning.

In recent years the role of the state has also changed, though in practice not (although often presented as such in liberal discourses) with the market as the ideal. In neoliberal politics, the state plays a much more influential, regulating part than it does in a classical liberal market ideology. With reference to Mark Olssen, Michael W. Apple argues that in contrast to the negative image of state power in classical liberalism, neoliberalism represents a much more positive conception of the state's role as the provider of the conditions, laws and institutions necessary for its operation. According to Apple, this involves the establishment of the conditions to create individuals who are enterprising and competitive entrepreneurs (Apple, 2006; Olssen, 1996). To quote Olssen:

> It is not that the conception of the self-interested subject is replaced or done away with by the new ideals of 'neo-liberalism', but that in an age of universal welfare, the perceived possibilities of slothful indolence create necessities for new forms of vigilance, surveillance, 'performance appraisal' and of forms of control generally. In this new model the state has taken it upon itself to keep us all up to the mark. (Olssen, 1996, p. 340)

Though Olssen's discussion addresses individuals, his point also concerns changed perceptions of institutions. The neoliberal ideology considers institutions as instruments of upbringing and controlling individual behaviour, and of preventing social problems. As pointed out by Nikolas Rose, the neoliberal ideology implies the emergence of a range of novel practices, which seek to shape individuality. 'Liberal strategies of government thus become dependent upon devices... that promise to create individuals who do not need to be governed by others, but will govern themselves, care for themselves' (Rose, 1996, p. 45). Kindergartens can be seen as such devices, aimed at transforming children into flexible and responsible, self-regulating citizens adjusting their behaviour to institutional guidelines.

Institutions are responsible for giving guidelines to individuals in order to prevent social problems. To ensure that they actually comply with the political requests, a variety of evaluative and regulatory means are applied, both at the level of the institutions and in the municipalities that are obliged to enforce a specific educational agenda. As the state has a monopoly, it holds and exercises the authority both to define institutional purposes, obligations and commissions and to control and measure the effects and outputs. Contract managing has become the preferred tool in the public administration of municipalities with detailed specifications of the aims and objectives of the institutions. Financial management is the driving force, with economic rewards to institutions that fulfil the parameters of the contract. This mechanism has given what Apple terms the 'evaluative state' its increased power (Apple, 2006, p. 474).

In the area of early childcare in Denmark, these neoliberal tendencies have become particularly evident in the administrative structure. A heated debate concerning the returns of the financial investment has turned up with consequences for the institutional organization, in the form of demands of transparency, efficiency and enhancement of the quality of public services. Testing, regular procedures of evaluation and written documentation have been introduced as insurance against waste of public resources and means to control the outcome. Demands for detailed documentation, descriptions of objectives and pressure to organize daily activities in learning-centred ways are just some of the new initiatives that begin to alter the form and role of daycare in society. In this process, the notion of quality has changed to refer to a pre-described content that ensures a predictable result rather than the more open-ended humanistic focus of children's daily wellbeing. Institutional quality relates to efficiency in relation to more general mechanisms of society, especially the educational system, and not the comprehensive education of children with an emphasis on social inclusion and democratic skills, so praised in former times.

A new discourse on childcare institutions

In June 2007, a new law *Lov om dagtilbud* (Law on Public Day-Care) that concerns daycare institutions took effect. This brings together all former texts of law concerning nurseries, kindergartens and after-school institutions, reformulates the aims and obligations of early childcare, and integrates this in the overall educational structure. The orientation towards schools is now explicit. Kindergartens prepare children for schools with the aim of overcoming social differences. For that reason, children's fluency in Danish is to be tested at the age of three years in order to identify difficulties at an early age. The institutional environment is also to be regularly evaluated in relation to specific assessment standards. Institutions must submit an annual report on aims, methods, activities and reflections on outcomes and obstacles in order to ensure children's preparedness for school.

In the text, the governing principle seems to be an aim to enforce connections between daycare and the educational system, between daycare family and the labour market and between daycare and the Danish society in general. The purpose is, in other words, to comply with the interests of families, labour market and society (defined in a rather nationalistic way), apparently based on the conviction that these interests will be identical with those of children. The emphasis on social inclusion and programmes designed to stimulate play, fantasy and creativity, which used to dominate the preamble, is downscaled in favour of a predefined notion of children's needs. In the very first paragraph, it is stated that the main purposes of kindergartens are to offer the child a sound and stimulating learning environment, to overcome social inequalities in families, to ease the transition to schools and to facilitate families' relation to the labour market (Lov om dagtilbud [Law on Public Day-Care], 2007, §1). It is also stated that daycare institutions are obliged to give children a sense of community, to integrate them into and develop a mutual connection with the Danish society (ibid., §7, Subsection 4).

The labour market needs flexible, well-educated and committed workers, and daycare institutions are the first link in the chain of production. At the same time, they serve the contemporary workforce, and the law therefore underlines the obligation of municipalities to offer institutions with flexible opening hours and present families with choices of types of daycare that suit different needs. The economic support for childcare within the family is extended, except for people who have lived in the country for less than seven years (unless they are European

Union citizens) (Lov om dagtilbud [Law on Public Day-Care], 2007 §87). This exception is worth noting, as the law consolidates a practice to enrol immigrant children into daycare. Politically, early childcare institutions are ascribed a central role in the processes of upbringing and integrating into society. While the law facilitates the option of taking care of ones' own children by giving economic support, it also states that only people with the right affiliation to society are entitled. In relation to children of economically deprived newcomers, daycare seems to be regarded as the best means of upbringing, which explains why these children are given priority access as early as possible (Gulløv, 2008).

The law presents a break with the former division between the state (defining the structural frames of organization) and the individual institution (deciding programmes, methods and pedagogical visions). With this law, purpose and content are much more centrally defined, leaving less space to institutions to develop their own educational focus. The pedagogical methods are still locally determined, as are the choice of materials and planning of the days, but with new demands on evaluation, reports and close correspondence with municipality workers, combined with much more detailed economic regulations, the institutional autonomy has diminished.

Though continuity can be identified, new lines of management are slowly about to alter the ways in which institutions and societal upbringing are conceptualized. These new forms have to do with the way children and daycare have moved from the margins into the centre of the political debates. With the neoliberal, and neo-national, currents, much more political attention has been assigned to education (Olssen, 1996, pp. 339–340). As in other countries, discussions have concerned the content and outcome of the institutional effort, but as the traditions, purposes and programmes are not identical in different countries, neither are the processes of reform. In Denmark, with its long history of state intervention in early childcare, the increased regulation by the state has, interestingly enough, not caused protest. Criticism has been raised against the workload, especially in relation to evaluation and testing procedures, but the decrease in local influence on general matters has not been opposed. This could be explained by the subtleness of state governing; a lot of procedures are decentralized so institutions have to regulate their own work, which makes the management of the state less visible. Whatever the cause, the centrally defined aims and obligations have smoothly been incorporated into educational discourses and practices, gradually altering the purpose and scope of the institutions.

The idea of social education for all preschool children is still prevalent, but the notion of 'the social' is changing. From a focus on social competencies and relations, the focus now seems to be on developing the individual child's ability to manage itself in accordance with a specific vision of society that stresses national cohesion (rather than social cohesion). Thus, even the youngest children are now part of the new management strategies permeating public institutions with consequences for notions of childhood, education, kindergartens and the role of society and state.

Conclusion

In this chapter, I have tried to outline the continuity in the history of the Danish kindergarten and to reflect upon changes in contemporary society. Following Borchorst, I have argued that the degrees of state intervention, universalism and social education, rather than formal teaching, are distinctive features of the Danish model of early childcare. Despite many changes in recent years, these features still characterize daycare, though all of them are in a process of alteration. Thus, daycare in Denmark is still characterized by a high degree of state intervention, although this intervention has become much more radical during the period of institutional expansion, especially during the last ten years. The boundaries of the political field have been extended into new areas. From a state primarily occupied with the frames of organization and economic guidelines, the new political attention concerns the priorities of the educational content and the role of institutions to prevent and solve politically predefined problems (Gulløv, Chapter 5).

Universalism in the sense that daycare institutions are for everybody seems more salient than ever before, especially for families that stray from defined social standards of citizenship. There is a significant pressure on parents to enrol their children in daycare institutions if they are suspected of not having the right attitude to or relationship with society. Daycare is an option, though more optional for some than for others, as it is regarded as the prime agent of socialization into society. Flexibility in relation to the labour market has been emphasized in order to ensure that daycare is actually an option for every child. Children go to daycare institutions in order to become active learners and self-manageable individuals.

The principle of social education still exists, but the meaning is changing. Kindergartens are now obliged to focus on outcome, and to ensure that children have the skills and competencies to manage themselves in accordance with dominant norms of the educational system and society in general. The emphasis on democratic skills, inclusion and tolerance is downscaled in favour of an outcome-oriented focus where demands of transparency, efficiency and enhancement of quality gradually change the agenda.

References

Apple, M. W. (2006) 'Producing Inequalities: Neo-Liberalism, Neo-Conservatism, and the Politics of Educational Reform' in H. Lauder, P. Brown, J. A. Dillabough and A. H. Halsey (eds) *Education, Globalization, and Social Chance* (Oxford: Oxford University Press).

Bennett, J. (2005) *Where Does Denmark Stand?* (Paris: OECD/BUPL).

Bloch, M., Popkewitz, T., Holmlund, K. and Moqvist, I. (2003) *Governing Children, Families and Education: Restructuring the Welfare State* (London: Palgrave Macmillan).

Borchorst, A. (2000) 'Den danske børnepasningsmodel – kontinuitet og forandring' (The Danish model of childcare – continuity and change), *Arbejderhistorie*, 4, 55–70.

Borchorst, A. (2005) 'Nøglen i de rigtige hænder. Lov om børne- og ungdomsforsorg 1964' (The key in the right hands. The childcare Act of 1964) in J. H. Petersen and K. Petersen (eds) *13 reformer af den danske velfærdsstat* (13 Reforms of the Danish Welfare State) (Odense: Syddansk Universitetsforlag).

Christiansen, N. F. and Markkola, P. (2006) 'Introduction' in N. F. Christiansen, K. Petersen, N. Edling and P. Haave (eds) *The Nordic Model of Welfare* (Copenhagen: Museum Tusculanum Press).

Coninck-Smith, N. de (1995) 'Byggeri for børn. Daginstitutionsbyggeri før, under og efter 2. verdenskrig' (Buildings for children. Day-care buildings before, during and after World War II), *Architectura*, 17, 7–30.

Fröbel, F. (1980) *Småbørnspædagogik* (The education of young children) (Copenhagen: Nyt Nordisk Forlag Arnold Busck).

Gordon, C. (1991) 'Governmental Rationality: An Introduction' in G. Burchell, C. Gordon and P. Miller (eds) *The Foucault Effect: Studies in Governmentality* (Chicago: University of Chicago Press).

Gulløv, E. (2008) 'Institutional Upbringing. A Discussion of the Politics of Childhood in Contemporary Denmark' in A. James and A. James (eds) *Culture, Politics & Childhood* (London: Palgrave Macmillan).

Lov om social service (Law on social service) (1997) nr. 454 10 June 2007, https://www.retsinformation.dk/Forms/R0710.aspx?id=85035#K3. Last accessed 25 March 2011.

Lov om dagtilbud (Law on daycare) (2007) nr 501, 06 June 2007, https://www.retsinformation.dk/Forms/R0710.aspx?id=32025. Last accessed 25 March 2011.

OECD (2001) *Starting Strong. Early Childhood Education and Care* (Paris: OECD).

Olssen, M. (1996) 'In Defence of the Welfare State and of Publicly Provided Education', *Journal of Education Policy*, 11, 337–362.

Rose, N. (1996) 'Governing "Advanced" Liberal Democracies' in A. Barry, T. Osborne and N. Rose (eds.) *Foucault and Political Reason* (London: UCL Press). Rose, N. (1999) *Governing the Soul. The Shaping of the Private Self* (London: Free Association Books).

Sigsgaard, J. (1978) *Folkebørnehaver og social pædagogik. Træk af asylets og børnehavens historie* (Folk-kindergarten and social education. Outline of the history of the asylum and the kindergarten) (Copenhagen: Forlaget Børn og Unge).

Shore, C. and Wright, S. (2000) 'Coercive Accountability. The Rise of Audit Culture in Higher Education' in M. Strathern (ed.) *Audit Culture. Anthropological Studies in Accountability, Ethics, and the Academy* (London: Routledge).

Skovgaard-Petersen, V. (1985) *Danmarks historie* (The history of Denmark), vol. 5 (Copenhagen: Gyldendal).

Skovgaard-Petersen, V. (2005) Om dannelse (On education), Unpublished paper (Copenhagen).

Statistisk årbog (Statistical yearbook) (2007) (Copenhagen: Statistics Denmark).

Tønsberg, V. (1980) 'Indledning' (Introduction) in F. Fröbel (ed.) *Småbørnspædagogik* (The education of young children) (Copenhagen: Nyt Nordisk Forlag Arnold Busck).

Weber, K., Rosenbeck, B., Christiansen, N. F., Kirkebæk, B., Andersen, M. and Kampmann, J. (eds) (2005) *Bag tallene. Humanistisk velfærdsforskning* (Behind the numbers. Humanistic welfare research) (Copenhagen: Danish Agency for Science, Technology and Innovation).

Øland, T. (2010) 'A state ethnography of progressivism: Danish school pedagogues and their efforts to emancipate the powers of the child, the people and the culture 1929–1960'. *Praktiske grunde. Nordisk tidsskrift for kultur- og samfundsvidenskab* (Practical Reasons. Nordic Journal of Cultural and Social Sciences , nr. 1-2, s. 57–90.

Part II

Flexible Spaces, Flexible Children? Contemporary Policy and Practice

6
'Child-Centredness' and 'the Child'
The Cultural Politics of Nursery Schooling in England

Allison James

Introduction

This chapter is concerned with exploring the ways in which ideas of 'childhood' and the 'child' are represented in the educational policies for children aged three to six years old, introduced in England in 1999, as an example of the ongoing construction and reconstruction of English childhood (James and Prout, 1997). However, the purpose of this chapter is not simply to document the particular conceptions and discourses of childhood that are embedded within these new educational policies; more importantly, it is to ask about the ways in which these may potentially shape the everyday experiences of children who attend the various institutions that are now obliged to work within this new regulatory framework. This chapter poses a set of critical questions, therefore, about the cultural politics of childhood (James and James, 2004) that is currently being promoted in England by asking about the kinds of childhoods that are being produced by and for children through these new policies. In some senses, the state's interests in children is always about the nation's future – for the future is, as Jenks (1996) notes, what children represent – and, as Hendrick argues with respect to the history of educational developments in the UK, educational policies have always built upon 'the value of children as investments in future parenthood, economic competitiveness and a stable democratic order' (Hendrick, 1997, p. 46). In exploring the implications for young English children of the recent introduction of a Foundation Stage curriculum, this chapter considers, therefore, how the state appears to be currently viewing the future. One answer appears to be is that it is with considerable anxiety; and that it is younger and younger children who are being made to carry the burden of this anxiety through the imposition of increasingly prescriptive ideas on children of what it is to be a child in order that their futures, as adults, might be secured. Indeed, the very introduction of this new curriculum suggests that the net of control that the government has sought to exert over English childhood over recent years is tightening still further (James and James, 2001).

'Early years' institutional life in England

Before exploring in detail some of the implications for children and childhood of this most recent educational initiative, it is necessary to sketch out the background of the institutional context within which this is taking place. Compulsory full-time schooling begins for children in England at the age of five. For younger children there is, however, a highly diverse set of institutional arrangements that provide both care and education, spread across the state and private sector, with the main ones being day nurseries and nursery schools. Day nurseries (both those provided by the state and those established within the private sector) care for children from birth to five years, with the costs being met by parents, unless children have special needs or are deemed at risk. In the latter case, provision is free or given at a reduced cost. By contrast, nursery schools, as the name suggests, are regarded as providers of early education, rather than care. They cater for children between three and five years old and since 1998, free, part-time access to nursery school has been available for all three- to five-year-old children, albeit limited to a two-and-a-half-hour session per day, five times a week, during the school term.

In the institutional provision it makes for young children, England draws, therefore, a particularly sharp division between 'care' and 'education'. Indeed, this has characterized the history of services to children in England, sitting in stark contrast with most other European countries where this distinction is often far more blurred (Penn, 1997). Unsurprisingly, these two English institutions turn out to be premised on rather different ideologies of what constitutes 'children's needs' and what is good for children. Thus, as discussed in detail elsewhere (James, 2008), this sharp differentiation between practices of 'care' and practices of 'education' have helped reinforce the diversity of English childhoods, sustaining, for example, differences between children along class and/or ethnic lines that help to identify some children as being 'at risk' and 'in need' of intervention by the state in order to ensure their future as responsible adult citizens.

Indeed, as Penn argues, until very recently the British Government has regarded 'the care of children [as] the responsibility of their parents', the implication being that 'no one else should be expected to carry the financial cost of that care' (Penn, 1997, p. 8). Reinforced by a vast array of policy initiatives – parenting classes in school that are designed to instruct young people about childcare before they have children, and parenting orders dished out to those parents who fail to care for their children properly once they have had them – the ideal location for childcare and child socialization in England remains firmly within the family. Thus, in England, it is only those children who are deemed to live in 'uncaring' families who are given free places in day nurseries, underscoring the idea that it is the job of these institutions to work as substitutes for 'proper' familial socialization. As Penn notes, the only 'publicly funded care services which do exist are welfare based, and cater for children in need, usually defined as children from highly distressed and vulnerable families' (Penn, 1997, p. 8). 'Care' in this context is thus delivered within a service that offers 'regular surveillance and protection' for children (Penn, 1997, p. 8).

In stark contrast to day nurseries, English nursery schools, on the other hand, are places that care for young children in a rather different way – traditionally, through the provision of an early education that replicates the kind of caring and educational environment characterized by the ideologies of middle-class family life (James, 2008). In a report of discussions held with government ministers over the implementation of 'early learning goals' for young children in 1999, this is made explicit:

> Children should start learning to read, write and count as young as three and should have mastered the rudiments before the end of their first year in primary school, the government said yesterday as ministers set out to bury the idea that early childhood is a time for carefree play.

Margaret Hodge, the education minister, said children from disadvantaged backgrounds 'deserved the well-structured nursery education that was seen as a matter of course in middle class homes' (*Guardian*, 23 June 1999).

It is therefore against this background of the separation between state provision for care and for education/schooling that the analysis of the cultural politics shaping current policies for three- to six-year-old children presented in this chapter has to be seen. As explored below, they are firmly part of an educational, rather than a care agenda, that is arguably oriented towards the achievement of the future economic goals of the state, rather than an agenda centred on the current needs and interests of children themselves.

Interrogating child-friendliness/child-centredness

The assertion just made that the current policy agenda for young children is not centred on the needs of children but focused, instead, more on the long-term needs of the state begs the question, however, of what is meant by being child-centred or child-friendly. Exploring this at the outset is therefore imperative. This is especially so given that these descriptions appear so commonsensical and everyday as to seem not to require much interrogation. Indeed, such is their common appeal that, in the context of the raised profile of children's rights, these phrases slip into a wide range of policy and practices arenas, as indicated below. And yet it is precisely such processes of 'naturalization' that lend them their power as particular kinds of discourses. This was, of course, Foucault's point about regimes of truth and, as Walkerdine (2001) has argued, an important feature of such regimes is the kind of subjectivities that they help establish. What Foucault called the 'microphysics of power' is the way in which these discourses 'produce and regulate what it means to be a subject within different social practices' (Walkerdine, 2001, p. 20).

> To understand the relation between subjectification (the condition of being a subject) and subjectivity (the lived experience of being a subject), it is necessary to examine what subject-positions are created within specific practices and how actual subjects are both created and live those diverse positions. (Walkerdine, 2001, p. 21)

The notion of subject position is therefore an important one, and, in Walkerdine's formulation, which makes lived experience a key component, it becomes particularly useful because she emphasizes that subject positions are not only created but also lived. This means that they are not fixed but remain potentially fluid and open to change. In this sense, children's subjectivities arise in and through the contextualized, ongoing everydayness of their lives. By interrogating the discourses around child-friendliness/child-centredness to be found in current policy agendas, it becomes possible to identify a range of subtly different subject positions being opened up for children.

Thus, for example, following the introduction of the new curriculum for three- to six-year-olds, which is the focus of this chapter, a new policy for child health was introduced in 2003. Outlined in a report from the Department of Health called *Getting the Right Start. National Service Framework for Children* (NSF), ostensibly this policy has the needs of children at its core, drafted as it was in quick response to the strong critiques made of services for children in England following the Kennedy report (2001) on Bristol Royal Infirmary. Thus, in the foreword to the NSF, Alan Milburn (the Secretary of State for Health) states explicitly the need for what he calls child-friendly hospitals: 'child-friendly hospitals recognize that children are not the same as adults' and he goes on to say that this 'means designing hospital services for children from the child's point of view' to ensure that 'the care that we deliver for children is genuinely child-centred'. Recent research by Birch et al. (2007) on children's perceptions of hospital space suggests, however, that from children's own perspectives these services have yet to adequately meet their needs.

One of the root causes of this failure to meet children's needs, other than the very practical issues identified by children, pertains, I suggest, to the ways in which the concept of 'child-centredness' is formulated within the policy itself. Thus, for example, in the passage quoted above, three different phrasings are used – child-friendly, child-centredness and the child's point of view – as if they are synonyms with one another, with scant regard for any potential differences in meaning. Indeed, as in other settings, the phrases 'child-centred', child-focused' and 'child-friendly' appear to form part of a panoply of buzz words that institutions now use to signal or validate their commitment to children – their desire to make children's lives somehow better, to make places suitable for children or simply to be nice to them. The uncritical use of these terms is, however, highly problematic because they are not without resonances of different kinds.

Take, for instance, the variety of meanings that attach themselves to the term child-friendly. In the USA, for example, there exists the Child-Friendly Initiative. This is described as 'a grassroots, non-profit organization dedicated to improving the lives of children' whose members are 'working to transform their neighborhoods and communities into places that honor and respect children and support families', the intention being to build 'stronger neighborhoods, healthier communities and well-adjusted children who become caring citizens in the world' (Child-Friendly Initiative, 2006). Child-friendly here seems to be about ensuring that children's everyday lives are better so that they prosper, in the future, as adult citizens.

Childfriendly.net in the UK, on the other hand, is a watchdog website. It is a forum that encourages people to recommend 'child-friendly places in [your] locality to other parents to make their lives easier'. Here, then, the service is actually for parents, not for children, with children being regarded, in some senses, rather negatively through the suggestion that it is children's particular needs that make life difficult for parents. Indeed, children find themselves somewhat demonized – the website cites, approvingly, a quote from Phyllis Diller 'always be nice to your children because they are the ones who will choose your rest home' (Child-Friendly Initiative, 2006).

Finally, there is the United Nations Children's (Emergency) Fund (UNICEF) initiative for child-friendly cities, which aims to establish in cities 'a local system of good governance committed to fulfilling children's rights'. The intention is to enable children to be 'actively engaged in fulfilling the right of every young citizen' not only 'to influence decisions' about their city but also to 'express their opinion on the city they want' and to ensure that basic needs for safety, education, health and socializing are provided. UNICEF goes on to specify in detail what this kind of urban environment might actually look like and, although this list is phrased in terms of a children's rights agenda, it seems to incorporate what should be a right for everyone living in a city, whether they are children or adults. In this usage of 'child-friendly', children are seen as having needs and rights that match those of adults.

The conceptualization of 'child-friendliness' embraces, therefore, a range of rather different, yet very familiar, subject positions for children. First is the suggestion that children are different from adults and that they need rather different things from the physical and social environment; second, is the idea that children are becomings, and that attention needs to be given to making environments better for children now if the future is to be guaranteed (Lee, 2001); and third, there is the idea that children should be able to express opinions and influence decisions about things that concern them *as* children. Interestingly, therefore, it is only within the interpretation of the notion of child-friendliness found in the UNICEF example that a subject position enabling children's agency is opened up (Mayall, 2002).

Within the field of education it is this latter interpretation of the concept 'child-friendly' within different policy and practice discourses that would seem to encompass some of the features of what has been traditionally regarded as a 'child-centred' approach. However, as the next section explores, the educational conceptualization of 'child-centredness' has, itself, been open to different interpretations, interpretations that again have invoked a range of subject positions for children. Thus, in exploring what the cultural politics of the new curriculum might mean for three- to six-year-old children in England, it is important to consider exactly what kind of discourses children may be becoming subject to in English nursery schools.

Child-centredness in education – a disputed history.

In their exploration of the history of the meaning of child-centredness in the USA, Chung and Walsh (2000) plot the many twists and turns through which this concept developed. Beginning from its roots in Froebel's work in the early nineteenth century through to its implementation in the 1930s as a form of progressive education, backed by the emergence of developmental psychology, they reveal a range of different subject positions that were opened up for children. These form a recognizable and familiar continuum: at one end, 'the child' is positioned as a social actor and agent, and at the other, the child's present life takes on importance in terms of their child's future citizenship status. Recurring time and again, including in relation to the new educational policies introduced for young children in England, these subject positions constitute an important part of the lexicon of early childhood education around which debate flourishes. They are, therefore, integral to its cultural politics.

Subject position 1: The child as agent

The term child-centredness can be traced as far back as the eighteenth century when, in his description of the education of *Emile*, Rousseau laid out a scheme of learning that argued for children's innocence and for the need to protect children from the social world. Rousseau argued that children should learn according to their nature, by their experience in and with the world, rather than through direct instruction. By the nineteenth century, as Chung and Walsh (2000, p. 217) describe, Froebel had developed this idea further by arguing that children needed a special kind of education because of their limited intellectual ability. In their view, children would gradually, and naturally, develop abilities through their ongoing engagement with the world, a process to be facilitated largely by play, rather than formal schooling. Play, it was suggested, enables children to act directly upon their environment and to engage with it and, through this, they would learn. Out of this, Froebel argued, an experientially based and growing self-consciousness would develop since the child would be at the centre of its own learning. In Froebel's view, children had a 'divine essence' that was 'in need of cultivation and protection rather than interference' (Soler and Miller, 2003, p. 59).

Subject position 2: The child as individual

The rise of developmental psychology, with its focus on surveillance and measurement and the use of scientific principles to judge a child's development, led to a second kind of subject position being opened up for 'the child' within early educational philosophies through providing a developmental yardstick against which individual children might be measured. This led to a new centring on the needs of individual children, so that a child's unique and personal development might be nurtured. Writing in 1919, Catherine Watkins described this in the following manner:

'the child . . . with his awakening powers has become the centre and the nurture and development through self-activity, rather than the pouring of instruction, has become the generally accepted idea. (cited in Chung and Walsh, 2000, p. 225)

Thus, by the mid-twentieth century, under the rubric of what became known as progressive education, the idea of the child as the agent of their own learning (subject position1) appears in a somewhat modified form in relation to the idea of a child-centred curriculum. Promulgated by educationalists such as Montessori in Europe and Dewey in the USA, the emphasis had shifted from notions about the value of children of free and unstructured play to a focus on 'building a curriculum around the activities and interests of children' (Rugg cited in Chung and Walsh, 2000, p. 226). As Soler and Miller note, now the adult was to be the 'guide and moderator' of children's play so that the 'child's real needs and learning patterns' could be built upon and exploited to facilitate learning (Soler and Miller, 2003, p. 59). Although, according to Dewey, children remained at the centre of their own learning, the ways in which children contributed to their learning environment also shaped their experience. Importantly, within this subject position, children's agency is somewhat reduced for, as Norquay argues, 'child-centred pedagogy, sustains [a] focus on the unique individual by linking behaviour to personality and predetermined developmental appropriateness' (Norquay, 1999, p. 189). It thereby also sidelines the effects of structural conditions and social contexts that can work to shape any particular child's learning, behaviour and experiences and which are critical to the cultural politics of childhood (James and James, 2004; Stephens, 1995).

Subject position 3: The child as future citizen

As Chung and Walsh document in relation to the USA, a competing Hegelian perspective on child-centredness was in circulation in the late nineteenth century. This argued that 'in kindergarten children begin to become conscious and intellectual members of society' (Chung and Walsh, 2000, p. 219) and, since the child was by nature savage, its intellect needed to be controlled by learning the art of self-activity. Thus, rather than the kind of natural unfolding of self-consciousness being advocated by Froebel, educators such as Harris argued that the independent thinking that the nation required of its adult citizens could only occur through a more controlled regime designed to *produce* citizens who were independent:

> We desire in our systems of education to make the citizen as independent as possible from mere external prescriptions. We wish him to be spontaneous – self active – self-governing. The government of the United States becomes better in the ratio that the citizen becomes self directive. (Harris 1870 cited in Chung and Walsh, 2000, p. 220)

Here then it was the state's interests rather than the child's that were the focus of this version of child-centredness. Although the child here was visualized as being at the centre of the future of society, children now occupied a position that was subject to regimes of surveillance and control that were designed to ensure that they were fit for the future. When combined with the influence of developmental psychology, this produced what Chung and Walsh identify as the drive for social efficiency that was so characteristic of the early twentieth century: the emergence of a curriculum that would train children's developing capacity efficiently, by setting out a curriculum that contained specific activities that needed to be accomplished at particular ages. As Bertha McConkey wrote in 1911:

> The kindergarten is not an experiment .... It has come to stay for it meets a need that no other agency can meet so well. It lays broad and deep foundations for virtuous and effective living and cannot therefore be spared from any complete system of education. (cited in Chung and Walsh, 2000, p. 224)

As Chung and Walsh observe, 'for efficiency-minded educators...a curriculum based on children's natural order of development was wasteful. The curriculum should be composed of concrete activities selected from adult living and organized according to individual abilities' (Chung and Walsh, 2000, p. 224). Buttressed by systems of testing and measurement that had become part of the panoply of new 'scientific' approaches to child study, the focus fell on age-based assessments of what children need for their future wellbeing. Thus, in this subject position, the child also has little agency, since its present needs are defined through reference to the future.

In sum, then, these three subject positions constitute a continuum of subtly different ideas of child-centredness – from the child as actor and agent, through the child as individual, to the child as future citizen. Vestiges of all of these are to be found in the ways in which policies for early education are currently being framed in England. However, that some rather than others have come to predominate reflects the contemporary cultural politics of early childhood education.

Schooling the nursery child

As noted above, in the English context, all children aged three to five years do have free part-time places at nursery schools, although not during school holidays, underscoring the strong link between nursery *schools* and the education sector as a whole. Indeed, what young children now have to do, while at nursery school, can increasingly be described as a new form of 'schooling' and not as, formerly, preschool activities that are about learning through play. Since 1999, nursery schools have had to embrace the foundation level of the National Curriculum, which has its own 'early learning goals' spread across six areas and assessed on a 13-point scale: personal, social and emotional development; communication, language and literacy; mathematical development; knowledge and understanding of the world; physical development; and creative development.

The tension between the different kinds of child-centred subject positions that have been opened up for young children within this new policy was apparent from the outset, with the child as agent (subject position 1) being displaced by the child as future citizen (subject position 3). In an account of the ways in which the new curriculum plans were greeted by early educationalists, for example, these opposed positions are clearly represented:

When first introduced in 1999 these goals were met with a hail of criticism from the heads of 16 of the 18 nursery schools that [were] identified as centres of excellence. They said children under six should not be forced into formal learning of literacy and numeracy, but be allowed to develop social skills and learn through play. Otherwise too many youngsters – particularly boys – would 'learn to fail' at an early age. (*Guardian*, 4 October 1999)

However, it was also quite clear that from the government's perspective the most important subject position that was to be made available for children, within this new framework, was subject position 3 – the child's future must take precedence over the child as active agent. Margaret Hodge, a government minister, was quoted as saying:

I am fed up of hearing how unstructured play and free activity are all that a young child needs.... Many children start nursery at the age of three unable to speak properly or communicate. They can't concentrate; they lack confidence and show no enthusiasm for learning; they don't know their colours, they are unfamiliar with numbers and they have rarely seen a book. Of course we don't want three-year-olds to sit in rows learning Latin. But equally if we do not structure the activities, the play and the learning they enjoy in their nursery setting, children will not develop the skills they need to succeed in life and at school. (*Guardian*, 4 October 1999)

And she continued:

Play in playgroups and nurseries should be 'purposeful'. The days of toddlers 'colouring, cutting and pasting' are over. Before the age of six, all children should be able to recognise numbers, count to ten, understand adding and taking away, know the alphabet and read a range of common words. I don't accept, as some from advantaged backgrounds seem to be arguing, that we are being over-formal. If the well-to-do expected these standards of attainment by their children, how could the government deny them to poorer children for whom education is the best hope for a better life? (*Guardian*, 4 October 1999)

Thus, the guidance notes that accompany the framework (QCA, 2000) and the aims for the Foundation Stage state explicitly that what children need 'is a well-planned and resourced curriculum to take their learning forward and to provide opportunities for all children to succeed in an atmosphere of care and feeling valued' (QCA, 2000, p. 8). Indeed, that the policy set out 'early learning goals' already suggests that there are targets to be achieved, orienting the child not only towards the future but also towards specific pre-identified ends. In addition, it should be noted in the above extract that it is the *curriculum* that will 'take the child's learning forward'. Children themselves seem redundant except as the vehicles for learning.

Although at first glance the set of principles guiding the Foundation Stage curriculum appear child-centred/child-friendly in terms of, for example, social inclusivity – it aims to ensure that all children feel included, secure and valued – in only one guiding principle is the child recognized explicitly as an active agent (subject position 1) when it is stated that 'early years experience should build on what children already know and can do'. Overwhelmingly, the other principles of the framework are outcome based (subject position 3) in terms of what the individual child (subject position 2) will achieve: 'well planned, purposeful activity and appropriate intervention by practitioners will engage children in the learning process and help them make progress in their learning' (QCA, 2000, p. 11).

The other guiding principles for the curriculum are that 'effective education requires both a relevant curriculum and practitioners who understand and are able to implement the curriculum requirements'; that 'effective education requires practitioners who understand that children develop rapidly during the early years – physically, intellectually, emotionally and socially'; and that early education 'should also encourage a positive attitude and disposition to learn'. In addition, it is noted that 'to be effective, an early years curriculum should be carefully structured' and that there should be three strands that provide for 'the different starting points from which children develop their learning'. Finally, it is suggested that there should be 'relevant and appropriate content that matches the different levels of young children's needs' and that children should be directed towards 'purposeful activity that provides opportunities for teaching and learning, both indoors and outdoors'. Thus, although the guidelines occasionally nod in the direction of child-initiated activity, which the teacher then develops, this agentive subject position is rarely glimpsed within the guidance notes for the delivery of the Foundation Stage curriculum.

Subject positions 2 and 3 – the subjection positions oriented towards the individual child as future citizen – also dominate in the goals that have been specifically constituted as a set of targets that individual children should reach. In relation to reading, for example, it is stated that by the time they enter primary school aged five, all children should have, at the very least, developed an interest in books, should know that print conveys meaning and they should be able to recognize a few familiar words. Most children should, in addition, know that in English, print is read from left to right and top to bottom, show an understanding of elements of stories, and read a range of familiar words and simple sentences independently; they should be able to retell narratives in the correct sequence, drawing on language patterns of stories, and have an understanding of how information can be found in non-fiction texts to answer questions about where, who, why and how. The more advanced five-year-old will, however, have reached point nine on the predetermined scale and by five will be able to read books of their own choice with some fluency and accuracy.

The regular monitoring of children is also mandatory during the Foundation Stage and here subject position 2 becomes critical through the attainments that are recorded in the Foundation Stage Profile that must be completed for every child. Any child who has attended a nursery school will thus enter primary school, at the age of five, with an individual assessment profile, compiled through a range of monitoring processes and, as Norquay (1999) points out, those who fail to reach certain targets are liable to have their 'failures' explained away as individual failings (subject position 2) rather than the failings of a system whose interest does not centre on the child as an active agent in its own learning (subject position 1).

Although Soler and Miller suggest that the later guidance notes that were issued for the Foundation Stage partly mollified the opposition to the proposals mounted by the early childhood community (QCA, 2000), careful scrutiny of the guidance still reveals little evidence of subject position 1 – the position that might encourage children to be seen as agents of their own learning – being opened up for children. This is despite the fact that in the guidance, the 'goals' are redescribed as a set of 'learning opportunities and experiences considered to be appropriate for young children' and also that the focus on 'the achievement of outcomes' is somewhat reduced (Soler and Miller, 2003, p. 61). As Soler and Miller comment:

> Despite the intervention of the early childhood community and subsequent collaboration with government agencies, the early learning goals were shaped by the need for pupils to attain clearly prescribed outcomes. (Soler and Miller, 2003, p. 62)

Thus, for example, there are a series of stepping stones, identified for staff to enable children to succeed. These are set out with a series of pre-determined outcomes, and it is the teacher, rather than the child, who is represented as the main facilitator of these opportunities, with the child's own agency rarely being acknowledged. At age three the advised stepping stone is to:

> provide activities that give children the opportunity and motivation to practice manipulative skills, for example cooking and playing instruments. (QCA, 2000, p. 67)

This leads to a later stepping stone:

> provide opportunities for children to develop fine motor control by for example pouring water into tiny cups, finger games and setting out cutlery. (QCA, 2000, p. 67)

And this strategy ends with advice to:

> Intervene to help children hold a pencil effectively. Use opportunities to help children form letters correctly, for example, when they label their paintings. (QCA, 2000, p. 67)

It is the teacher who provides the opportunities for the most part. On only one occasion is the opportunity for learning created by the child when, for example, the child is encouraged to name their paintings. However, this is, most likely, an activity that the teacher had originally provided children with the opportunity to do.

Conclusion

In stark contrast to the kind of 'self-realization' dreamt of by Froebel for children at the end of the nineteenth century and discussed by Kjørholt (2005) in relation to Norway in the twenty-first century, this analysis of the cultural politics surrounding the education of young children in England suggests that the new Foundation Stage curriculum represents an insidious form of governmentality. Through the very limited subject positions that are made available to children within the guidelines and framework of the early years' curriculum that focus on child-centredness largely in relation to outcomes, children are taught – by adults – to govern themselves. And they are being taught do so, according to Dahlberg and Moss (2005), in order that the state might have the kind of flexible individual who is necessary for the neoliberal state. With its focus on outcomes and measurement, the Foundation Stage curriculum, in both its design and its delivery, threatens to leave little room for the agentic child. As Dahlberg and Moss note, it is not only the regulatory apparatus that works in this way to shape what teachers do. As this policy starts to be fully implemented, everyday life in nursery schools will begin to:

> inscribe a certain way of reasoning, which has very practical consequences: systems of categorization and norms, for example, [will be] brought to bear on children through observation and assessment procedures and systems of ideas [will] construct an understanding of who children are and whom they should become. (Dahlberg and Moss, 2005, p. 19)

And, in line with Grieshaber's discussion of comparable changes taking place for preschool children in Queensland, Australia, this will involve the reinvention of the preschool child 'according to the logic of outcomes and industry' (Grieshaber, 2000, p. 270). As in England, the kind of child-centredness characteristic of an earlier era, which encouraged children's development socially, emotionally, physically and cognitively through play, is being replaced by a new curriculum that is 'reducing the distance between the preschool child and the school child' and centring on children's needs largely in terms of their future contribution to the state (Grieshaber, 2000, p. 277).

However, since a recent report yet again documents the poor literacy levels of many English children and young people, pointing out that one in six are leaving school 'unable to read, write and add up properly' (HMSO, 2006, p. 4), it is not clear whether further reducing children's opportunities to exercise their agency within the education system, at still younger ages, will solve the state's anxieties about the skill level of the future workforce. The introduction in 1988 of a National Curriculum framework for older children, that many children now experience as boring and disempowering and far from child-centred (Christensen and James, 2001), appears not to have had the desired effect. It is doubtful, therefore, whether a policy directed at making ever younger children the focus of such attention will fair any better.

References

Birch, J., Curtis, P. and James, A. (2007) 'Sense and Sensibilities: In Search of the Child-Friendly Hospital', *Built Environment*, 33, 4, 405–416.

Child-Friendly Initiative (2006) http://www.childfriendly.org/ (home page), accessed 25 May 2006.

Christensen, P. and James, A. (2001) 'What Are Schools For: The Temporal Experience of Learning' in B. Mayall and L. Alanen (eds) *Conceptualising Child-Adult Relations* (London: Falmer Press).

Chung, S. and Walsh, D. J. (2000) 'Un-packing Child-Centredness: A History of Meanings', *Journal of Curriculum Studies*, 32, 2, 215–234.

Dahlberg, G. and Moss, P. (2005) *Ethics and Politics in Early Childhood Education* (London: RoutledgeFalmer).

Department of Health (2003) Getting the Right Start. National Service Framework for Children (London: Department of Health Publications).

Grieshaber, S. (2000) 'The State Reinventing the Preschool Child', *Discourse: Studies in the Cultural Politics of Education*, 23, 3, 269–281.

Hendrick, H. (1997) 'Constructions and Reconstructions of British Childhood: An Interpretive Survey, 1800 to the Present' in A. James and A. Prout (eds) *Constructing and Reconstructing Childhood: Contemporary Issues in the Sociological Study of Childhood* (London: Falmer Press).

HMSO (2006) Leitch Review of Skills: Prosperity for All in the Global Economy World Class Skills (Norwich: HMSO).

James, A. (2008) 'Day Care or Early Education? Perspectives on the Institutional Construction of a "Good" Childhood for Young Children in UK?' in G. Robinson, U. Eickelkamp, J. Goodnow and I. Katz (eds) *Contexts of Child Development: Culture, Policy and Intervention* (Darwin: CDU Press).

James, A. L. and James, A. (2001) 'Tightening the Net: Children, Community and Control', *British Journal of Sociology*, 52, 2, 211–228.

James, A. L. and James, A. (2004) *Constructing Childhood: Theory, Policy and Social Practice* (Basingstoke: Palgrave Macmillan).

James, A. and Prout, A. (eds) (1997) *Constructing and Reconstructing Childhood: Contemporary Issues in the Sociological Study of Childhood* (London: Falmer Press).

Jenks, C. (1996) 'The Post-Modern Child' in J. Brannen and M. O'Brien (eds) *Children in Families* (London: Falmer).

Kennedy report (2001) Learning from Bristol: The Report of the Public Inquiry into Children's Heart Surgery at the Bristol Royal Infirmary 1984–1995 (Bristol: Bristol Royal Infirmary).

Kjørholt, A. T. (2005) 'The Competent Child and "the Right to be Oneself": Reflections on Children as Fellow Citizens in an Early Childhood Centre' in A. Clark, A. T. Kjørholt and P. Moss (eds) *Beyond Listening: Children's Perspectives on Early Childhood Services* (Bristol: The Policy Press).

Lee, N. (2001) *Childhood and Society* (Buckingham: Open University Press).

Mayall, B. (2002) *Towards a Sociology of Childhood* (Buckingham: Open University Press).

Norquay, N. (1999) 'Social Difference and the Problem of the "Unique Individual": An Uneasy Legacy of Child-Centred Pedagogy', *Canadian Journal of Education*, 24, 2, 183–196.

Penn, H. (1997) *Comparing Nurseries: Staff and Children in Italy, Spain and the UK* (London: Paul Chapman Publishing).

Qualifications and Curriculum Authority (QCA) (2000) *Curriculum Guidance for the Foundation Stage* (London: Qualifications and Curriculum Authority).

Soler, J. and Miller, L. (2003) 'The Struggle for Early Childhood Curricula: A Comparison of the English Foundations Stage Curriculum, *Te Whariki* and Reggio Emilia', *International Journal of Early Years Education*, 11, 1, 57–67.

Stephens, S. (ed.) (1995) *Children and the Politics of Culture* (Princeton: Princeton University Press).

Walkerdine, V. (2001) 'Safety and Danger: Childhood, Sexuality and Space at the End of the Millenium' in H. Hultqvist and G. Dahlberg (eds) *Governing the Child in the New Millennium* (London: RoutledgeFalmer).

7
Governed Markets and Democratic Experimentalism*
Two Possibilities for Early Childhood Education and Care

Peter Moss

> The world suffers under a dictatorship of no alternatives. Although ideas all by themselves are powerless to overthrow this dictatorship we cannot overthrow it without ideas.
>
> (Unger, 2005a, p. 1)

I had originally expected this chapter to be a case study of applying market logic to early childhood education and care (ECEC) in one country, England. But as I proceeded I found it necessary to counterpoint this case, of what I term governed markets, with another case, this one more imaginary – though not without some actual examples – and offering an alternative possibility for providing ECEC, what I have termed democratic experimentalism. The reason I have done so is because the English case demonstrates, inter alia, the dangers of non-democratic policy development, by which I mean the absence of any debate or enquiry into alternatives, so that one way of doing things becomes taken for granted. For if democracy is to mean anything, it should be its capacity to disturb such taken-for-grantedness, Unger's 'dictatorship of no alternatives', offering citizens instead the prospect of real alternatives inscribed with distinct values, purposes and goals.

---

* This chapter was written in 2008. It does not, therefore, take account of recent economic and political events, including a new Conservative-led government in the UK following the May 2010 election.

England: A case study in governed markets

England offers a stark example of one approach to the marketization of ECEC, what might be termed strongly governed markets. This approach combines a reliance on markets as a mechanism for the supply and delivery of services, while at the same time governing them in the interests of certain national goals so as to restrict their scope for diversity and to mediate the provider/purchaser relationship at the heart of the market. The English governed market in ECEC offers important insights into both the rationality of neoliberalism and the will to control, both of which have proved irresistible to successive English governments over the last 25 years (see James' Chapter 6, this volume, for further discussion of recent developments in ECEC in England).

As in many English-speaking countries, ECEC was low on the policy agenda in England for decades after the Second World War. In a typical male breadwinner society, only a minority of women with preschool-age children were employed, most part time; 'childcare' was mainly a matter of informal arrangements, such as grandparents or fathers caring for children while mothers worked evenings or weekends. Formal services – officially termed 'daycare' – were largely private, supplied predominantly by 'childminders' (family daycarers), with a few nurseries. Many public nurseries were closed soon after the war, and those that remained became increasingly 'social welfare' services for children deemed to be at risk or in need.

Alongside 'daycare', some services existed primarily to provide education to three- and four-year-olds. Playgroups, set up to fill the gap left by patchy public provision, were mainly run by non-profit 'voluntary' organizations, often local parent-led groups. Nursery classes were provided in some primary schools, whose first 'reception' class took increasing numbers of four-year-olds, entering primary school before the compulsory school age of five years. School-based provision was completed by a small number of separate schools dedicated to three- and four-year-olds, 'nursery schools'. Provision in school varied from place to place, nursery education being widespread in left-wing local authorities but far less common elsewhere. Both playgroups and nursery classes offered predominantly part-time attendance, ranging from a daily morning or afternoon session to just two or three sessions a week.

Things began to change in the second half of the 1980s, the decade of Thatcherite rule. The number of employed women with young children, and the number working full time, began to increase, reflecting a new group of well-educated women who resumed employment after maternity leave (Brannen and Moss, 1998). One response was the beginning of a rapid increase in day nursery provision, nearly doubling in England between 1989 and 1994 (from 75,400 to 147,600 places). Moreover, these nursery places were provided by a particular sector: private, for-profit providers. During this five-year period, places in public nurseries fell from 28,800 to 22,300, while private places nearly trebled, from 46,600 to 125,300 (The Stationery Office, 1999, table 2).

By 2008, private for-profit providers dominated the nursery scene; in January of that year, there were an estimated 736,000 places in the UK for children from birth to eight years in nearly 16,000 settings (Laing and Buisson, 2008b). An indication of this dominance, but also of the taken-for-grantedness of market discourse in contemporary England, comes from the following excerpt from an article in a monthly magazine, *Nursery & Childcare Market News*, reporting on the 2008 edition of the *Children's Nurseries UK Market Report*. The report is produced annually by a company that describes itself, on its website, as 'the leading provider of authoritative data statistical analysis and market intelligence on the UK Healthcare Community Care and Childcare sectors' and which advertises the report as bringing 'key activity indicators, market trends, and market projections for input into your business planning and strategy' (Laing and Buisson, 2008a).

> Laing & Buisson estimates the value of the UK children's day-care nursery market at £3.8bn for the calendar year to 2007. As in previous years, private for-profit businesses generate the lion's share of this income, totaling a shade over £3bn. (Laing & Buisson, 2008b, p. 9)

Policy attention turned to early education in the 1990s. Towards the end of the Conservative government, in 1996, a commitment was made to increase provision for three- and four-year-olds. To create a market, with a mix of providers (a 'mixed economy'), a voucher system was proposed, which parents could use to purchase nursery education of their choice up to the value of £1100 per year; this was taken as far as piloting in four local authorities. The Labour government, returned in 1997, took forward the Conservatives' belated interest in early childhood by introducing a universal entitlement to free part-time early education (12.5 hours per week initially, to be extended to 15 hours by 2010) for all three- and four-year-olds.

The Labour government scrapped the voucher proposal but retained the Conservatives' faith in markets and a mixed economy. Under Labour, a range of providers – public, voluntary and private; schools, nurseries, playgroups and childminders – have been encouraged to offer 'early education' for three- and four-year-olds, receiving a 'nursery education grant' if they meet certain conditions; for example, working with the National Curriculum. Today, attendance is almost universal for three- and four-year-olds (97 per cent). Though most provision for four-year-olds is in maintained schools, most three-year-olds receive their early education in the private sector, in nurseries, playgroups or schools (Department for Children, Schools and Families, 2008).

Despite administrative responsibility for all ECEC services being integrated into education since 1998, and a number of subsequent integrative measures (such as a single system of standards, curriculum and inspection), these services in effect remain split between 'childcare' and 'early education'. The former is dominated by private for-profit nurseries and childminders, relies on 'childcare workers' with relatively low levels of qualification and poor pay, and is treated as, first and foremost, a private responsibility of parents. In 2007, two-thirds of nursery income came from parents, the remainder from employers and government grants for providing early education; lower-income parents can receive government subsidies, in the form of tax credits, and these account for a quarter of the fees paid by parents (Laing and Buisson, 2008b). 'Early education', by contrast, is dominated by schools, especially for four-year-olds, includes a substantial proportion of graduate teachers with relatively good pay and is considered a public responsibility, with direct funding of services.

However, what both parts – 'childcare' and 'early education' – share is a market approach. I turn now to consider its development and rationale.

The market approach

While the post-1997 Labour government has undoubtedly given much greater policy attention to ECEC, compared with previous governments, many policies adopted by Labour have much in common with their Conservative predecessors. In education, the 1986 Education Act is widely seen as a landmark measure starting a major process of reform, including an emphasis on diversity of provision, school autonomy and parental choice. Whitty et al. (1998) have described the result as 'quasi-markets', seeking to make public services behave like the private sector, in particular through state-funded schools competing with each other. In nursery education, not only were state-funded schools to compete but successive governments, Conservative and Labour, actively enabled private sector services to enter the fray, turning a quasi-market into an actual though, as we shall see, heavily regulated market.

While the development of market approaches in early education policy can be clearly documented and dated, the process is less clear in 'childcare', at least initially. There is no one point in time when government explicitly determined on a market approach in 'childcare', no policy document where different options were considered and the market approach preferred, no parliamentary debate on the subject. Yet by 2008, a senior civil servant could state in a public presentation that a 'diverse market [is] the only game in town' (Archer, 2008). What happened over a period of years is a shift from implicit acceptance of the market to active encouragement.

Post-war governments, of Left and Right, viewed mothers' employment with either hostility or indifference; either way, 'childcare' was deemed a purely private matter, except for basic regulation of all 'daycare' services to ensure minimum standards. There was a small market, and this was never questioned as the means to provide what was variously termed 'daycare' or 'childcare'. It was, one might say, a market by default. This remained the case in the late 1980s and early 1990s as maternal employment and private nursery provision began to grow. The first glimmer of more active policy, in the final years of the Conservative administration, was the introduction in 1994 of the 'childcare disregard', a modest system of demand subsidy, significant as a form of funding linked to market approaches, its rationale being to enable low-income consumers to enter the market from which they might otherwise be priced out.

The new Labour administration broke with the past by adopting wholehearted support for maternal employment and prioritizing policies to increase such employment. 'Childcare' (a term and concept to which the government has remained attached despite transferring responsibility for daycare services from health to education) was to be stimulated as part of a 'Childcare Strategy', and this was to be achieved by encouraging private providers into the market and by active state stimulation of the market. This stimulation has taken three main forms. First is developing an extensive tax credit scheme, a demand subsidy approach to funding, intended to enable lower-income parents to pay nursery and childminding fees. Second is providing start-up support for private providers in poor areas where markets struggle to get established. Third is facilitating the functioning of markets: in 2006 the government stated that 'there is already a diverse market in childcare, in which the private, voluntary and community sectors play a major part. But gaps remain, and we need to develop in every area a thriving childcare market which will respond to parents' needs' (Department for Education and Skills, 2006, p. 3). The Childcare Act 2006 required local authorities to actively manage the 'childcare' market to secure sufficient childcare for working parents. A government summary of the act states that the 'key provisions' of Sections 6, 8–11 and 13 propose that:

> local authorities take the strategic lead in their local childcare market, planning, supporting and commissioning childcare. Local authorities will not be expected to provide childcare direct but will be expected to work with local private, voluntary and independent sector providers to meet local needs. (Department for Children, Schools and Families, 2006, no page)

The extreme reluctance to allow the public sector to participate in this market is readily apparent: a diverse market, therefore, meant a market of private providers, mainly operating as for-profit businesses, with the local authority left to act as the provider of last resort.

Why a market approach?

In studies of the welfare state, England, like other English-speaking countries, is usually allocated to the category 'liberal welfare regime', characterized by Esping-Andersen as having three core elements:

> It is, firstly, residual in the sense that social guarantees are typically limited to 'bad risks'.... [It] is, secondly, residual in the sense that it adheres to a narrow conception of what risks should be considered 'social'.... The third characteristic of liberalism is its encouragement of the market. (Esping-Andersen, 1999, p. 75)

In the 1980s, Thatcherite Britain, along with Reaganite America, went into a period of hyper- or neoliberalism: there was a 'dramatic consolidation of neoliberalism as a new economic orthodoxy regulating public policy at the state level' (Harvey, 2005, p. 22). The rationality of neoliberalism placed even higher value on targeting, reducing social risks and markets, as well as emphasizing other values, including individual choice, flexibility, competition and private provision of services (and an accompanying suspicion of anything public). Markets gave expression to these values, facilitating choice, competition and flexibility through the diversity and responsiveness of private providers. The citizen-subject of neoliberalism was the autonomous consumer, able and willing to assume personal responsibility for a wide range of risks and able to flourish in the market by using information and calculation to find best value for money, keep providers on their toes and drive down costs.

Another feature of neoliberal rationality was a somewhat divergent attitude to 'care' and 'education'. 'Education' could be seen as a public good, something clearly necessary to economic success and the production of the citizen-subject, able to practice freedom and flexibility; education services, therefore, might be delivered through the market, but the state would be justified in funding them. 'Care', however, whether 'childcare' or 'eldercare', was seen as a private responsibility, remaining so when transferred from the domestic to the public sphere, an essentially private commodity to be subsidized by employer or government only to the extent they calculated it in their interests to do so. Thus, though public expenditure on 'childcare' services, mainly through the tax credit system, has increased considerably under Labour, the proportion of costs borne by government remains low, compared both with early education and with countries, such as the Nordic states, which have fully integrated care and education and accepted ECEC as a public responsibility (OECD, 2006).

To fully integrate 'childcare' into the education system and to create a single system, as, for example, characterized the ECEC systems in the Nordic states by the 1980s, made no sense from a neoliberal perspective. It would only serve to muddy the waters, creating unnecessary additional public expense, both by putting the funding of what had been 'childcare' on the same footing as 'early education' and by calling into question the low levels of qualification and pay of 'childcare workers'. From the neoliberal perspective, low pay is not a contentious issue of power and injustice but results from market valuation of the work involved, in this case based on paid workers simply undertaking for money what women do unpaid and unqualified in the home.

Regulated markets

While markets, operating with a mixed economy of providers, have been a driving principle of English ECEC policy since the 1990s, they have taken a very particular form: highly regulated by a powerful central government. What has emerged has been described in the educational field as 'quasi-markets' combined with 'an evaluative state' (Whitty et al., 1998, p. 20). The state has argued the virtues of choice and diversity, on the one hand, while, on the other hand, it has introduced an array of agencies and mechanisms that have given it unparalleled control over education and childcare.

What are these agencies and mechanism? First, they have developed a highly prescriptive curriculum covering the early years, most recently in the form of the Early Years Foundation Stage (EYFS). In two volumes – a statutory framework and practice guidance – running to 160 pages, the EYFS sets out 69 early learning goals, educational programmes for each of 'six areas of learning and development' and assessment arrangements, culminating in the Early Years Foundation Stage Profile. The profile involves assessing children on 13 scales, each divided into nine 'points', with the procedure specified in detail in a handbook running to 90 pages. This dense and detailed network of norms and criteria leaves little scope for interpretation or supplementation and is very much in the tradition of what Bennett (2006) refers to as the 'pre-primary approach':

> Each child is expected by the final year to have reached pre-defined levels of learning in subject areas useful for school.... A cognitive curriculum is drawn up at central level, with the assumption that it can be delivered uniformly in all preschools, often by teachers who are not certified in early childhood studies. (Bennett, 2006, public lecture)

This is in contrast to what the second report of the Organization for Economic Cooperation and Development (OECD) 'Starting Strong' review describes as a 'guiding framework' curriculum: 'Frameworks based on consultation allow local interpretation, identify general quality goals and indicate how they might be obtained' (OECD, 2006, p. 209).

Secondly, the implementation of this curriculum, and overall government monitoring and regulation of individual services, is assured by a state agency, the Office for Standards in Education, Children's Services and Skills (Ofsted), which inspects all ECEC services, including childminders. Ofsted is not only a key means of regulation but also an important part of the market system, since its reports on individual services are publicly available, providing parents acting as calculating and informed consumers with information on which to base their purchasing decisions.

Thirdly, through another agency, the Children's Workforce Development Council, a training system for 'childcare workers' is based on a detailed set of 'national occupational standards' broken down into elements, which in turn contain detailed criteria against which the performance of workers can be assessed. The work, in short, is conceptualized as a set of task-defined competencies and prescribed behavioural standards, and the qualified worker as someone who has demonstrated an ability to conform to these standards against defined performance criteria. Workforce development includes the goal of what is termed 'a graduate-led early years workforce', with nurseries and non-school settings to be headed by a graduate, the newly introduced role of the Early Years Professional (EYP), qualification for which requires meeting 39 defined standards (Children's Workforce Development Council, 2008). The EYP will lead a non-graduate work team (Children's Workforce Development Council, 2008). What is envisaged is a hierarchical workforce of technicians, led by the EYP, who will implement a detailed curriculum to produce predetermined outcomes, all to be monitored by a central government agency.

This system of standardization, surveillance and control has been constructed as part of an immense exercise in detailed policy making and direction by central government, expressed, communicated and directed through a mass of documentation. Consultation documents, policy documents, acts, guidance and advice, memoranda, letters to local authorities, reports and projects have poured forth, setting out in great detail how everything is to be done and what everyone is to do.

How and why has this happened? How has the English state espoused both neoliberalism and strong regulation? Why has it so qualified a belief in markets by creating this framework of managerial control?

At a somewhat superficial level, one explanation is that the state has done this because it could. England has long been one of the most centralized states in Europe. One of the achievements of the Thatcher government was to reduce or eradicate the influence of alternative centres of power to national government, what Rose refers to as 'intermediate enclaves of power: fiefdoms of local government, enclosures of professional expertise, the rigidities imposed on labour markets by trades unions' (Rose, 1999, p. 147). With its centralizing traditions and weak counterbalances, the English state was able by the 1990s, if it so chose, to exert detailed control over a burgeoning ECEC sector, albeit one that was split and made up of a myriad of providers.

But we must seek deeper levels of explanation if we are to answer the question: Why did a state committed to resurgent market liberalism choose to exercise its powers? Here two lines of explanation can be explored, though I do not pretend that they are the only possibilities on offer. One argues that neoliberalism is in tension with more conservative traits. Michael Apple, writing about the mixture of markets and management apparent in the US compulsory education sector (but redolent of both this sector and ECEC in England) has described an alliance – a 'new hegemonic bloc' – of neoliberals and neoconservatives, 'tense and filled with contradictory tendencies' but still capable of exerting leadership in educational policy and reform: the former emphasizing the relationship between education and the market, the latter agreeing with the neoliberal turn to unregulated markets, but seeking stronger control over knowledge, morals and values through curricula, testing and other means (Apple, 2004). More generally, Harvey has pointed to 'the increasing authoritarianism evident in neoliberal states, such as the US and Britain', equating this authoritarianism with a strain of neoconservatism that is:

> … entirely consistent with the neoliberal agenda of elite governance, mistrust of democracy, and the maintenance of market freedoms. But it veers away from the principles of pure neoliberalism and has reshaped neoliberal practices in two fundamental respects: first, in its concern for order as an answer to the chaos of individual interests, and second, in its concern for an overweening morality as the necessary social glue to keep the body politic secure in the face of external and internal dangers. (Harvey, 2005, p. 82)

The tensions between neoliberalism and neoconservatism are particularly acute within Conservative politics, and indeed reflect two different conservative constituencies, the first eager to engage with the demands and opportunities of global economic competitiveness and the preparation of citizens at ease with globalism and cosmopolitanism – the 'global middle class'; the other more traditional and local in perspective, 'who see their social reproduction in terms of traditional occupations and labour markets and whose sensibilities rest on a more stable English identity'.

But England's new-found policy interest in ECEC has mainly taken place during a Labour administration, within which the political dynamic is perhaps somewhat different. 'New Labour' – following a Third Way politics – adopted the market with enthusiasm and confidence, fending off the antipathies and doubts of a marginalized 'Old Labour' constituency that had its roots in declining heavy industry and a male breadwinner ideal and was attached to public sector provision of public services. Across a wide range of policy areas and services, New Labour has espoused the values of neoliberalism: individual choice, competition and entrepreneurship, and the ideal of the self-regulating and autonomous subject managing their own risk through informed and calculating engagement with the market.

At the same time, this strong espousal of what Rose terms 'advanced liberalism' does not preclude an active state. What is called for is, in the words of Giddens, 'a new mixed economy' (Giddens, 1998, p. 99), with a 'social investment state' replacing the welfare state, concerned less with redistribution 'after the event' and more with a 'redistribution of possibilities' through 'a cultivation of human potential', in particular through investment in education, also desirable to ensure national survival in an increasingly competitive global economy (see Strandell, Chapter 5, this volume, for further discussion of the social investment state). In the new mixed economy, the market is no longer subordinate to the state; it is instead harnessed so that its dynamism acts in the public interest, with a new synergy between public and private sectors.

The use of the market and private entrepreneurial flair in the provision and delivery of services is one of three main mechanisms for the 'social investment state'. The second is a strong technical role for research, research understood and deployed as 'a producer of means, strategies, and techniques to achieve given ends' (Biesta, 2007, p. 18). Such technical research provides clear 'evidence' of 'what works', to ensure effective investment in the best-performing technologies and to calculate the returns made from that investment. The third is new public management, inscribed with the ethos of business, the rationality of markets and the image of the citizen as customer, and providing the social investment state with an array of new technologies.

> In the new public management, the focus is upon accountability, explicit standards and measures of performance, emphasis on outputs, not inputs, with rewards linked to performance, desegregation of functions into corporatized units operating with their own budgets and trading with one another, contracts and competition, and insistence on parsimony maintained by budget discipline. This required a shift from an ethic of public service to one of private management. (Rose, 1999, p. 150)

With the use of markets, technical research and new public management, government is turned into a modern business organization, managing a wide array of production units at a distance, through setting objectives, allocating resources and endlessly auditing their attainment. Providers of services – production units – have greater day-to-day autonomy and freedom to compete with each other, freed as they are from direct bureaucratic management, yet do so within a highly prescribed framework of national standards and targets. Providers compete with one another, but as part of an internal market subsumed within a national corporate entity – England plc – which is engaged in competing with other similar national corporations.

Everything is dangerous

Michel Foucault comments that 'not everything is bad but that everything is dangerous'. Good intentions offer no escape from power relations and no safeguard against adverse consequences. This should serve as an urgent reminder to all involved in the development of early childhood services, itself part of a process of a growing institutionalization of childhood. Too often the advocates of early childhood services treat them as a purely technical matter, with self-evident purposes: the only issue is to ensure correct technology – 'high quality' – is applied to achieve predetermined outcomes (for example, developmental or learning goals), the only danger if children are exposed to wrong or incorrectly applied technology – 'low quality'. Who provides these services is immaterial; all that matters is how, and ensuring the effective workings of the market and individual choice.

But these services are deeply political. Their purposes and possibilities are not self-evident, but multiple and contestable. The dangers they pose include governing children ever more effectively, through applying increasingly potent 'human technologies' to achieve ever more strongly prescribed outcomes. Who provides them can matter very much if we understand them in a certain way, and collective choices may matter as much as individual choices.

The discourse of strongly governed markets constructs early childhood services as businesses, supplying a commodity for sale to parents; and as factories, applying technologies to children to produce predetermined outcomes. In this construction, children become objects of 'childcare' and 'education', parents become consumers and early childhood workers become technicians, whose task it is to apply technologies correctly. The role of the state has been to create conditions in which a market can develop and function effectively, delivering services, while at the same time ensuring the application of effective technologies and the auditing of their effects. It has also invested public money. This investment has been justified on two grounds: first, that 'childcare' is needed to increase maternal employment; and secondly, that early intervention will secure large long-term returns in a range of educational and social benefits, concentrated particularly on the large minority of economically disadvantaged children.

It is not my purpose in this chapter to question these grounds for investment, although neither should be taken for granted and accepted unquestioningly. Rather, I want to suggest that the discourse of governed markets and its rationale represents just one perspective on early childhood services, and that there are others that could inform and shape the institutionalization of childhood. I want, therefore, to relativize the discourse of governed markets in the interests of a democratic politics of childhood. I want to outline here just one other discourse, for purposes of illustration, without claiming that this discourse, which I term democratic experimentalism, is the only other possibility. I call it speculative because although I think examples exist of individual services, and even individual local authorities, working with this discourse, there are no systemic examples, at national or regional levels; what I am doing is exploring a possibility (for a fuller discussion of this discourse, with more examples, see Moss, 2008).

Democratic experimentalism: A speculative case study

The term 'democratic experimentalism' is borrowed from the work of the Brazilian social theorist Roberto Unger, who has the ambitious goal of imagining how to reform contemporary societies to empower humanity. He seeks an alternative to proposals for change that are either so radical as to appear unachievable or so incremental that they are achievable but trivial. He finds this alternative in what he has termed 'democratic experimentalism', which can, he argues, bring about major, long-term change through cumulative reforms, gradual and piecemeal. This strategy requires a desired direction for change, 'a credible image of change' – the central question is where to? – and the power of human imagination and hope, 'which helps form the possibilities it envisages'.

Unger extends the concept of experimentation to services, such as education, but makes it clear that experimentation is contingent on democracy:

> The provision of public services must be an innovative collective practice, moving forward the qualitative provision of the services themselves. That can no longer happen in our current understanding of efficiency and production by the mechanical transmission of innovation from the top. It can only happen through the organization of a collective experimental practice from below.... Democracy is not

just one more terrain for the institutional innovation that I advocate. It is the most important terrain. (Unger, 2005a, p. 179)

Other sources of inspiration are individuals, organizations and countries that have proposed democracy as a fundamental value in education. Dewey, for example, affirmed that 'all those who are affected by social institutions must have a share in producing and managing them' and elsewhere defines democracy as 'a way of life controlled by a working faith in the possibilities of human nature...[and] faith in the capacity of human beings for intelligent judgement and action if proper conditions are furnished' (Dewey, 1976, p. 225). The recent OECD thematic review of ECEC, the most important cross-national study in this field, concludes its final report with a call 'to aspire toward ECEC systems that support broad learning, participation and democracy'. This means 'an early childhood system founded on democratic values' that encourages 'democratic reflexes in children' and that recognizes the 'democratic dimension' in parental involvement, 'that is the exercise by parents of their basic right to be involved in the education of their children' (OECD, 2006, pp. 218–219). The report envisages 'early childhood services as a life space where educators and families work together to promote the well-being, participation and learning of young children...based on the principle of democratic participation' and notes that 'this principle can also work effectively in management' (OECD, 2006, p. 220).

At a national level, the Swedish national preschool curriculum states a clear commitment to democracy as the basis for ECEC services:

Democracy forms the foundation of the preschool. For this reason, all preschool activity should be carried out in accordance with fundamental democratic values. (Swedish Ministry of Education and Science, 1998, p. 6)

Other Nordic countries, too, pay explicit attention to the importance of democracy in their early childhood curricula. Wagner (2006) argues that democracy is central to the Nordic concept of the good childhood and notes, in support of this contention, that 'official policy documents and curriculum guidelines in the Nordic countries acknowledge a central expectation that preschools and schools will exemplify democratic principles and that children will be active participants in these democratic environments' (Wagner, 2006, p. 292).

This attention to democracy and also to decentralization, arguably a precondition for experimentation, gives the Nordic countries a strong potential for democratic experimentalism in ECEC. At the same time, there is evidence that they are being increasingly drawn in another direction, by the pull of neoliberalism, with heightened policy attention given to marketization, competition, individual choice, flexibility and private provision.

Democracy then is a fundamental value of the early childhood institution (for a further discussion of this idea and what it might mean in practice, see Moss, 2007). Experimentalism is also fundamental. This is far more than simply responding to market forces. It means services engaging with families – children and adults – in the creation or co-construction of new knowledge, new understandings and new desires. Services become like workshops or laboratories, where new theories can be created and tried, produced from the encounter of different perspectives and identities; in this way, participatory democracy is a condition for experimentation. The results of this experimentalism are what Hardt and Negri (2005) term 'immaterial production', which includes 'the production of ideas, images, knowledge, communication, cooperation, and affective relations... social life itself' (Hardt and Negri, 2005, p. 146). Such immaterial production, they argue, is based on cooperation, collaboration and communication – 'in short, its foundation in the common'. In the model, the immaterial products created by the experimentalism of early childhood services are not appropriated as private property but are made freely available for the common good.

So in a discourse of democratic experimentalism, early childhood institutions can be understood as places of encounter between citizens and as collaborative workshops, in which many projects are possible – social, cultural, ethical, aesthetic, economic and political. Here are just a few, hinting at the potential of these social institutions, not detailing a complete inventory:

- Construction of knowledge, values and identities.
- Researching children's learning processes.
- Community and group support and empowerment.
- Cultural (including linguistic) sustainability and renewal.
- Gender equality and economic development.
- Democratic and ethical practice.

The institution is a potential, a becoming, a place of possibilities; it produces outcomes and some may be predetermined – but many others will not be. Surprise, wonder and amazement are welcomed, the 'dictatorship of no alternatives' resisted.

Understanding an early childhood institution in this way is very different from understanding it as the provider of a private commodity to a customer or as an enclosure for applying technologies to predetermined normative ends. It is a public good and a public responsibility, an expression of a community taking collective responsibility for the education and upbringing of its young children. Services feel a responsibility for and wish to be open to all local families, not just for those wanting and able to pay for childcare; and because of their commitment to participation, these services want to be both inclusive and responsive to the needs of all families. In democratic experimentalism, early childhood services, along with schools, are recognized as uniquely important public institutions, since all citizens attend them on a regular basis for a considerable period of time.

The practice of democratic experimentalism is not easy and needs certain conditions in place to enable it, including certain understandings or images of the child, parent and educator; certain values; certain tools; educated workers; and time. I will consider each of these in turn.

Understandings or images of the child, parent and educator

The market model posits a utility-maximizing 'homo economicus', focused on individual (including family) needs and benefits, and freed 'from what are construed as the burdensome chains of social justice and social responsibility' (Davies and Saltmarsh, 2007, p. 3). This active and autonomous risk-managing subject is engaged in a calculative and contractual relationship with a commodity-providing and self-interested provider, kept up to the mark by the discipline of competition; without such competition, resources will be wasted and provision will be unresponsive. The model of democratic experimentalism, by contrast, presumes a subject who is capable and willing to adopt a public as well as a private role, with a sense of social justice and responsibility, and who is a citizen concerned with collective as well as individual wellbeing. This subject can be child or adult, children being viewed as agents and rights-bearing citizens in the here and now, whose views and experiences need full expression in the processes of democratic participation that are central to this model.

The *child*, in the model of democratic experimentalism, is understood not only as a competent citizen but also as an expert in their own life, having opinions that are worth listening to; they have the right and competence to participate in collective decision making. *Parents* are seen as competent citizens 'because they have and develop their own experience, points of view, interpretation and ideas...which are the fruits of their experience as parents and citizens' (Cagliari et al., 2004, p. 30). Last, but not least, *workers* are understood as practitioners of democracy. While recognizing that they bring an important perspective and a relevant local knowledge to the democratic forum, they also recognize that they do not have the truth or privileged access to knowledge. As Paulo Freire puts it, the educator may offer their 'reading of the world', but their role is to 'bring out the fact that there are other readings of the world' (Freire, 2004, p. 96), at times in opposition to their own.

Values

Democratic and experimental practice needs certain values to be shared among the community of the early childhood institution, including participation, dialogue, trust – and choice. The use of the word 'choice', in the context of this model, refers to the democratic process of *collective* choice or decision making, not only the *individual* choice of the market model: 'choice' is a value in both models, but understood in different ways. As a recent report on Britain's democracy puts it:

> We do not believe that the consumer and the citizen are one and the same, as the new market-driven technocracy seems to assume. Consumers act as individuals, making decisions largely on how an issue will affect themselves and their families. Citizenship implies membership of a collective where decisions are taken not just in the interest of the individual but for the collective as a whole or for a significant part of that collective. (Power Inquiry, 2006, p. 169)

Bentley makes a similar distinction and blames a shift from collective to individual choice-making for the contemporary crisis of democracy:

> Liberal democracy combined with market capitalism has reinforced the tendency of individuals to act in ways that reduce our ability to make collective choices. This is the underlying reason for the crisis in democracy...our preoccupation with making individual choices is undermining our ability to make collective choices. Our democracy is suffocating itself. (Bentley, 2005, pp. 9, 19)

Other values of particular importance include:

- *Respect for diversity*, through adopting a relational ethics that gives the highest value to diversity (see Dahlberg and Moss, 2005).

- *Recognition of multiple perspectives and paradigms*, acknowledging and welcoming that there is more than one answer to most questions and that there are many ways of viewing and understanding the world.
- *Welcoming curiosity, uncertainty and subjectivity*, and the responsibility that they require of us (see Rinaldi, 2006).
- *Critical thinking*, which is 'a matter of introducing a critical attitude towards those things that are given to our present experience as if they were timeless, natural, unquestionable: to stand against the maxims of one's time, against the spirit of one's age, against the current of received wisdom ... [it is a matter] of interrupting the fluency of the narratives that encode that experience and making them stutter' (Rose, 1999, p. 20).

Tools

Of particular importance is the tool of pedagogical documentation, by which practice and learning processes are made visible (for example, through notes or observations of children's work, videos or photographs, taped conversations, children's drawings or constructions in different materials) and then subject – in relationship with others – to dialogue, reflection, interpretation and, if necessary, democratic evaluation and decision making (for fuller discussions of pedagogical documentation, see Dahlberg et al., 2007; Rinaldi, 2006). Pedagogical documentation has a central role to play in many facets of the early childhood institution: ensuring that new knowledge is shared as a common good; evaluation as participatory meaning making; planning pedagogical work; professional development; and in research by children and adults. The contribution of pedagogical documentation to democratic practice in the early childhood institution cuts across these particular uses: 'Sharing the documentation means participation in a true act of democracy, sustaining the culture and visibility of childhood, both inside and outside the school: democratic participation, or "participant democracy", that is a product of exchange and visibility' (Rinaldi, 2006, p. 59).

Educated workers

Not only does democracy in the early childhood institution require workers who are understood, both by themselves and others, as practitioners of democracy 'with a professional obligation to create an educational environment which will sustain the development of democratic virtues and practices' (Carr and Hartnett, 1996, p. 195). It also needs a workforce whose initial and continuous professional development supports them in this role. This requires a capacity to work with uncertainty (Urban, 2008) and openness to other perspectives and knowledges – to the otherness of others. Fortunati, working in the ECEC services of the Tuscan town of San Miniato, describes the early childhood worker as needing to be:

> removed from the fallacy of certainties, [assuming instead] responsibility to choose, experiment, discuss, reflect and change, focusing on the organisation of opportunities rather than the anxiety of pursuing outcomes, and maintaining in her work the pleasure of amazement and wonder. [She must be able] to free herself from an outcome different from that which the children come up with as they construct their own experience. (Fortunati, 2006, p. 37)

Important, also, is the ability to discuss, exchange, reflect and argue, in short to be able to enter into dialogue. Dialogue, Paulo Freire says, is the way 'people achieve significance as human beings...It is an act of creation... [it is] founded upon love, humility, and faith' (Freire, 1996, p. 70); it cannot exist without critical thinking, 'thinking which perceives reality as process, as transformation, rather than as a static entity' (Freire, 1996, p. 73); 'it is the opportunity available to me to open up to the thinking of others' (Freire, 2004, p. 103).

Time

Democratic experimentalism in ECEC services, indeed anywhere (including schools), takes time – and time is in short supply. More thought needs to be given to the question of time, and how we might redistribute it across a range of activities and relationships; for example, to enable parents to participate in democratic and experimental early childhood institutions without foregoing participation in paid employment. Ulrich Beck addresses this issue with the concept of 'public work' that would provide 'a new focus of activity and identity that will revitalize the democratic way of life' (Beck, 1998, p. 60), and he suggests various ways of paying for public work. Unger argues that 'it is fundamentally important that every able bodied adult should have a position in both the production system and the caring economy...We have to try different things' (Unger, 2005b, p. 180). One direction to take might involve moving away from current parental leave policies, narrowly focused on providing full-time care for very young children or temporary care for children who are ill, towards a far broader 'time credit' policy, giving citizens the right to a certain amount of paid leave over a working lifetime, to use for a variety of purposes, including participation in children's services.

Nor is the need for time confined to parents. Workers in early childhood services need space in their working lives to devote to documentation and dialogue, not just to prepare future work but to be able to reflect upon, interpret, exchange and evaluate current practice.

Towards an experimental welfare state

One of the tricks of a discourse striving for hegemony is to claim a local, culturally specific idea as universal, timeless and inevitable – there is no alternative. This is the case today with the doctrines of markets (though whether it has been damaged in the long term by the 2008 financial crisis remains to be seen) and new public management. These doctrines increasingly pervade policy, provision and practice in ECEC, not just in their Anglo-Saxon heartlands but increasingly in other parts of the world.

But there are always alternatives, other ways of thinking and doing. I have tried to explore one such alternative for early childhood, an alternative that I would argue finds expression in a number of examples, albeit scattered. At a time when there is increasing recognition of the diversity and complexity in our world and our understandings of it, it is more than ever important to question dominant policy discourses that insist on the possibility of one right answer, and to explore the possibility of welfare states that welcome, promote and support experimentation and the idea that there are always multiple answers.

References

Apple, M. (2004) *Ideology and Curriculum*, 3rd edn (London: RoutledgeFalmer).

Archer, M. (2008) Childcare and Early Years Provision in a Diverse Market – the Government's Approach, http://www.uel.ac.uk/icmec/seminar/index.htm, accessed 29 September 2008.

Beck, U. (1998) *Democracy Without Enemies* (Cambridge: Polity Press).

Bennett, J. (2006) ' "Schoolifying" Early Childhood Education and Care: Accompanying Pre-School into Education', public lecture given at the Institute of Education, University of London, 10 May.

Bentley, T. (2005) *Everyday Democracy: Why We Get the Politicians We Deserve* (London: Demos).

Biesta, G. (2007) 'Why "What Works" Won't Work: Evidence-Based Practice and the Democratic Deficit in Educational Research', *Educational Theory*, 57, 1, 1–22.

Brannen, J. and Moss, P. (1998) 'The Polarisation and Intensification of Parental Employment in Britain: Consequences for Children, Families and the Community', *Community, Work and Family*, 1, 3, 229–247.

Cagliari, P., Barrozi, A. and Giudici, C. (2004) 'Thoughts, Theories and Experiences: For an Educational Project with Participation', *Children in Europe*, 6, 28–30.

Carr, W. and Hartnett, A. (1996) *Education and the Struggle for Democracy* (Buckingham: Open University Press).

Children's Workforce Development Council (2008) Guidance to the Standards for the Award of Early Years Professional Status, http://www.cwdcouncil.org.uk/assets/0000/2398/EYP_Guidance_to_standards_web.pdf, accessed 29 September 2008.

Dahlberg, G. and Moss, P. (2005) *Ethics and Politics in Early Childhood Education* (London: Routledge).

Dahlberg, G., Moss, P. and Pence, A. (2007) *Beyond Quality in Early Childhood Education and Care; Languages of Evaluation*, 2nd edn (London: Routledge).

Davies, B. and Saltmarsh, S. (2007) 'Gender Economies: Literacy and the Gendered Production of Neo-Liberal Subjectivities', *Gender and Education*, 19, 1, 1–20.

Department for Children, Schools and Families (2006) Summary of Childcare Act 2006, http://www.everychildmatters.gov.uk/_files/7D318642AFE510D3C215793486082610.doc, accessed 26 January 2009.

Department for Children, Schools and Families (2008) Provision for Children under Five Years of Age in England: January 2008 (SFR 12/2008), http://www.dcsf.gov.uk/rsgateway/DB/SFR/s000790/SFR12-2008.pdf, accessed 29 September 2008.

Department for Education and Skills (2006) Choice for Parents, the Best Start for Parents: Making it Happen (London: Department for Education and Skills).

Dewey, J. (1976) 'Creative Democracy: The Task Before Us' in J. Boydston (ed.) *John Dewey: The Later Works, 1925–1953, volume 14* (Carbondale: Southern Illinois University Press).

Esping-Andersen, G. (1999) *Social Foundations of Postindustrial Economies* (Oxford: Oxford University Press).

Fortunati, A. (2006) *The Education of Young Children as a Community Project: The Experience of San Miniato* (Azzano San Paolo: Edizioni Junior).

Freire, P. (1996) *Pedagogy of the Oppressed* (London: Penguin Books).

Freire, P. (2004) *Pedagogy of Hope* (London: Continuum).

Giddens, A. (1998) *The Third Way: The Renewal of Social Democracy* (Cambridge: Polity Press).

Hardt, M. and Negri, A. (2005) *Multitude* (London: Penguin Books).

Harvey, D. (2005) *A Brief History of Neoliberalism* (Oxford: Oxford University Press).

Laing & Buisson (2008a) Independent Health Data Mailing Lists, Newsletters, Market News Reports Surveys, http://www.laingbuisson.co.uk, accessed 29 September 2008.

Laing & Buisson (2008b) 'Demand Outstrips Supply for the First Time According to Leading Report', *Nursery & Childcare Market News*, 7, 2, 8–9.

Moss, P. (2007) 'Bringing Politics into the Nursery: Early Childhood Education as a Democratic Practice', *European Early Childhood Education Research Journal*, 15, 1, 1–16.

Moss, P. (2008) Early Childhood Education: Markets and Democratic Experimentalism, http://www.bertelsmann-stiftung.de/bst/de/media/xcms_bst_dms_24015__2.pdf, accessed 29 September 2008.

OECD (2006) Starting Strong II (Paris: OECD).

Power Inquiry (2006) *The Report of Power: An Independent Inquiry into Britain's Democracy* (London: The Power Inquiry).

Rinaldi, C. (2006) *In Dialogue with Reggio Emilia: Listening, Researching and Learning* (London: Routledge).

Rose, N. (1999) *Powers of Freedom: Reframing Political Thought* (Cambridge: Cambridge University Press).

The Stationery Office (1999) Children's Day Care Facilities at 31 March 1999 England, http://www.archive.official-documents.co.uk/document/dfee/daycare/cdc-03.htm, accessed 29 September 2008.

Swedish Ministry of Education and Science (1998) Curriculum for Preschool (English translation) (Stockholm: Swedish Ministry of Education and Science).

Unger, R. M. (2005a) *What Should the Left Propose?* (London: Verso).

Unger, R. M. (2005b) 'The Future of the Left: James Crabtree Interviews Roberto Unger', *Renewal*, 13, 2/3, 173–184.

Urban, M. (2008) 'Dealing with Uncertainty: Challenges and Possibilities for the Early Childhood Profession', *European Early Childhood Education Research Journal*, 16, 2, 135–152.

Wagner, J. T. (2006) 'An Outsider's Perspective: Childhoods and Early Education in the Nordic Countries' in J. Einarsdottir and J. T. Wagner (eds) *Nordic Childhoods and Early Education: Philosophy, Research, Policy and Practice in Denmark, Finland, Iceland, Norway, and Sweden* (Greenwich, CT: Information Age Publishing).

Whitty, G., Power, S. and Halpin, D. (1998) *Devolution and Choice in Education* (Buckingham: Open University Press).

8
Daycare, Flexible Workers and the Combination of Work and Childcare

Birgitte Johansen

Introduction

Time has become the focus of attention since both mothers and fathers, more than previously, have to divide theirs between vital caring duties and their responsibility to earn a living in a flexible work life. Together, the 'stacked' responsibilities are often regarded as constituting a 'time bind', particularly for women (Hochschild, 1997). Publicly funded daycare is depicted as a solution to this situation (Carnoy, 2002; Esping-Andersen et al., 2002; Fraser, 1994; Gornick and Meyers, 2003), and one that is within reach of most Norwegian parents. Accordingly, this chapter will explore the situation of parents participating in the new work life using daycare for their children. Important questions that will be discussed are how these parents experience the combination of a flexible work life and the use of daycare and whether daycare resolves their likely time bind.

These questions are actualized by contradictory research on the temporal consequences of work-life 'flexibilization' for caring during the last decade (Brannen, 2005; Jacobs and Gerson, 2004). On the one hand, flexibility in work life, particularly more flexible working hours, is regarded as a solution for combining caring and working and is frequently seen in organizational work-life balance policies (Fleetwood, 2007; Perrons et al., 2005); for example, in combination with daycare (Gornick and Meyers, 2003). Often work-time flexibility is compared with standardized work time, ignoring different temporal outcomes of flexibility. Part-time work as care-friendly flexibility is, however, criticized by feminists as a gendered work-time strategy that reproduces a gendered economical inequality (Kitterød, 2007).

On the other hand, flexibility can produce temporal obstacles for carers. Flexible working hours become employer-led (Fleetwood, 2007; Rubery et al., 2005) and expand through work-life intensification. We witness a situation of general individualization of the responsibility for handling the risks and insecurities produced by flexible labour markets for workers (Beck, 2000; Brown et al., 2003). Workers' abilities to be flexible and to answer the needs of the labour market and work organizations thus become an important investment asset for the individualized career and mere survival in the flexible labour market (Carnoy, 2002; Crompton, 2006). Consequently, a 'flexibilization' of family policy arrangements, such as parental leave, has been questioned because it requires adapting care to the temporal demands of work life (Brandth and Kvande, 2009).

Flexible work time is potentially both greedy and generous regarding the opportunities it may provide for combining care and work. Yet daycare opening hours in Norway remain standardized. The sector has abandoned the short-time offers of the post-war period (Korsvold, 2008), but the opening hours of daycare centres in Norway have not followed the potential 24 hours of work time. Daycare centres normally close between 16.30 and 17.00 hours. User adaptability to the issue of opening hours in Norwegian public documents has focused on adapting part-time places to the cash-for-care arrangement (St. meld. nr. 27, 1999–2000). Against this backdrop I will present a qualitative analysis of interviews from an empirical study conducted with parents working in jobs representative of the flexible labour market, such as freelancers and knowledge workers in different professional fields. I argue that flexible labour markets produce risk and insecurity that interacts with different positions and strategies of parents. This process generates differing types of flexible working hours. The varying types of work-time flexibility represent differing potentialities and limitations for the organization of care and also the use and need of daycare. The analysis encourages a discussion of the suitability of daycare for flexible parents and their children in the context of flexible labour markets lacking responsibility with respect to the provision of care.

Time, work and daycare

The analyses focus on different temporal outcomes of flexibility with different potentialities and limitations for the organization of care in the data; I therefore apply the concept *temporal opportunity structure for caring*. This is a hybrid concept merged by 'structure of opportunities' used by Ellingsæter (2006, p. 122) for family policy and Adam's (2004) concept of *timescape*. Part-time work produces a different temporal opportunity structure for caring, such as delivering and picking up children in daycare, compared with full-time work. The temporal organization of daycare centres in terms of opening hours produces yet another temporal opportunity structure for caring. In Norway this is rather set and standardized.

The temporal dimension of opportunity structures for caring build on the works of Barbara Adam on timescapes (Adam, 2004). Timescapes offer a sociological way of conceptualizing time and the integration of time in social analysis derived from the landscape metaphor. Time, as a landscape, has different dimensions and Adam (2004, p. 144) separates them and turns them into empirical operational notions suitable for analysis: *time expansion* (operationalized as duration, continuity), *time past, present and future* (operationalized as understandings of time horizons), *tempo* (operationalized as pace and intensity) and *time sequence* (operationalized as rhythm and periodicity). The dimensions of timescapes show how temporality is integrated into work-life flexibility and the production of temporal opportunity structures for caring through the duration of work days, the tempo of tasks to be solved, and the rhythm of careers in terms of job shifts. Likewise, the integration is shown in the need to invest time in the present to reduce insecurity and risk in the future. The different dimensions of temporality might vary and enable a study of different temporal outcomes of work-life flexibility, hence also for the temporal opportunity structures for caring.

Adam (2004) perceives the present-day work time as a 'public industrial timescape' where time is woven into power relations through its commoditization rooted in a 'time is money rationality'. Economically irrational use of time, such as unpaid care, is valueless according to this rationality. Acker (2006) understands the 'time is money' rationality in terms of a gendered substructure of labour markets producing the normal, model worker as a non-carer. The model worker is gendered since care responsibilities are defined as female (Acker, 2006), which suggests a gendering of temporal opportunity structures for caring. As competition increases, the model workers are those who never sleep, consume or have children (Carnoy, 2002, p. 143). The model worker must be understood against the backdrop of neoliberal rationalities permeating advanced liberal democracies where a privatization of the responsibility for risk management is central (Rose, 1996). Individualized risk management of self-provision through the labour market is best handled by the 'model individual' of neoliberalism, which has the attributes and interests of a male entrepreneur. The model worker is globally dispersed by competition in the globalized economy (Connell, 2000, p. 51). The analysis will discuss the model worker related to the temporal opportunity structures for caring and the use of daycare.

Method

To explore and understand the temporal opportunity structures for caring and the role of daycare for parents working in flexible labour markets, I analyse material consisting of in-depth interviews with 11 parents working in jobs representative of the 'new work life'. The aim has been to study the combination of paid work and care by parents working in segments of the labour market that experience a high degree of individualized responsibility for self-provision in a situation implying individualized risk taking. Knowledge work and individualized risk are traits of the new work life described in general terms (see Beck, 2000). However, this is better articulated among freelancers and/or contract workers. In terms of time use, independent workers have the longest working days in Norway (Bø et al., 2008). Yet previous findings on female freelancing also suggest it to be a strategy to handle caring and work (Parker, 2004). Freelancers are therefore an interesting case.

I made a strategic selection (Hammersley and Atkinson, 1995) of freelancers anticipating the processes of competition, insecurity and risk being evident. Based on previous research in the field of advertising (Rasmussen and Johansen, 2005), I wanted to interview freelancers in this area. I understood them to be a critical case (Cresswell, 1998) that would enable the extension of a logical generalization. Yet, it was hard to find freelancing parents with young children using daycare. Musicians and a journalist entered the material for this reason and by the snowball method of recruiting (Cresswell, 1998). For the same reason, some also informed retrospectively about their experiences of having children in daycare, having somewhat older children (first- or second-grade class, that is, age five to seven years) at the time of the interview.

Themes in the interviews were the parents' careers, their experiences of working, of becoming parents, the combination of care and work, and the use of daycare. Evidently, their careers were marked by frequent job-shifts, alternating between or combining freelancing and employment. There were different work-life experiences to consider, not only those of freelancing.

Through analysis, the material was coded in order to reflect on and explore the data (Coffey and Atkinson, 1996). A within- and cross-case analysis (Miles and Huberman, 1994) enabled the identification and explanation of three types of work-time flexibility (*regular long hours, irregular hours* and *flexible part time*), of which the risk generated by the flexible labour market stood central. Some parents had worked under all three types of work-time flexibility. These three were in turn defined along a dimension of greedy/generous, inspired by Coser's (1974) metaphor 'the greedy institution'. The three types of flexibility produced different temporal opportunity structures for caring, framing the parents' encounters with daycare differently. The analysis presents each type of work-time flexibility together with a related section where the parents' experiences of daycare are elaborated. A name with the initial 'M' indicates that the informant is a musician, while those with the initial 'A' worked in advertising, and 'John' was a journalist.

Greedy flexibility: Regular long hours and use of daycare

Regular long hours is the first type of work-time flexibility in the material. As time expansion it represents long durations of work hours over an extended period of time. Long working days are the rule. The concept of regular long hours displays a 'greedy flexibility' consuming parents' time, rendering the temporal opportunity structure for caring limited.

Regular long hours were generated by different factors. The work process itself, such as coming up with a good idea, could be unpredictably time consuming. Also the pleasure gained from the work sometimes resulted in long hours being worked. Yet much of the regular long hours were rooted in insecurities and the possibilities produced by flexible labour markets wherein the parents make their living. It was vital to avoid a non-income situation. The parents applied different strategies to reduce the risk of ending up jobless and to generate future income in a competitive and shifting market; for example, using time to make good products, and becoming and remaining visible and available to clients or colleagues, as well as by networking. The future in terms of possible contracts and income sources had to be constantly borne in mind. These efforts resulted in long hours and were understood as vital to make a living, to reduce risk and to grasp or create opportunities. The long working hours can be regarded as 'time rules of the game' and consequently not questioned by the parents in the interviews. There was a general understanding of the 'way it works here'. As an example, the problem of being away for longer periods of time was affirmed as something one simply adapted to. This resembles the time norms that Epstein et al. (1999) found in organizations employing professionals where working long hours was the sign of a serious and committed employee. In their study, part timers became time deviants in the organizations and were accordingly cut off from career opportunities. For the parents in this study, the general norm of extensive time use is directly related to being a successful market operator. According to this 'time is money' rationality, renouncing on time investments positions market players as 'risk-deviants' as they set themselves apart from the most rational thing to do in order to reduce risk, namely, to invest time in working. Central to the parents' stories was taking personal responsibility to make a living, earn money and continue to make a living selling one's services directly to a client or to a firm. To be a family provider was part of this picture.

The element of risk and provision and how to handle this was articulated by Miranda. She had worked as a freelance jazz singer for years, having started as a music student, before she had children. She had invested time and effort in minimizing risk by generating commission and income. Being visible, alert, available and taking initiative are central and time consuming elements in her story, which in many ways is a 'success story' since she was a known singer. Miranda described her feeling of insecurity as a 'new' freelancer:

> Then you become like...you are drifting without anchorage in the ocean. It takes time to get used to that feeling....That is the feeling I was so afraid of in the beginning. I took everything I could get, I mean EVERYTHING. I think that I was about to work myself to death, I just didn't realize it....I don't know how many per cent I worked, but I was teaching in five different places and played in three different bands. I was constantly thinking that if I don't go for it all the time, I will not have anything to eat next month, so I was never at ease. You become more at ease after a while working as a freelancer....It is about positioning. And before you get a position, you stress around. And I see now the market is becoming more and more saturated. I have the luxury that many people know who I am.

Apparently, the reduction of future risk is related to building oneself as a brand. There is also a link to the relationship between the job and work as an identity project (Giddens, 1991). Freelancers' personal identities are strongly linked to their work, and regular long hours enable them to show themselves as serious players in the market and good enough to be employed. There is an understanding, particularly among musicians, that freelancing is the only way of making a living based on your personal musical interests. This strengthens the tolerance to long hours and simultaneously confirms them as purchasable actors in the market. Miranda was no longer in an underprivileged position and she was in demand. Still, as a freelancer, it is not smart to rest on one's laurels, and the phone soon stops ringing if one says 'No' too many times.

Regular long hours are also worked by parents who are permanently employed in advertising and/or design agencies. Similarly, the element of personal responsibility for the result is apparent here, but as an organizational strategy to handle competition by increasing the tempo and workload on the one side and structuring of career paths on the other. Adele, who was married to a graduate engineer, had gone through higher education in the arts abroad. In her interview she was expecting her second child. Adele had moved between advertising agencies abroad and those at home in Norway. She had been working regular long hours for several years before she became pregnant for the first time. In her previous job she had worked as an art director. She explained:

> No one cares about every hour you use. You just have to deliver.... [Making] creative suggestions [to a customer] is in itself hard to do from eight in the morning to four in the afternoon, always. The industry has been pressured very hard during the last five years. So there is a tendency to do more than one necessarily has to do, or to expect oneself to do more.

Interviewer: Because of the competition in the market?

> Yes, or to say 'Yes' to all the demands of the customer, like 'OK. Can this be finished by tomorrow?' – 'Yes'. Only that we don't really have the capacity to do so, we have four large commissions to run already, but we just have to solve it...and this becomes a vicious circle because everybody underbids the others in a relatively small market [thereby] contributing to pressure....And it is not calculated into working hours....so, in a way, you get fewer and fewer hours to do more and more work.

Thus, the tempo of work in terms of intensity and pace is increased in order to be able to do more in a shorter time, maximizing economically useful time. However, the standard for the product remains unchanged. To deliver good products is important both for the firm and also for the worker since it plays a role of door opener for further contracts:

The jobs I have done in my career are the references to secure contracts today. So you depend upon them to be good enough to show to potential clients. You therefore put in extra effort to make it into something special. And it can be hard to predict the time it takes for you to have a good idea. ... there is no set answer as to when something is finished; it's when you think it is yourself. That is a matter of experience. (Adele)

The product's quality can be experienced as a personal responsibility because the work result is tied personally to the worker, a well-known strategy used by organizations to control workers (Rasmussen and Johansen, 2005). The result represents the workers' abilities almost in moral terms, and this generates long hours for the employee, yet at the same time they are profitable for the employee:

It is individualized, because it is the project of the agency, and it is the project of the customer, but how good I am becomes very evident. ... When, for example, I design a cool milk container, then people know that I did it. (Adele)

Regular long hours are greedy in terms of the time left for caring. Especially advertising markets operate within a strong 'time-is-money' rationality. The person fitting the normal player in these markets is not a carer but a person with the attributes and interests of the male entrepreneur (Connell, 2000). The temporal opportunity structure for caring becomes limited but still forms the contexts for the parents' encounters and experiences regarding the use of daycare, as will be discussed in the following section.

Rushing to reach daycare centres

The limited temporal opportunity structure for caring frames care in general and the parent's encounter with daycare centres in particular. Having a child represents a dramatic change in one's organization of time and this is particularly felt when the period of paid leave ends and the combination of care and work is about to be practised. From being able to answer to the demand for extensive hours both from organizations and from the market for freelancing, the opening hours of daycare centres come to represent a challenging temporal limit for parents. When acting in accordance with the needs of children and the standardized opening hours of daycare centres, parents become less flexible and more rigid in the face of demands for regular long hours:

> The largest transition is time – that you are not that flexible on the time anymore.... then you have to dare say [to talkative colleagues], 'You know what? I just have to leave for the day-care centre', because they could easily sit there till eight in the evening. It was hard to combine this with fetching my child in day care. (Adele)

The limited temporal opportunity structure created by regular long hours conflicts with the daycare centres' standardized opening hours; they are not synchronized. This is particularly the case in the afternoon and evenings, the period of the day when the work day is often extended. Daycare is vital in combining work and care but often work days extend the opening hours of daycare centres. Matthew was a lone father and claimed that he seldom worked less than 60 hours a week as an event organizer. He questioned the tempo of work and the consequences for his son:

> What worries me now is that he, at the age of five, has, to a certain degree, to follow me and my pace. We have determined now that it is not good. There are quite simply too many days each week I pick up my son at day care and I say to him: 'You and I, the two of us, we're going to stop by Daddy's office'. Then we spend a rather long time there.... In the worst case, he maybe gets too little sleep because I have to bring him with me to work as I do not have anyone who can relieve me, to put it like that. If my baby sitter can't come or my neighbour has gone, and things like that, then I have to bring him with me to work and the clock will be eight, rather than six, before we go home. Then he will be too late in bed, and maybe I have a meeting in the morning so that we have to wake up at six – this is the worst case, however, it is not normal, but it might happen. That exhausts him.

In Matthew's case the provider and care responsibility, in combination with regular long hours, intensified the work-care dilemma. The limited temporal opportunity structure for caring is clear. On the one hand, he had sole care responsibility and no family to help him, and on the other hand, he felt that he had to stick to his job even if it created a limited temporal opportunity structure for caring. Working part time was not an option for him because, first, he did not see how the work tasks could be shared due to the organization's budget and, secondly, he needed the money from a full-time position. When the care assistance from daycare ended, his work days continued.

The age at which children are supposed to start in daycare is synchronized with the paid leave arrangement, for approximately one year. This can be a problem for parents working in a competitive situation where presence is weighted or necessary, or, as in the case of Agatha, they return early to work for economic reasons. Agatha loved her job. She was working as a freelance engineer in advertising, focusing more on programming than design. She had worked freelance nearly her entire career, and had three children who at the time of the interview ranged in age from early twenties to early primary school age. For long periods of time she had been a single mother and she stressed the provider element of parenting. At the time when Agatha unexpectedly became pregnant with her third child, she was already divorced. She did not live with the expected child's father. Due to her late response to the organization of leave for independent workers, she was denied sufficient paid leave that would enable her to support her family financially. Her freelance work meant she had a good income for her family, enabling her to afford an expensive home loan. She had become dependent on this income; she was a 'provider mum'. The additional child meant a situation of reduced wage income and also the absence of daycare since the child was too young. The situation forced her to continue working for provision:

> It was stressful because of the uncertainty of whether I would be able to cope with the situation. I just had to decide I was going to make it. The child should be allowed to come. So I went some rounds with myself. I made a deal with my present agency that I was to come and go as I pleased, bringing the child with me. And the boss there, he gave me the largest office, a baby cradle, a baby chair, you name it. Everything was ready for me.... I think it is all about attitude. I am normally an optimistic person. (Agatha)

When the child reached the age of 7.5 months, Agatha hired a private nanny (*dagmamma*). First, this exceptional case shows us the importance of daycare for work organizations portraying a situation without this offer at hand. Secondly, it exemplifies the need for a care offer for babies if parents are to be model workers in the flexible labour market, since long absences turn them into 'risk deviants'. Public daycare releases organizations from the responsibility for caring.

This supports Ellingsæter and Solheim's (2002) argument that welfare state arrangements might keep the care-work dilemma out of the work sphere, thereby reproducing what Acker (2006) calls a labour market's non-responsibility towards caring.

Greedy and generous: Irregular work hours and daycare

The second type of work-time flexibility is *irregular work hours*. Here the time sequence of working time is more varied, as parents work periodically long hours, oscillating between periods with greedy flexibility and generous flexibility. Accordingly, the temporal opportunity structures also shift between being both limited and extended towards caring. Muriel described it as follows: 'From time to time it feels like I work a lot. Then again in periods it is calmer.' In periods with much work, parents with irregular work hours experienced similar challenges towards caring as those who worked regular long hours. Still, there are some particularities with this flexibility which I will focus on below.

Those in a situation of irregular hours periodically had fewer commissions as freelancers, particularly the musicians. Their situation was marked by a higher degree of insecurity and unpredictability regarding income and work. They had to jump at chances more when they occurred, as it was a buyers' market; examples included commissions involving touring, which could suddenly obtain public funding, or an event that needed entertainment. Combining different sources of income – such as conducting, singing at funerals or teaching music at a public music school for children – was a strategy for handling the risk produced by the flexible market. Practising such multiple activities resembles what Beck (2000) has described as a 'Brazilianized' work situation. For Muriel, the unpredictable situation in terms of economy was hard to combine with responsible parenting and the provider role. She had become a freelancer before she had children, but concluded:

I do not think I would have chosen the same [job], having children. Because having such an insecure and unstable economy and at the same time knowing that you have the responsibility for children, yes, I think that would have been a totally different situation.

Despite much work in periods, the temporal shifts open for 'Holes other than summer holidays', as Margaret, a singer, described them, thus pointing to the double-edge of work-life flexibility related to care. This type of flexibility is organized more around the pendulum of greedy and generous. Michael, a father of two girls, explained the generosity/greediness as follows:

> Like today, I have this day, I am my own man, you can come here and interview me, and afterwards I can be home receiving a serviceman. Otherwise, I will use my day practicing and then I will make dinner for my family. Of course, that is family friendly? But, then again, I might be touring. For example, this February I will be away for weeks on end.

In this case, the model worker of irregular work hours is also the non-caring entrepreneur. The period where the work time was generous towards caring was not a result of a care-friendly market, but of a market where such workers are not in demand. Irregular work hours produced a particular temporal opportunity structure for caring characterized by both limitations and possibilities following the rhythm of variable workloads.

Shifting needs of daycare

The temporal opportunity structure for caring frames the organization of care and parents' use of daycare. In periods, the flexibility is generous in relation to time for caring and how parents made use of daycare. The extended opportunity structure for caring allows for time to be spent with children, slowing down the tempo of everyday life. Muriel had combined an extended temporal opportunity structure for caring with a combination of cash-for-care and part-time daycare, thereby reducing the hours her children spent in daycare. In this situation, the opening hours of daycare centres were not a problem. However, when the pendulum swung towards regular long hours, evening work or periods involving parents touring, work limited the temporal opportunity structure for caring. Then, organizing care appeared more like a jigsaw puzzle where daycare could be a part of the solution or actually not fit with the needs at all. As Muriel said:

> There has never, for us, been enough of the public care service, precisely because we have flexible jobs. We have always had to organize with a private nanny, with my mother-in-law, my mother, or an aunt...a person that has travelled with us or stayed here with the children. As the children have grown older we have also sent them to an aunt who is a housewife and lives in the countryside. We have been totally dependent on private people giving us a hand.

Travelling shows us how parents' need for assistance in the form of care is unsynchronized with the opening hours of daycare centres. This actualizes a 24-hour daycare service. Yet, when faced with this issue, the parents said they preferred using family, friends and nannies to cope with the situation. The idea challenged their understanding of daycare as a supplement to informal care. Thus, an offer of this kind would lead to an unwelcome extension of the institutionalization of their children's lives.

Generous flexibility: Flexible part-time and daycare

The last type of work-time flexibility is *flexible part time* where work hours have a shorter duration compared with the normal work day. The time sequence of flexible part time, shown through its rhythm, is adapted to care responsibilities. This is a generous flexibility related to caring, producing an extended temporal opportunity structure for caring. It is not standardized in the sense of having one day off each week.

In contrast to the other two types of flexibility described, this is a work-time flexibility driven by the care needs of the family. It is important to have in mind the Norwegian contexts on part-time work. Part-time work is a common strategy used by Norwegian mothers to combine care and work (Bø et al., 2008). The possibility of adapting work hours to care responsibility is institutionalized by law. Despite the legal regulation of part-time work, in Norwegian knowledge-based organizations part timers can become 'time deviants'. This was the experience of Adele, who did not even consider working part time as an option in the organization in which she worked. Hence, she chose to become a freelance designer as a way of 'exiting' (Hirschman, 1970) a situation marked by regular long hours and a limited temporal opportunity structure for caring:

> There are many girls who start their own sole proprietorship and I think it has something to do with the everlasting time pressure. There are surely many girls that cannot handle both that and a family. (Adele)

In this way, freelancing became an individualized strategy for moulding an extended temporal opportunity structure for caring flexible to shifting care-tasks. This happened by reducing one's availability to clients:

When I don't have anybody expecting me to be somewhere at a given point of time, that is the way I become flexible. Or that is the way I become available for caring. (Miranda)

Thus, from the study sample it was evident that freelancing for women working in advertising became the 'mummy track', a second-rate way for women to establish their own business compared with men. As they do not fit into the entrepreneurial model worker of advertising, they apply this strategy to be able to combine care and work. For men, entrepreneurship signalled initiative and creativity when starting up a competing agency with its own 'look', which often resulted in a situation of regular long hours. This was confirmed by Axle's and Andrew's stories. Hence, freelancing as a part-time strategy came at a cost, namely, the risk of being positioned as second best, as part-time workers renounced their availability and visibility, thereby breaking with the expectations based on the model worker. Thus, by working part time they became 'risk deviants' according to the 'time is money' rationality. However, this risk was outweighed by having a partner to share the risk with. Having a partner with a remunerable income enabled the mothers to take such risks because their family would still be provided for if commissions failed. This enabled Agatha to consider: 'Once in a while, I just halt, reflecting on how it works with the relation between living and working, and I will reconsider taking a job or not.'

Hence, the mothers working flexible part time diverge from single parents for whom the theme of provision is more outspoken. It is harder for sole providers to work part time than for those whose risk can be shared. In the light of Acker's (2006) gendered substructure, we can see that using time to care is problematic for parents earning a living in flexible labour markets. Because care practices are gendered, this becomes a specific problem for women. Some, capable of risk sharing, can choose caring and a part-time path that is already defined as normal for women.

Flexible part time affects the frames in which mothers can define their motherhood in terms of time use. Andrea, for example, worked flexible part time as a freelance designer in what she reckoned to be a 70 per cent position. For her, motherhood and time use was closely interwoven with the moral question of deciding to have children and, not least, being responsible for them.

I reason like this: I myself have chosen to have children, so then I have to spend time with them, not work long hours, like 'Monday I work over time, Tuesday it is your turn'. [Those kinds of families,] they are hardly together. I know couples who live like that, but it is not my cup of tea.

This form of motherhood differs from the 'provider mum' represented by Agatha. Agatha, however, neither had the financial opportunity nor the wish to position herself as a 'time-for-children mum'. Still, a generous flexibility led to an extended temporal opportunity structure for caring that framed the use of daycare.

Slowing down the tempo of everyday life

Flexible part time generates an extended temporal opportunity structure for caring. Among the informants, released time was used for caring, in a broad sense also affecting the use of daycare. Organizing everyday life to avoid friction, being at home with ill children, shopping, making dinner, cleaning and organizing children in the mornings was part of this. Adele stressed that it also gave her time on her own. Central was the issue of slowing down the tempo of everyday life, especially for their children, exemplified by enabling them to sleep longer and eat breakfast at home as well as being picked up early. This affected the use of daycare in temporal terms, as the parents used flexible part-time working as a means to reduce the hours their children spent in daycare. A full-time position was often paid for, but used flexibly:

> We never deliver the children before eight o'clock. I think that is early enough. I am rather set on that. And I fetch them from the day-care centre no later than four in the afternoon. But earlier on, we delivered at eight and picked them up at quarter to three or twelve thirty, and last year mostly at one thirty, but that was rather short.... I think that from seven in the morning till four or half past four in the afternoon is too long. (Andrea)

Comparing this temporal opportunity structure to the others already described, having time to care becomes somewhat a token of surplus, a kind of extravagance compared with those not having the possibility to choose caring for economic reasons. It is striking that this child-oriented and female-practised flexibility is the only one falling into the standardized opening hours of daycare centres.

Concluding discussion

This chapter started with the question of whether daycare can ease the inherent temporal dilemma between participating in flexible labour markets and caring for children, in a Norwegian context. The analysis has shown three types of work-time flexibility in the study sample, generating different temporal opportunity structures for caring and use of daycare that can shed light on the question of regular long hours, irregular hours and flexible part time. There are different processes generating these types of flexibility, but they are in one way or another linked to the risk produced by flexible labour markets and the strategies and possibilities for handling the risk. A central theme in the analysis has been the individualized responsibility for handling provision and caring in a work life whose model worker is a person without care responsibilities: the non-caring entrepreneur.

The first two types of flexibility generate a temporal opportunity structure for caring that is not synchronized with the opening hours of daycare centres. So, the dilemma of working and caring is eased, but not resolved by daycare. Only the mothers in flexible part-time work have an extended temporal opportunity structure for caring that coincides with the opening hours of daycare centres. This was due to their ability to share risk with a partner and follow the normalized work-time practice of part-time work for working mothers in Norway. Daycare centre's opening hours are clearly synchronized with standardized work time. The focus has been on the parents. However, it would be of interest to study the temporal opportunity structures for caring as frames for modern childhood more profoundly. Further studies on the relation between work-life flexibility and the timescapes of childhood should be carried out.

The analysis presented here has been based on a small sample of working parents. Yet the practices of the parents in the study sample represent a general trait linked to the neoliberal rationalities permeating advanced liberal democracies: the privatizing of risk and responsibility (Rose, 1996) and the 'individual' of neoliberalism having the attributes and interests of a male (or non-caring) entrepreneur (Connell, 2000). Such model workers are globally dispersed by competition in the globalized economy and are therefore interesting as a general phenomenon. Against this backdrop, the analysis has demonstrated the challenges facing welfare states in tailoring a family policy fitting the model player in the flexible labour market. This is a model player without care responsibilities, generating an everlasting need for removal of care loads by daycare centres. A solution could be to extend daycare centre's opening hours to a 24-hours service and to receive infants. A relevant question concerns whose interests that would serve. No doubt the beneficiaries of the market would gain, including the welfare state itself. More questionable is the parent–child relationship and the wellbeing of children.

The unit of change in this solution comprises daycare, parents and children, not the market or work organizations. A non-responsibility for care in market standards would be reproduced. It therefore seems like the heart of the problem lies within the workings of markets and their non-responsibility towards caring. Central questions are how welfare states could enable parents with care responsibilities to work less without turning them into 'risk deviants' and also how this could be approached on a policy level.

References

Acker, J. (2006) *Class Questions: Feminist Answers* (Oxford: Rowman & Littlefield Publishers).

Adam, B. (2004) *Time* (Cambridge: Polity Press).

Beck, U. (2000) *The Brave New World of Work* (New York: Polity Press).

Bø, T. P., Kitterød, R. H., Køber, T., Nerland, S. and Skoglund, T. (2008) Arbeidstidmønstre og utviklingstrekk (Worktime patterns and developments), Report 2008/12 (Oslo: SSB).

Brandth, B. and Kvande, E. (2009) 'Free Choice or Gentle Force? How Can Parental Leave Change Gender Practices?' in A. T. Kjørholt and J. Qvortrup (eds) *The Modern Child and the Flexible Labour Market. Child Care Policies and Practices at a Crossroads?* (London: Palgrave Macmillan).

Brannen, J. (2005) 'Time and the Negotiation of Work Family Boundaries. Autonomy or Illusion?', *Time and Society*, 14, 1, 113–131.

Brown, P., Hesketh, A. and Williams, S. (2003) 'Employability in a Knowledge-Driven Economy', *Journal of Education and Work*, 16, 107–126.

Carnoy, M. (2002) *Sustaining the New Economy. Work, Family and Community in the Information Age* (New York: Russel Sage Foundation).

Coffey, A. and Atkinson, P. (1996) *Making Sense of Qualitative Data. Complementary Research Strategies* (Thousand Oaks: Sage).

Connell, R. W. (2000) *The Men and the Boys* (Cambridge: Polity Press).

Coser, L. A. (1974) *Greedy Institutions: Patterns of Undivided Commitment* (New York: The Free Press).

Cresswell, J. C. (1998) *Qualitative Inquiry and Research Design. Choosing Among Five Traditions* (Thousand Oaks: Sage).

Crompton, R. (2006) *Employment and the Family. The Reconfiguration of Work and Family Life in Contemporary Societies* (Cambridge: Cambridge University Press).

Ellingsæter, A. L. (2006) 'The Norwegian Child Care Regime and Its Paradoxes' in A. L. Ellingsæter and A. Leira (eds) *Politicising Parenthood in Scandinavia. Gender Relations in Welfare States* (Bristol: The Policy Press).

Ellingsæter, A. L. and Solheim, J. (2002) 'Makt, kjønn og arbeidsliv: teoretiske landskap' (Power, gender and work life: Theoretical landscapes) in A. L. Ellingsæter and J. Solheim (eds) *Den usynlige hånd. Kjønnsmakt og moderne arbeidsliv* (The invisible hand. Gender power and modern work life) (Oslo: Gyldendal Akademisk).

Epstein, C. F., Carol, S., Oglensky, B. and Saute, R. (1999) *The Part Time Paradox. Time Norms, Professional Life, Family and Gender* (New York: Routledge).

Esping-Andersen, G., Gallie, D., Hemerijk, A. and Myles, J. (2002) *Why We Need a New Welfare State* (Oxford: Oxford University Press).

Fleetwood, S. (2007) 'Why Work-Life Balance Now?', *International Journal of Human Resource Management*, 18, 387–400.

Fraser, N. (1994) 'After the Family Wage: Gender Equity and the Welfare State', *Political Theory*, 22, 591–618.

Giddens, A. (1991) *Modernity and Self-Identity. Self and Society in the Late Modern Age* (Cambridge: Polity Press).

Gornick, J. C. and Meyers, M. K. (2003) *Families that Work. Policies for Reconciling Parenthood and Employment* (New York: Russell Sage Foundation).

Hammersley, M. and Atkinson, P. (1995) *Ethnography. Principles in Practice* (New York: Routledge).

Hirschman, A. O. (1970) *Exit, Voice and Loyalty. Responses to Decline in Firms, Organizations and States* (London: Harvard University Press).

Hochschild, A. R. (1997) *The Time Bind. When Work Becomes Home and Home Becomes Work* (New York: Metropolitan Books).

Jacobs, J. A. and Gerson, K. (2004) *The Time Divide. Work, Family and Gender Inequality* (Cambridge: Harvard University Press).

Kitterød, R. H. (2007) 'Fremdeles et tosporet foreldreskap? Mors og fars yrkesarbeid i barnefasen' (Still a two tracked parenthood? The work life participation of mothers and fathers during childhood years) in E. Kvande and B Rasmussen (eds) *Arbeidslivets klemmer. Paradokser i det nye arbeidslivet* (Feeling the pinch. The paradoxes of the new work life) (Bergen: Fagbokforlaget).

Korsvold, T. (2008) *Barn og barndom i velferdsstatens småbarnspolitikk. En sammenlignende studie av Norge, Sverige og Tyskland 1945–2000* (Children and childhood in welfare states' child-policies. A comparative study of Norway, Sweden and Germany 1945–2000) (Oslo: Universitetsforlaget).

Miles, M. B. and Huberman, A. M. (1994) *Qualitative Data Analysis. An Expanded Sourcebook* (Thousand Oaks: Sage).

Parker, S. C. (2004) *The Economics of Self-Employment and Entrepreneurship* (New York: Cambridge University Press).

Perrons, D., Fagan, C., McDowell, L., Ray, K. and Ward, K. (2005) 'Work, Life and Time in the New Economy: An introduction', *Time and Society*, 14, 1, 51–64.

Rasmussen, B. and Johansen, B. (2005) 'Trick or Treat? Autonomy as Control in Knowledge Work' in R. Barrett (ed.) *Management, Labour Process and Software Development* (New York: Routledge).

Rose, N. (1996) 'Governing "Advanced" Liberal Democracies' in A Barry, T. Osborne and N. Rose (eds) *Foucault and Political Reason. Liberalism, Neo-liberalism and Rationalities of Government* (London: UCL Limited Press).

Rubery, J., Ward, K., Grimshaw, D. and Beynon, H. (2005) 'Working Time, Industrial Relations and the Employment Relationship', *Time and Society*, 14, 1, 89–111.

St. meld. nr. 27 (1999–2000) Barnehage til beste for barn og foreldre (Day care in favour of children and parents) (Oslo: Barne- og Familiedepartementet).

9

Kindergarten as a Bazaar

Freedom of Choice and New Forms of Regulation

Anne Trine Kjørholt and Monica Seland

Introduction

The point of departure for this chapter on the kindergarten as a social space for childhood and children's everyday lives is discourses on flexibility and user orientation. *Time* and *place* are important dimensions of the social space that is constituted by political discourses, since they represent and produce images of childhood and what it means to be a child, as well as particular understandings of learning, knowledge and care. Teachers and staff in kindergartens, like the children themselves, are also active participants in (re)constructing time and space through everyday social practices.

As elaborated in several other chapters in this book, *user adjustment* and the notion of *choice* and *flexibility* as key values have assumed great influence in developments in and reforms to kindergartens in Norway in the last ten years (Kjørholt, Rantalaiho, Chapters 1 and 4). Discourses on flexibility are also reflected in recent changes in the architectural style of kindergarten buildings and the organization of place (Kjørholt and Tingstad, 2007; Seland, 2009). Changes in the organization of place are followed by a change in organization of time, structuring professional practices and daily life for both children and staff in the kindergarten. The changes in the organization of time and place reveal how these institutions seem to be embedded in discourses of flexibility and individual choice in particular ways. *Flexibility* is thus a key term in the new discourses on both kindergarten policy and the new design of kindergarten buildings (Kjørholt and Tingstad, 2007; Seland, 2009).

Compared with other Nordic and European countries, until 1990 the percentage of children in Norway below school age with access to a place in a kindergarten was low, in spite of the official goal of a kindergarten place for all. According to reports to the Norwegian parliament (*Storting*), it was the municipalities that were made responsible for establishing kindergartens for all by the end of 2007. The different municipalities were faced with many challenges in order to fulfil these goals, not least financially. Reducing the cost has therefore been an important part of the process of extensively increasing the number of kindergartens for many municipalities. The cost of a traditional kindergarten place is largely connected to the ratio of the number of children per kindergarten teacher and the number of staff. New, creative, flexible ways of organizing time and space have therefore been introduced, focusing on 'the competent child' and 'modern pedagogical ideas', and emphasizing children's freedom of choice and rights to influence their everyday lives in the kindergarten (Kjørholt, 2005; Kjørholt and Tingstad, 2007).

The term 'new kindergarten building' occurs in several political documents produced locally from early 2000. One of them is entitled the *Function and Area Programme for Municipal Kindergartens in Trondheim,* adopted by the Trondheim City Council (Trondheim municipality, 2005). The document presents guidelines for the design of the kindergarten building, emphasizing the importance of its architecture. It presents a framework, or model, describing local standards for how kindergarten buildings in the municipality will be designed. The quotation below shows that the new kindergarten building reflects new visions about everyday life in the kindergarten:

> When you are planning the communication area in a kindergarten, it can be inspiring to think of the bazaar as a metaphor. The building has several functions that should be easily accessible, like shops and workrooms in a bazaar. (Trondheim municipality, 2005, p. 12)

In this quotation we see that the new design of the kindergarten is connected to the metaphor of a *bazaar*. This is interesting from many points of view. Traditionally, kindergartens in Norway have been associated with the *home* as a metaphor for quality (Korsvold, 1998). This shift in metaphor from the home to the bazaar opens up many questions. The aim in this chapter is to discuss the kindergarten as a social space for children, with an emphasis being on children as social participants and their everyday lives within the new space of the kindergarten. The chapter includes an analysis of the political discourse connected to the new kindergarten building, anchored in a previous analysis of discourses on flexible places and the kindergarten building (Kjørholt and

Tingstad, 2007) and an ongoing PhD study (Seland, 2009).[1] A pertinent question to be addressed is what kinds of individual freedom of choice and social life are being offered to both children and adults by the new architecture. Based on an analysis of political documents and data from fieldwork in a kindergarten in one of the largest towns in Norway, we will discuss how children and adults are affected by the new discourses. We argue that there is a dynamic interconnectedness between discourses on children as competent subjects with rights to participation and neoliberal discourses on flexibility and individual choice. These discourses represent an increasing market orientation that constructs children as customers. Furthermore, these discourses are connected to contemporary discourses on the kindergarten as a space for learning.

From kindergarten as a home to kindergarten as a bazaar

Traditionally, kindergartens have been divided into separate sections or units, organized for a particular and fixed group of children and adults. Kindergartens vary in size, consisting of one to eight units (normally between two and five), and each with a fixed group of children. Every unit has own defined playing area, which usually consists of a large play room, a smaller one where it is possible to have a sleep, a room for cooking and a wardrobe where every child has their own shelf and peg for clothes, shoes and other personal belongings (Kjørholt and Tingstad, 2007).

The term 'new kindergarten building' was initiated by the 'Large City Network', which was established to encourage cooperation among the larger cities in Norway with regard to kindergarten policy and practice. The point of departure for the Large City Network project was that the 'traditional' manner of organizing physical place and the use of rooms according to fixed and stable groups of children do not permit the flexibility required in terms of indoor space and staff (Kjørholt and Tingstad, 2007). The document *Function and Area Programme for Municipal Kindergartens in Trondheim* (2005) describes new ways of organizing children in kindergartens in this community: groups of children are separated into several so-called 'bases', instead of fixed sections or units. We argue that in many ways the document represents new discourses about children and the kindergarten as a social space for young children. The new kindergarten has several 'base areas' where a particular group of children, normally 18, eat and gather together in the mornings and afternoons. During the rest of the day, all the other rooms are used jointly and in flexible ways by different groups of children belonging to the different 'bases'. This implies a shift from organizing the children in fixed and stable groups to a more flexible organization of children (Kjørholt and Tingstad, 2007; Seland, 2009).

In accordance with the new architectural model, the kindergarten where the fieldwork was conducted had a joint space with a long corridor (termed a communication area in the document) and a lot of separate rooms designed for special activities, such as painting, building with wooden blocks, drama and music activities, or reading books in the library (for further description, see Seland, 2009). In the political document, the metaphor of the bazaar is further elaborated in this way:

> The building has many functions that provide great accessibility, like shops and workshops along a street in a bazaar. Here we are thinking of the kindergarten's common room, joint play rooms and workshops. The meeting rooms also require a high degree of accessibility. Doors can be open on to the street, or they can be closed. Activities that usually take place along the street, like cafes and shops in the city, may be moved out into the street if need be. (Trondheim municipality, 2005, p. 12)

A bazaar is a particular market place for buying and selling things, first and foremost associated with the Middle East. In a market, individuals are customers or consumers who are free to move around and buy whatever they want. There are numerous different shops offering a variety of goods, such as spices, furniture, food, clothes and jewels. Historically, bazaars can be traced back to the beginning of the 1600s in the Middle East. Socially, bazaars are associated with a pulsating life involving a myriad of different people, who are often unknown to each other. Aesthetically, there is a richness and variety involving different senses, such as the smells of spices, the colours of hand-dyed textiles and many different sounds. A traditional bazaar is in many ways totally different from a home, which in a Norwegian context is associated with stability and a close-knit relationship among a few well-known family members.

This shift of metaphor, from a home to a bazaar, is interesting in many ways. We ask whether the use of the bazaar metaphor represents a step towards an increasing emphasis on children as individual customers or consumers in an institutional setting. By choosing this metaphor, which can be transformed into the less exotic metaphor of a 'shopping centre', the document indicates that new experiences, play and social relations are like 'goods in a market', to be selected by children's individual choices. From this perspective, participation is connected to the child's right to choose between different types of offering, and the child becomes a consumer in the kindergarten's own bazaar or shopping-centre. It then appears that discourses on children's right to participate are intertwined with market-oriented discourses in which the child is constructed as a customer or a consumer. Accordingly we ask whether, and in accordance with this shift, members of the staff are themselves transformed from teachers into producers or 'salespersons' offering different kinds of activity. The new kindergarten requires new professional roles, flexible and ready to adjust to the customer's wishes and needs. We therefore see the outline of a new mode of childcare based on other values and qualities than those we know from the traditional Norwegian kindergarten (Kjørholt and Tingstad, 2007).

The use of the bazaar as a metaphor for the new kindergarten and its association with shopping and a high degree of flexibility and freedom of choice contributes to a picture of institutional life as exotic and exciting. The shift of metaphor from home to bazaar also reflects a political desire to transform the aim, content and curriculum of this institution for small children. The style and atmosphere in the new kindergarten is not supposed to be homelike and cosy anymore, but a public institution for small children's learning (for further elaboration of this point, see Seland, 2009). The quotation below illustrates this shift:

> The aesthetics of the home has traditionally been the norm for kindergartens. Now a greater emphasis on the kindergarten as an institution in a positive sense is the aim of the kindergarten as a public space. The kindergarten of today will be influenced by good architecture, equipped with good-quality furniture and modern design. (Trondheim municipality, 2005, p. 7)

Seeing the kindergarten as a bazaar is further characterized by highlighting workshops, art studios and rooms designed for special activities, such as sports and gymnastics, while the former so-called 'family space' designed for symbolic play no longer seems to have the same priority. This was a main concern of the 'traditional' kindergarten, which greatly emphasized 'free play' and 'children's own culture'. When the term 'play' is mentioned in the political document, it is first and foremost connected with terms like learning and aesthetics; that is, play is a tool with which to explore. However, the change from kindergarten as a home to kindergarten as a bazaar, with a shift from fixed units to bases with a room designed for special activities and learning, is first and foremost connected to children's right to freedom of choice (Kjørholt and Tingstad, 2007).

While the metaphor of a home connotes a private space, the bazaar belongs to the public space. The shift of metaphor from home to bazaar can therefore also be connected to discourses of ('the good') childhood in Norway, which values the private sphere and the home as an ideal place to which children belong. Play and activities with friends in the home and close environment, in particular in nature and outdoors, are core ingredients of a 'proper' Norwegian childhood (Gullestad, 1992; Kjørholt, 2004; Nilsen, Chapter 11). One of the reasons for the small number of kindergartens and institutional care for children below school age in Norway until the 1990s was the strong emphasis on children belonging to the family and the private sphere, as well as the constructed dichotomy between public and private.

Children's meeting, flexibility and freedom of choice

The organization of place in the kindergarten, governing everyday life for children and adults and expressed by the 'new kindergarten architecture', is also followed by a change in the way time is organized. We will now give an overview of the daily time structure (*dagsrytmen*) – a fixed timetable – before we continue with a presentation of data on how the new structure of time and place affects social practices among children and adults (Seland, 2009). Which positions do the new discourses create for children as social participants during the day? What are the possibilities and limitations of activities and social relations among children and between children and adults? In particular, we will describe the 'Children's meeting', which aims to promote children's rights to actively participate in everyday life and provide them with an influence in decision-making processes in the kindergarten. The Children's meeting is particularly connected to discourses on children's right to freedom of choice.

Daily timetable
06.30: Kindergarten opens. Breakfast and 'free play'
09.00: Children's meeting and thereafter selected activities
10.45: Assembly
11.30: Lunch
12.00: Outdoor play
14.30: Fruit time and thereafter 'free play' inside or outside
17.00: Kindergarten closes.

Interestingly, following the change in the organization of time and place in the kindergarten, new concepts and words have been brought into use. One such concept often heard during fieldwork was 'focal time' (*kjernetid*), used by the staff to refer to the time of day when those activities they perceive as the most important take place, normally between 09.00 and 14.00 hours every day. The Children's meeting is an important aspect of this 'focal time'. Below we present an excerpt from the field notes on the Children's meeting:

The Children's meeting

It is nine o'clock in the morning, and the time has come for the daily Children's meeting. All 80 children, 40 from each base, are sitting on benches in the wardrobe area. The time has come for the children to make individual decisions about which room they want to stay in for the next couple of hours. As usual, Kari, the kindergarten teacher, opens the meeting by shouting each and every child's name to see who is present and ticking them off the attendance sheet accordingly. Then she explains that today all the three year olds are going to have a club meeting in the Arts and Crafts Room, so this room will not be available to the other children. Nor will the Painting Room be available, since there are not enough staff members on duty today to keep it open. While Kari is telling the children this, I can see Albert, a five year old boy, making a whispered agreement with Karen and Anna that they will choose the Drama Room and play together there today. After all the three year olds have left the room where the Children's meeting is taking place, the teacher continues: 'Who wants to go to the Construction Room?' Some of the children raise their hands and are then allowed to go to the room. 'Who wants to go to the Drama Room?' Albert, Karen and Anna raise their hands quickly and shout, 'I will, I will!' Today many children wish to play in the Drama Room, but only four from each base are allowed to do so because there are restrictions on how many children are allowed to play in each room so that rooms do not become too crowded. The teacher points to Karen, Anna and two other children, and they then leave to go to the Drama Room with a smile on their face. Albert sits there on the bench, watching them pass. Kari continues to call out the name of the rest of the rooms, ticking everyone's name off the sheet as they make their individual choice about where to stay. When she has finished, Albert and some other children still remain. 'Where do *you* want to be, then?' asks Kari. 'You can choose to play outdoors, or read books in the library', she suggests. 'All the other rooms are now filled up. If you can't decide, I'll just have to place you somewhere,' Kari points out. Albert says that he wants to play outdoors, and with a resigned look in his face walks slowly out of the room, and starts to put on his outdoor clothes. (Seland, 2009)

The Children's meeting forms part of the discourse emphasizing children's right to participate in everyday life in kindergarten. The construction of small children as claimers of rights and citizens within kindergartens in Norway can be traced back to 1999, and has since then become increasingly powerful. The National Curriculum, White Papers and political documents produced both locally and nationally construct small children as competent subjects with rights to influence and have a say in daily life in the kindergarten (Kjørholt, 2005). In the documents related to the Large City Network, it is argued that the new model enables the staff to be more flexible in organizing children into different and flexible groups in order to promote increased freedom of choice for individual children by giving them a broader range of activities to choose from (Kjørholt and Tingstad, 2007). It is further argued that this promotes children's abilities to make their own decisions regarding activity and playmates during the day (Kjørholt and Tingstad, 2007, p. 10). In reports written by teachers in several of these 'new kindergartens', individual freedom of choice is underlined as an important aim, connecting flexible places to increased freedom of choice for the children (Kjørholt and Tingstad, 2007). The quotation below shows this view being further developed in the political document by means of the bazaar metaphor:

The current conceptualization of children is characterized by seeing children as competent, active, creative and explorative, being in need of a stimulated environment with many options to choose from regarding experience, activity and learning. The environment needs to be characterized by the fact that children are going to participate in and actively influence everyday life. The design and furniture have to be planned in a way that promotes competence and own individual choice (taken by children). (Trondheim municipality, 2005, p. 16)

This construction of children as competent social actors with rights to participate in and influence everyday life has been a factor in both policy and research since the late 1980s (Clark et al., 2005; James et al., 1998; Kjørholt, 2004). In Nordic countries, discourses on children as autonomous and competent claimers of rights have been particularly powerful (Brembeck et al., 2004; Gulløv, 2003; Kampmann, 2004; Kjørholt, 2005). Neoliberal discourses on participation as freedom to choose are evident here, in line with earlier research in Nordic countries interpreting rights to participate and citizenship as self-determination, and rights to individual freedom of choice (Clark et al., 2005; Kjørholt, 2005). Jan Kampmann argues that this is characteristic of the second period of institutionalization of children below school age (Kampmann, 2004).

The connection with freedom of choice for the individual child with the concept of learning in the quotation above is interesting. In the political document, the term 'the third pedagogue' is also used, referring to the physical place and design of the kindergarten. This shows that discourses on the new kindergarten architecture are connected to discourses on learning influenced by the philosophy of thinking from 'Reggio Emilia'.[2] These discourses have become increasingly powerful in relation to policy and practice in kindergartens in Sweden and Norway in recent years.

Regulation and control: Changing social practices

However, the case study of the 'new kindergarten building' also reveals that there seem to be certain paradoxes and challenges connected with the construction of the kindergarten as a flexible place, and of children as subjects with increased freedom of choice. From the observation made during fieldwork in the kindergarten, we can see that Albert was not in a position to choose either where to stay or whom to play with. Albert was not alone in this experience, which happened every day for some of the children. In order to create a good atmosphere for learning, the teachers had decided to restrict the maximum number of children in each room to eight, while only four children were allowed in the Family Room[3] because of its small size. This meant that only four out of 80 children could play with dolls and other forms of family-oriented activities in the Family Room each day. Combined with the architecture, these restrictions represented a major practical limitation to the children's freedom of choice. Because of the furnishing in this new kindergarten, which allowed the children access to nearly all the cupboards and drawers with teaching materials, the teachers had introduced a rule that required a staff member to be present in each room because, as one of them explained: 'We don't want things to be messed up or broken in there.' So if there were not enough staff members on duty, rooms had to be closed. The only exception was the small Family Room, which was open almost all the time.

The staff member in each room either has a planned pedagogical programme or is just *present* as an available, sensitive, playing or observing adult. To indicate to the children whether a room was opened and accessible, or closed, the staff put a sign on each door showing either a green, happy face or a red, sad face. The red signs were those that were visible most of the time, except for the one-and-a-half hours after the Children's meeting. In the early mornings and the afternoons, the Construction Room and sometimes the Drama Room were opened. The other rooms could only be chosen for this period after the Children's meeting. The children were then obliged to play in the base area or outdoors. The reason for this, the staff explained, is a time pressure and the need to use the time for other important activities, such as meetings, supervision and lunch breaks.

As one of the staff members explained, if the children were 'floating freely around' in all the rooms in the kindergarten, control by the staff would be undermined, and neither they nor the parents would know whether the children were enjoying themselves and whether they had had the expected learning outcome. Thus, this shift from small, fixed groups to larger and flexible groups of children represents a challenge for the staff with regard to fulfilling the aim of ensuring learning for each child, as stated in the National Curriculum. Learning requires close contact with and knowledge about the individual child, their experience and abilities. Documentation is an important part of the staff's daily obligations, being seen as a valuable tool to communicate to the parents the children's activities during the day. A documentary log is hung on the wall in the base area every day. It contains the names of the children who have been present in the room and a short report on the activities they have been engaged in.

Documentation has become increasingly powerful in discourses related to pedagogical theory and practice in early childhood education and care, influenced among others by the tradition in 'Reggio Emilia' institutions (Rinaldi, 2005). This documentation is closely connected to assessment and may thus also be seen as an instrument of regulation and control in a regime that is flexible regarding time and place. The practices of the Children's meeting in the new kindergarten reveal, on the one hand, increased emphasis on participation and freedom of choice for children in an open 'flexible place', and, on the other hand, increased control and regulation. This confirms empirical studies of children in daycare institutions in Denmark. Eva Gulløv argues that this combination of children being constructed as self-managing subjects while at the same time being controlled and protected points to an unresolved conflict regarding children's social position (Gulløv, 2003, p. 24). From this ambivalent social position of children within the new social space of the kindergarten follow certain paradoxes and dilemmas for the professional staff concerning pedagogical practices and responsibilities. Before turning our attention to this, however, we will look more closely at children's experiences related to freedom of choice in the new kindergarten. Below we present an excerpt from a dialogue between Monica Seland and a small group of five-year-old children:

> *Monica*: Tell me about the Children's meeting.
> *Marius*: It's boring. We have to sit in our own places and say where we want to be.
> *Ola*: I just want to be everywhere – in all the rooms! And then we have to answer [...he continues] and listen. And there are many children who fool around. We have to raise our hands very quickly if we're going to get the room we want!
> *Monica*: Tell me about the former kindergarten you went to [a traditional kindergarten with two fixed units or sections and fixed groups of children, 16–18 in each]. What was it like there?
> *Lise*: We didn't have a Children's meeting there.
> *Monica*: How did you decide where to be, then?
> *Anna*: We didn't have to choose a room – we could just move around and play a little here and there and there...Everywhere!
> *Monica*: Were you allowed to go to the other unit or section?
> *Anna*: We could move and be where we wanted.
> *Lise*: Sometimes I get sad at the meeting when we're not allowed to go in the room we want.
> *Anna*: Many kids do!

This excerpt clearly reveals the limitations on freedom of choice that the children are faced with in the new open landscape. Another example that illustrates the same point is the following observation, taken from field notes:

> It's morning. All the children, apart from Nina and Peter, are present at the Children's meeting. The whole group of 40 children has come together in one of the two base areas to make their choices of where to stay and play. Since it is the end of November, it is still twilight outside and the ground is covered with a thin white layer of snow,

like a carpet. The first snow of the winter season has come and Kari, the teacher, asks with a smiling face: 'Who wants to join me out in the snow today?' Most of the children raise their hands and shout eagerly: 'I do (*æææ*)'. Both children and adults are happy and excited, looking forward to going outside in the snow, and they start putting on their outdoor clothes in the wardrobe. However, after a while one of the staff from the other base enters and says: 'You can't allow so many children to play outdoors since that will require more staff outside. As a result, there'll be a lack of staff for the special rooms and we'll have to close some of them. Then the children from our base who have chosen to play indoors won't be able to have their choice.'

This example reflects the dilemmas and paradoxes involved in organizing and coordinating staff for the large group of 80 children in the two bases. Professional practices that are intended to be exercises in freedom and flexibility may, on closer examination, turn out to be new forms of regulation and control. If four of the staff members are outdoors looking after 30 children from one of the two bases playing in the snow, the implication is that four rooms have to be closed, thus restricting freedom of choice for those who want to play indoors. On the other hand, if the staff choose to be indoors to fulfil the choices of those who want to play in one of the rooms on the bazaar street, the children who have chosen to be out in the snow will have to suffer. These observations from the ethnographic study in the new kindergarten (Seland, forthcoming) thus support earlier reports made by teachers in other base-organized kindergartens (Kjørholt and Tingstad, 2007). Practical solutions introduced to cope with larger and more flexible groups of children seem to imply a high level of regulation. It is interesting to note the new term 'the principle of sluicing' (*sluseprinsippet*) in the reports of teachers referring to new forms of regulation, which means that in early mornings and late afternoons half the base must be closed in order to enable the staff to monitor fully what is going on and to make tidying up easier. The paradox is that, in order to provide individual choice, flexibility and self-determination, staff members feel obliged to organize strictly (Kjørholt and Tingstad, 2007).

The social space of the new kindergarten consequently opens up new professional positions for the staff. One significant change is the larger number of children and adults they have to relate to. The flexible organization of place and child groups requires new forms of cooperation among the staff. As we see from the excerpt above, time is spent daily in negotiations and discussions regarding the organization distribution of staff in the physical landscape. On the one hand, the extended social network that is created represents a potentially more stimulating and cooperative space for the staff. On the other hand, this requires new forms of competence. One of the teachers in the kindergarten argues that, if the municipality is going to continue establishing these new and flexible kindergartens, and organizing the children in flexible base-oriented groups, then the curriculum and profile of kindergarten teacher training in the university colleges must be changed. She continues:

> Kindergarten teachers need better competence in organization theory and stuff. I feel more like a traditional principal of a kindergarten, who is responsible for the administration and organization of activities and has an overview. Monica: Do you feel more like an administrator than a teacher? Teacher: Yeah, I just walk around because the kids are moving all the time.

The changes in the 'new kindergarten' are also connected to recent reforms regarding management of welfare services, including early childhood education and care (ECEC); that is, new public management. Drawing on Nick Rose, Peter Moss argues that new public management implies a focus on outputs, not inputs, standards and measures of performance. He states that new public management is: '... inscribed with the ethos of business, the rationality of the markets and the image of the citizen as a customer' (Moss, Chapter 7, this volume, p. 138). In a dialogue with one of the assistants who has worked in kindergartens for 12 years, she reflects on the difference between the traditional kindergarten with fixed units, where she worked earlier, and the new kindergarten with flexible place and child groups:

> I think there was more freedom to make spontaneous decisions regarding different things during the day in the 'traditional' kindergarten than I feel in the new kindergarten. It's a stricter and more fixed time structure now. Time now governs daily life in the kindergarten more than ever, leaving little room for children's spontaneous activities.

She further explains that in the more 'traditional' kindergarten where she worked previously, they discussed the importance of a flexible time structure that allowed room for spontaneity, care, play and close contact with the children. These experiences represent a contrast with the way the new kindergarten is presented in the political document. As we have seen, one important argument for the new model is that it is supposed to enable staff to be more flexible in their organization of children into different, more flexible groups in order to promote increased freedom of choice for individual children. (For further description of how public management affects the 'new kindergarten', see Seland, 2009.)

However, the fact that flexible organization and new professional practices that are required are demanding is reflected in an increased rate of sick leave among staff. From 2004 to 2007 the rate increased from approximately 10 per cent to 13 per cent. Apart from having a negative impact on the staff, causing stress and requiring increased effectiveness among those at work (Seland, 2009), the effect on children is also significant. Whereas the social network in the traditional kindergarten, which uses the home as an ideal, can be described as fixed, simple and stable, emphasizing close social relations and care within close-knit communities, the social network offered to children in the new kindergarten, which uses the bazaar as a metaphor, can be described as larger, more flexible and more multifaceted.

'The kindergarten of the future and childhood as an investment'

The term 'kindergarten of the future' is often repeated in the political document *Function and Area Programme for Municipal Kindergartens in Trondheim*, in which it is stated that the kindergarten of the future requires a high degree of adaptability to changing needs in a rapidly changing society. Furthermore, it is argued that this rapidly transforming society requires a kindergarten building that is open to a diversity of challenges and new needs from different users. It is stated that we do not know what these changes are, but we ought to have a kindergarten building that can easily adapt to new needs. This is further connected with the 'generality, flexibility and elasticity of the building' with respect to the main constructions, the technical installations, and the design of the rooms and furniture (Trondheim municipality, 2005).

From a discourse perspective, it is interesting to note other ingredients in the argument for the reorganization of the physical place in the political document. The new architecture is also presented as more *effective* because a larger group of children can utilize the 'special rooms', such as the room for drama and symbolic play. This means one can have just one room for each activity and thereby avoid many small wooden block rooms, many doll rooms and so on. Flexibility according to place is a key term that is supposed to create meeting places for groups of children of any size. These flexible meeting places are also described as being more *functional,* creating greater *availability, openness* and *transparency.* However, fieldwork data call into question this assumption, which is made in the political discourses connected to the new kindergarten architecture.

As we have seen, the 'new kindergarten' represents a new and different space for both children as social participants and for the staff and the professional practices they develop. As elaborated in several chapters, this space reflects the new demands of a flexible working life (Brandth and Kvande, Chapter 3; Johansen, Chapter 8; Jurczyk and Lange, 2007). Furthermore, the transformation towards greater flexibility points to new demands for 'flexible identities' in a (post)modern society, as well as new forms of government through self-determination and freedom of choice (Fendler, 2001; Hultqvist and Dahlberg, 2001). There is a dynamic connectedness between the upbringing and socialization practices of children, on the one hand, and the demands of society, on the other. The neoliberal trends characterized by increased market orientation and flexibility in working life also require flexible workers who are easily able to adapt to shifting and changing demands and social relations in a rapidly changing environment. The transformed space of the new kindergarten reveals how, from an early age, children are prepared for future life, being brought up to be flexible and competent workers in a market-oriented society.

This case study from Norway also confirms the increasing emphasis in many European societies on children seen as human capital and childhood as a space for investment in future workers, as discussed in Chapter 1. As reported in several chapters, there seems to be a shift towards a growing accent on ECEC services as a place for learning and a cognitive-oriented curriculum, first and foremost, which is also clearly evident in Nordic countries with a tradition connected to social pedagogy, play and 'children's own culture' (see Gulløv; Moss; Strandell, Chapters 5, 7 and 12). An important question is how these discourses on ECEC services and childhood as an investment interact with rights discourses on children as citizens, emphasizing children as competent social actors.

Concluding discussions

This aim of endorsing children's rights to influence and to social participation embedded in global rights discourses constituted by the United Nations Convention on the Rights of the Child has been used as a basis for granting children the status as citizens. However, this status is associated with a lack of clarity regarding what it means. This ambiguity can be traced back to a lack of theorizing as well as to a lack of knowledge regarding how rights to participate are interpreted and implemented in different social contexts. For a long time, the question of what it means to be a child citizen was hardly addressed in either policy or research. However, since 2000 in particular, interesting theorization has contributed to illuminating the complexities in questions regarding children and citizenship. Perspectives building on feminist critiques of liberal theories of citizenship have generated new understandings. Instead of linking participation to individual autonomy, rationality and freedom of choice, rights are seen as being embedded in and practised within a complex web of social relationships (Kjørholt, 2004; Lister, 2008; Moosa-Mitha, 2005; Smith and Bjerke, 2009). Children's rights to participate, so often interpreted as self-determination and individual freedom of choice, including in early childhood education and care in Nordic countries (Kjørholt, 2005), is thus being questioned. By linking participation to social relationships, interdependencies and belonging, relational theories open up for new approaches and social practices embracing emotional and sensual expressivity, aesthetic practices, care and a variety of different forms of participation. The kindergartens are thus constituted as spaces for learning and creativity in a broad sense, opening for a variety of different forms of participation, and promoting integrated communities and dialogues among children, as well as between children and adults.

The idea of the kindergarten as a bazaar and the new practices of participation for children and adults within the flexible time and place regime in Norway clearly demonstrate the dynamic interconnectedness between neoliberal and market-oriented policy discourses, on the one hand, and discourses on children, learning and institutional care, on the other. As we have seen, the Children's meeting that takes place every day aims to give children individual freedom of choice by letting them express their desires regarding where to stay and play. This means constructing children as *choice-makers* and *consumers,* first and foremost oriented towards choosing among the different offers available on the bazaar street. We argue that this construction of children as consumers in the new kindergarten reflects how market-oriented discourses are expanding and intruding into fields of human life other than the economic sphere. It has been argued that market-oriented discourses are increasingly powerful in modern societies, since they are also invading our minds and ways of thinking and acting outside the market (Tranøy, 2006). Thus, this expansion also implies the spreading out of a particular understanding of what it means to be a human being – first and fore-most an 'economic man', acting on the basis of rationality, autonomy and free choice. In the kindergarten context, this requires children to be aware of their own wishes, and that they have the ability to verbally express their rational will from an early age. Contemporary discourses on ECEC reflect the rationality of the market and an image of the citizen as customer (see Moss, Chapter 7). Provocatively, we may then ask if the discursive shift from children as dependent, vulnerable and in need of care, embedded in developmental psychology, to children as competent claimers of rights and citizenship paradoxically has the effect of delimiting children's space for participation by reducing children, first and foremost, to consumers and customers. If so, we will argue, this indicates a need for a critical investigation into the ethical and ideological values connected with the kindergarten as a space for children and childhood in modern welfare societies.

Notes

1. Seland's study forms part of the research programme entitled 'The Modern Child and the Flexible Labour Market' (see also Qvortrup and Kjørholt, 2004). It is Seland's PhD fieldwork in a daycare centre from which this chapter draws.
2. This pedagogical tradition is traced back to kindergartens in Reggio Emilia in Italy, influenced by Malagucchi. It emphasizes art, aesthetics and children's abilities to explore and learn through their own activities and using their 'hundred languages'.
3. The Family Room was furnished with a small kitchen, dolls and clothes, trolleys, teddy bears and so on.

References

Brembeck, H., Johansson, B. and Kampmann, J. (eds) (2004) *Beyond the Competent Child: Exploring Contemporary Childhoods in the Nordic Welfare Societies* (Roskilde: Roskilde University Press).

Clark, A., Kjørholt, A. T. and Moss, P. (2005) *Beyond Listening. Children's Perspectives in Early Childhood Services* (Bristol: The Policy Press).

Fendler, L. (2001) 'Educating Flexible Souls: The Construction of Subjectivity through Developmentality and Interaction' in K. Hultqvist and G. Dahlberg (eds) *Governing the Child in the New Millennium* (New York: RoutledgeFalmer).

Gullestad, M. (1992) *The Art of Social Relations. Essays on Culture, Social Action and Everyday Life in Modern Norway* (Oslo: Scandinavian University Press).

Gulløv, E. (2003) 'Creating a Natural Place for Children: An Ethnographic Study of Danish Kindergartens' in K. F. Olwig and E. Gulløv (eds) *Children's Places. Cross-Cultural Perspectives* (London: Routledge).

Hultqvist, K. and Dahlberg, G. (2001) 'Introduction' in K. Hultqvist and G. Dahlberg (eds) *Governing the Child in the New Millennium* (New York: RoutledgeFalmer).

James, A., Jenks, C. and Prout, A. (1998) *Theorizing Childhood* (Cambridge: Polity Press).

Jurczyk, K. and Lange, A. (2007) 'Blurring Boundaries of Family and Work – Challenges for Children' in H. Zeiher, D. Devine, A. T. Kjørholt and H. Strandell (eds) *Flexible Childhood. Exploring Children's Welfare in Time and Space. Vol. 2 of COST A19 Children's Welfare* (Odense: University Press of Southern Denmark).

Kampmann, J. (2004) 'Societalization of Childhood: New Opportunities? New Demands?' in H. Brembeck, B. Johansson and J. Kampmann (eds) (2004) *Beyond the Competent Child: Exploring Contemporary Childhoods in the Nordic Welfare Societies* (Roskilde: Roskilde University Press).

Kjørholt, A. T. (2004) *Childhood as a Social and Symbolic Space. Discourses on Children as Social Participants in Society* (Doctoral Thesis) (Trondheim: Norwegian University of Science and Technology).

Kjørholt, A. T. (2005) 'The Competent Child and "the Right to be Oneself". Discourses on Children as Fellow Citizens within a Danish Day-Care Centre' in A. Clark, A. T. Kjørholt and P. Moss (eds) *Beyond Listening. Children's Perspectives in Early Childhood Services* (Bristol: The Policy Press).

Kjørholt, A. T. and Tingstad, V. (2007) 'Flexible Places for Flexible Children? Discourses on New Kindergarten Architecture' in H. Zeiher, D. Devine, A. T. Kjørholt and H. Strandell (eds) *Flexible Childhood. Exploring Children's Welfare in Time and Space. Vol. 2 of COST A19 Children's Welfare* (Odense: University Press of Southern Denmark).

Korsvold, T. (1998) *For alle barn! Barnehagens framvekst i velferdsstaten* (For all children! Kindergarten in the welfare state) (Oslo: Abstrakt Forlag).

Lister, R. (2008) 'Unpacking Children's Citizenship' in A. Invernizzi and J. Williams (eds) *Children and Citizenship* (London: Sage).

Moosa-Mitha, M. (2005) 'A Difference-Centred Alternative to Theorization of Children's Citizenship Rights', *Citizenship Studies*, 9, 369–388.

Qvortrup, J. and Kjørholt, A. T. (2004) 'Det moderne barn og det fleksible arbeidsmarked' (The modern child and the flexible labour market), *Barn*, 1, 22, 7–26.

Rinaldi, C. (2005) 'Documentation and Assessment: What is the Relationship?' in A. Clark, A. T. Kjørholt and P. Moss (eds) *Beyond Listening. Children's Perspectives in Early Childhood Services* (Bristol: The Policy Press).

Seland, M. (2009) *Det moderne barn og den fleksible barnehagen. En etnografisk studie av barnehagens hverdagsliv i lys av nyere diskurser og kommunal virkelighet* (Doctoral Thesis) (Trondheim: Norwegian Centre for Child Research, NTNU).

Smith, A. B. and Bjerke, H. (2009) 'Children's Citizenship' in N. Taylor and A. B. Smith (eds) *Children as Citizens? International Voices* (Dunedin: University of Otago Press).

Tranøy, B. S. (2006) *Markedets makt over sinnene* (The market governing the souls) (Oslo: Aschehoug).

Trondheim municipality (2005) *Funksjons- og arealprogram for kommunale barnehager i Trondheim* (Function and area programme for municipal kindergartens in Trondheim) (Trondheim: Trondheim municipality).

10

Children's Sense of Place

Aspects of Individualization, Flexibility and Free Choice within the Preschool Context

Gunilla Halldén

Introduction

In the book *The Century of the Child*, written in 1900, the Swedish author Key argued that the twentieth century should be the century in which we learn to let children develop as individuals and not simply be 'bad copies' of each other (Key, 1900). This was an attack on the kindergartens and schools of that time, which she saw as contributing to the brutalization of children. Children need free space and stimulation, she argued, not institutions where they are all cast in the same mould. Key argued in favour of a school where children had the possibility to choose subjects to study and to find their own interest and path through the curriculum. She was involved as a teacher in a school that used a progressive pedagogy and was one of those that introduced new ideas in the area of education. At the end of the century, when many scholars were engaged in summing up the changes that had occurred during the century, she was quoted frequently, and scholars and political decision-makers questioned whether this had really been the century of the child (Stafseng, 1996) and, if so, how this new childhood was constructed.

Modern childhood is, according to Jens Qvortrup, characterized by the 'Three Is' – individualization, institutionalization and individuation. This goes beyond a discussion of what goes on in a given institution and takes into consideration the relationship between processes that are important in order to understand childhood's position in the civilization process (Qvortrup, 1994, p. 9). Institutionalization is linked to a process of individualization where children are looked upon as individuals, not as representatives of a family. They are registered as individuals, and their individual development is supervised and controlled by health check-ups and in organized 'parental talks' in the preschool. This institutionalization and individualization paves the way for an individuation process, whereby all children are given the same rights because they all belong to the same category and must be treated equally. The rights and support in the welfare state are given to individuals, not to a household or a family; the individual is the basic unit. Elisabet Näsman states, drawing on Ulrich Beck, that this individuation process is in fact a 'restriction of the autonomy caused by the standardization and competitiveness in the midst of all increased opportunities' (Näsman, 1994, p. 178). In order to explore how the 'Three Is' influence everyday life but also are challenged by children's activities, I will draw on a study of children's lives in preschool. I will use the concepts of place and space in order to discuss how children use the physical locality that is arranged for them, and make it into a meaningful place. The empirical data illustrate how preschool as an institution positions children, but also how children find ways of using the institution for their own projects and act against the institutional order. This chapter is organized accordingly. First, I will give a short introduction to the Swedish preschool system, after which I will discuss place and space and then go on to use these concepts in the analyses of three ethnographic examples. The examples are used to explore how we can understand the meaning of the institution from children's perspectives.

Preschool in Sweden – a part of the school system

The preschool is an important institution in Sweden, and children join from an early age. The term preschool was introduced as the including concept for half and full daycare provision back in 1972 and the pedagogical aspect was emphasized. The reform that introduced a curriculum and made preschool part of the school system in 1998 has increased the individualization process in terms of emphasizing children's individual rights and choices. Today preschool is part of Swedish childhood, and although attendance is not compulsory, it is compulsory for local governments to arrange childcare services for all children. According to the Act on Preschool Education of 1998, children from the age of one year, whose parents are working or studying, have a right to this service. In addition, all four- and five-year-olds are able to attend preschool free of charge for three hours a day during the school year. The law stipulates that municipalities are obliged to offer this service, but that parents are free to decide whether their children are to take part or not.[1] The tendency now is that the earlier system of so-called family daycare (*familjedaghem*), whereby someone, most often a woman, took care of children in their own home, is replaced by preschools. Preschools are now considered to be part of children's life-long learning and not primarily a nursery arrangement vital to the labour market. However, since women in Sweden are part of working life, and families need childcare services, preschools are also part of Sweden's labour market policy.

The election in Sweden, in autumn 2006, which brought right-wing parties to power, has opened up a so-called free choice in relation to childcare services. This means that municipalities can choose to offer a 'cash for care' system instead of preschool places to parents with small children under the age of three. The amount of money is, however, so small that it is an impossible offer for single parents to accept. The fact that parents in Sweden favour dual-earner parenthood implies that it would not be an option for other parents, either. This renders the idea of free choice an illusion. The fact is that few municipalities have chosen to introduce this 'cash for care' system and few parents have chosen to use it.

Children's practices and the issue of place

In this section, I want to discuss how the preschool, as an institution and an important arena where modern childhood is lived, can be used by children in their daily lives and formed into the children's place, and not only a place for children (Olwig and Gulløv, 2003). The intention is to take a child's perspective and try to show how children actively give meaning to different places and create a peer culture and/or a private space within the institution. I will draw on a project entitled *Changing Preschool and a New Meaning of Childhood*, with ethnographies of children's everyday lives in preschool (Halldén, 2001).

More specifically, children's sense of place will be in focus, which means that I will show how children in our ethnographic studies use places in flexible ways in relation to what they need to form a child culture. In line with William Corsaro, child culture is understood as a result of children's interpretative reproduction (Corsaro, 1993). The process of interpretation is dependent on children's peer relations and the creation of interactive spaces; that is, spaces that protect children's interaction (Corsaro, 1997). The physical arrangement in the preschool is important and is used by children in order to establish interactive spaces in certain places. Different areas in the preschool can be analysed in terms of the facility to help children protect their play and, through that process, they are turned into places with meaning. Children's use of such places can be understood as a meaning-making process. One aspect of the physical arrangement is the artefacts that can be used by children in their creation of an interactive space. Peer relations in preschools are dominant, but it is also possible to see how children use places and artefacts to create a refuge and a place to be alone. A place can have a personal meaning for one child or a group of children.

The issue of place and space has been discussed by many scholars (see, for example, Olwig and Gulløv, 2003; Rasmussen, 2004, who draws on Tuan, 1974). The two concepts are tied together, but it is emphasized that a physical locality can be undifferentiated without any personal meaning. It is when it is used and a personal meaning is attached that it has the qualification of being a place, in Tuan's meaning. A place can perform the functions of a locality, with the potential of being a place for interaction or privacy. In analysing children's everyday lives in preschool from a place/space perspective, processes are identified when children create free spaces where they, and not the adults present,[2] are in control. This is why I want to analyse how children establish a sense of a place and defend the place as theirs. This connects to the issues discussed in this book, namely, *flexibility, individuality and user orientation*, but it does so from the children's perspective. Preschool is an important institution that hugely influences children's lives; it is the embodiment of institutionalized childhood, and it seeks legitimacy through a strong rhetoric of individuality. However, preschool is also an institution that is used by children, and from this perspective it is possible to highlight children's agency in the regulation of everyday life. The questions I want to raise are: Is it possible to be an individual in the collective of the preschool group? Is it possible to use the physical environment in a flexible way? Is it possible to defend the preschool as a children's place, in the meaning that they are the users of the institution? The discussion of children's places can then be related to the broader discussion of the institutionalization process and its meaning from a child's perspective.

Three ethnographies

Three examples will be used: the place where private and public meet, which is the hall; artefacts as tools in creating a place; and the possibility of establishing interactive spaces or privacy in relation to art activities. The examples come from three subprojects (Änggård, 2005; Markström, 2005; Simonsson, 2004). Each is based on ethnographic studies carried out in two preschools, which give us data from six institutions, all of which are located in different areas in a medium-sized Swedish town. The researchers used a similar approach in taking field notes, recording video and audio taping the activities, and interviewing children and adults. The length of the fieldwork varied with respect to each preschool, from five weeks to six months.

The two preschools where the longest periods of fieldwork were carried out had groups of 25 and 42 children, respectively, aged one to six years. The focus of this subproject was daily life and negotiations between home and preschool. The two other subprojects focused on special activities, namely, children's use of picture books and children's art activities. For these projects, four preschools with children aged three to five years were chosen, and the groups contained between 19 and 31 children. Consequently, the child's perspective was most often adopted in the projects that focused on art activities and the use of picture books, while the project that studied negotiations also considered the opinions of the parents and the professionals, and how they established routines and relationships. In this context, I will use the three subprojects and their findings as a starting point for a discussion on how the institution is used by children, and highlight how a place is given meaning.

The hall

The hall is the place where one enters the preschool, and it can be characterized as a place where something changes and where a border is marked. In using Bakhtin's framework, we can talk about it as a threshold chronotope, where the threshold is a metaphor for important divisions of time and place (Holquist, 1981). When making detailed analyses of the negotiations in the hall, it became obvious that the area was a domain between home and preschool. The parents represented the home and the teachers represented the institution. Ann-Marie Markström (2005) discusses the hall as a key symbol for the transition between those who care for children during daytime and who have a pedagogical role, and those who have the main responsibility in their role as parents. It was found that being a transit place gave the hall a special meaning for children, and the ethnography made it apparent that children made use of the fact that the hall was an area where their individuality could be exposed. In this area of transition between the private and the public, children have places that are their own.

This is unique in the preschool, which is guided by an idea that all spaces and all toys are to be used by everyone and nobody can claim them as their own. Contrary to the fact that the institution has an individualized rhetoric, there is a dominance of collectivism with regard to spaces. Everything is to be used by everyone and it is not possible to claim that something is private. The hall is an exception. Here, each child has a shelf with their name on it and a box or a drawer in which to put personal things. It is in this area that children keep favourite things that they have brought to the preschool, but which they are not allowed to play with during the day. As a transit area, the hall is not always under the surveillance of the adults. This gives children the opportunity to use the forbidden personal items and also to engage in private and forbidden activities, such as eating sweets. Some children use the hall to be alone or to play with friends.

We can talk about the hall as an important place from the children's perspective. It has a special meaning as an ambiguous space that is not home and yet not institution – something in between the private and the public. Although there are rules that are meant to prevent children from spending time in the hall, children always break the rules and use the area as a place of their own. Mary Douglas describes ambiguous spaces as dangerous areas where the borders are blurred, and states the need for rituals to handle this ambiguity (Douglas, 1966). The adults' rule, with the intention of keeping children away from the hall, can be looked upon as their way of controlling children, while children's use of the hall opposes this control. Children's preferences for playing in the hall can be understood as indicating that this area is out of institutional control and possible to use as place; that is, a space given special meaning and a possibility to protect a link to an identity outside the institution. It is an interactive space but has connotations due to the fact that it is related to the private sphere.

The picture book as a place

Maria Simonsson (2004) videotaped all the activities that involved children and picture books, and in analysing the data she could see how the book was used as a focal point for the children, both as part of play and interaction between peers, and as a legitimate reason to be alone. The children used books in very different activities. Two boys used one picture in a book as a scene in their play, and they acted out a sort of role play on the basis of the castle, the knight and the princess that were depicted in the book. They defended the place, and other children were kept out of the scene and were not allowed to take part in the role play. The official rule in the preschool was that all children could take part and that no items were private but should be shared. Contrary to this, the two boys used the book as their private world. The picture was turned into a place that had borders that other children were not allowed to cross, an arena where no one else could enter and with rules that were not explained or introduced to the other children. This was a way to establish an exclusive friendship that was based on the fact that no one else could know the rules – namely, an interactive space (Corsaro, 1997).

Other children were 'reading' to their peers and, when they were sitting together, a place of cosiness was created. For the children, reading books was a traditional part of the preschool routine. The adults gathered a group and used books as a way to calm the children down and introduce them to a cultural canon. These sessions were often held after lunch, when the children were supposed to rest. Some children acted as more competent readers and let the book have the role at the centre of an interactive space aimed at drawing children together in a caring interaction.

The possibility of forming a place characterized by care was also used by children who were sitting alone with a book. They were creating a 'reading bubble' around themselves and the book, and in doing that they also created a place where they were allowed to be alone. As shown in the hall example, the preschool is an institution for collective lives, although there is the rhetoric of the individualized institution. Children are supposed to be glad to be part of the group. The competent child is also interpreted as an active child, which means that the child is to take part in organized activities. A child who is sitting alone can be a threat in relation to the idea of the importance of social competence. Sitting alone with a book, however, is a legitimate way to establish a private arena in the collectivism of the preschool.

Using books as the focus of observations, Simonsson showed how children let books form places that were given personal meaning. When children were sitting with a book, it could be seen as an invitation for their friends to take part in role play or just to sit and listen to the child who 'read' the book, but it could also be a sign of privacy. In all of the studied situations, children used the book to mark a place, but the places created around the artefact had different meanings.

The possibility of establishing interactive spaces and/or privacy

When Eva Änggård (2005) studied how children make pictures, she saw that this was part of children's play world and peer culture. However, her ethnography also illustrated how, for example, the physical arrangements for painting activities could be discussed as a place with special meaning for the children involved. As discussed in the afore-mentioned examples, there is a collectivistic ideology in the preschool, which means that no one should be left alone. It is also part of the adult's duty to supervise the children and see that the rules are kept. Änggård identified two stations where picture making took place: one was a special painting room that was remotely situated, and the other was a table in the centre of the preschool where children passed through and the adults had their office with a desk in the corner.

When the adults organized painting activities in the remote room designed for them, the children had to follow rules about how to use the materials, and there were instructions to not waste paper or mix the colours. In the canon of how to allow the artistic child to emerge, there is emphasis on creativity and authenticity. However, there are also ideas of the importance of carefulness and prudence. The artistic child is enclosed in an ideology of neatness. In the painting room in the studied preschool, there was a range of different colouring materials, glittery paper and pencils, and water was also available. The children were allowed to use these materials but with care. Children's art activities were praised and seen as important, but also surrounded by restrictions. This area was characterized as a place for creativity, but not without boundaries. Children, however, had access to this room without any supervision and could then use the materials in ways that were not eval-uated by the adults. In doing this, they were, in different ways, crossing borders. Sometimes the activities resulted in chaos and in the children challenging the rules and becoming overexcited. The fact that the room was remotely situated made this possible. The control was not absolute.

Picture making was, however, an activity often done at a table in the centre of the preschool. The activity was open for all to join, and no negotiations were needed in order to start drawing. All children had access to the place. The fact that this activity was not organized by adults and not dependent on rules among the children made it an open activity but also flexible: the children came and went. This was also the reason why some children used the table as a sanctuary; it was possible to just sit there and have some peace. The remote painting room had a capacity to be used for carnivals, and the table in the centre was impor-tant in another way. Being under the supervision of the adults and not 'owned' by a group of children made the table a secure place and also a haven for refuge.

Focusing on an activity such as picture making presents and opportu-nity for a discussion on how different areas are used, and how children transform a place into an interactive space for protecting their play, or as a place that allows them to be part of an activity, but at the same time to secure some privacy.

Place and space – three studies and a common theme

When analysing children's opportunities to establish free zones, it is obvious that it is not easy for children to find such areas. In parallel to the rhetoric of individualization, we can find a strong ideology of collectivism. As pointed out at the beginning of this chapter, and referring to Näsman (1994), an institution such as the preschool can be described as part of the individualization process as well as a collectivization of the individual, or as Jan Kampmann (2004) phrased it, an institutionalized individualization. The 'Three Is' (individualization, institutionalization and individuation), which were introduced at the beginning of the chapter, involve a dilemma. Individuation means equal conditions, which at the same time turn into standardization. In that sense, individuation is connected to collectivism. What we can see in the ethnographic data is that children oppose the standardization and in doing so also oppose the collectivism.

What is obvious in the three ethnographies referred to here is that physical arrangement is important for children's opportunities to attach a sense of meaning to places. The peer culture involves an exploration of borders and of what it is possible to do in different areas. When discussing these issues and using the concept of place as an analytical entrance, we can see that different places are given different meanings. Some of them are children's places and used in order to form an interactive space protecting their play, while other places are used by the children in their defence of a refuge from collectivism.

When analysing the examples, it is useful to relate to the distinction between places for children and children's places. This is a different distinction from that between place and space. Earlier, I used place/space in order to see how children can use a place in order to create an interactive space and/or a refuge from collectivism. Places for children can thus be used in different ways, and detailed ethnographies of institutions for children have shown how children can turn such localities into places of their own (Olwig and Gulløv, 2003). However, the places arranged for children constitute important frameworks. Olwig and Gulløv refer to James, Jenks and Prout when stating that 'the child's freedom to move around and define places for themselves is embedded in new forms of power-knowledge relations, where children are at once being controlled by others and enjoined to regulate their own behaviour' (James et al., 1998, p. 8). This means that although we cannot say that the institution determines children's lives, we need to acknowledge the influence of structural frames and the power of artefacts and their governing of children's everyday lives.

When Kim Rasmussen discusses how children make use of the places that adults have arranged for them, he relates to Edward Relph, who states that a place is given meaning by the people who use it (Rasmussen, 2004, p. 165). Thus, a physical locality takes on existence and character. This is in line with Yi-Fu Tuan, who argues that an undifferentiated space becomes a place when one gradually experiences a setting, comes to know it better through lived experiences and attributes meaning to it (Tuan, 1974). If we discuss place from a phenomenological perspective, we must make a distinction between places for children and children's places. Rasmussen uses this distinction in relation to pictures that children have taken of their places. According to the Swedish sociologist Johan Asplund, place is in contrast to 'placelessness', a feeling of distance and a lack of possibility to have influence or to participate. Asplund also draws on Relph (1976) and Tuan (1974) when he states that place is more than the physical locality (Asplund, 1983). A place is social, and it has a meaning in a community when it is opened up for people's participation.

When studying children's places from this perspective, the concept of place is reserved for areas that have meaning for children and with which children become attached. Children use a physical locality and, in using it, also transform it into a meaningful place. These places often have an inconsistency and are transient, such as a den built by the children or the lines made with chalk on the schoolyard where children play hopscotch. Some places, however, can be given a meaning for children over a period of years (Kylin, 2003). Place is then a physical locality that is given meaning by children, and not all places for children are children's places. The concept 'place' is here used in two meanings: on the one hand, a physical locality, on the other hand, a meaningful place used to protect interactive or private spaces. In the example of the hall, we could see how the children made use of a place that was private and used it as a refuge from collectivism. We could, however, also look upon the preschool as an intermediate domain where private and public meet.

The preschool as an intermediate domain between public and private

Returning to the question I posed at the beginning of this chapter, regarding the role of preschools in the construction of childhood in

Sweden today, I argue that preschool is characterized as a domain between the private and the public. The institution is state organized and state supported, but it is closely linked to the private lives of children and their parents. As shown in the study of the changing preschool, which I conducted together with Ann-Marie Markström, the institution is influenced by the children, their parents and the pedagogical staff involved (Markström and Halldén, 2008). Children eat, sleep and play, and they go to the toilet or have their nappies changed. Childcare is to a great extent about the body. Much of what we refer to as private business is publicly handled in the preschool. This puts preschool staff in an intimate relationship with the children under their care and, because of this, also with their parents. The suitability of clothes, acceptable levels of hygiene and appropriate language are aspects of private life that are open to exposure in preschool. The preschool can be described as an intermediate domain where negotiations take place. It has its curriculum and educated staff, but the accomplishment of everyday life is a result of how the actors in the scene interpret the meaning of different places. The preschool is influenced by the adults as well as by the children, and the processes influence the childhood that is made possible.

Berry Mayall has accounted for the importance of the negotiations between paid and unpaid women that take place in an intermediate domain as 'an arena where state/public interests and family/private interests intersect' (Mayall, 2002, p. 11). The concept of an intermediate domain is not a specific place, but a space where unpaid work is a prerequisite for the paid work and where distribution of the work is negotiated. Everyday life in preschool is dependent on the work done by parents and children as well as by paid staff. Mayall uses the concept of intermediate domain to discuss how state-organized sectors, such as schools and health services, rely upon unpaid and also hidden work. She draws on feminist research on women's work as carers within paid and unpaid work, and in conceptualizing these processes the dichotomy between private and public is dissolved. When applied to the preschool, we can account for processes where ideas of an ideal childhood held by adults meet neoliberal ideologies of a flexible labour market and user orientation. Preschool is, on the one hand, a place for children, and the rhetoric emphasizes the pedagogical aspects. On the other hand, it is a service for parents in the labour force.

The preschool is a daycare service and an absolute necessity for the realization of dual-earner parenthood. However, it is also presented as being in the child's best interest and part of the school system and life-long learning. Parents' need for care services is transformed into the use of a school for small children, and in the negotiations between the adults around the child the contradictory interests must be disguised. The discourse of the preschool in contemporary Sweden is dominated by a learner perspective and the need for care, and the fact that children sometimes do not want to be in preschool is not possible to handle within this discourse. By using the concept of intermediate domain, it is possible to highlight the negotiations that take place and the various meanings of the preschool. In this intermediate domain, different actors meet with sometimes contradictory interests.

According to this perspective, the preschool as institution is an intermediate domain where young children live part of their daily lives, and where (unpaid) parents and (paid) staff meet. A child perspective on preschool entails accounting for the intersection between the interests of children, their parents and the preschool teachers. It also involves accounting for children's peer relations and the child culture that is created in preschools. Our understanding of the meaning of preschool must be informed by an analysis of the ideas favoured among the adults who are mandated to act in the best interests of the child. Yet it must also be informed by studies of children's experiences. A child's perspective on the study of the intermediate domain elucidates how children are important not only as passive receivers of care but also as active partners in a dialogue. Such a perspective can also show us how flexibility, individualization and choice are understood from a bottom-up perspective.

The preschool has an ambiguous character, being, on the one hand, connected to the labour market and a service for parents, and, on the other hand, an institution where children live their daily lives and establish peer relations and a child culture. Eva Gulløv discusses this ambiguity as related to the fact that placing children is never a neutral practice: 'This means that the question of where to place the youngest members of society is related to the individual parent's life situation, choices and possibilities, as well as more general assumptions' (Gulløv, 2003, p. 25). When most children are placed in preschool it is related to the need for care, but also to ideologies about how childhood should be lived. These ideologies are contradictory. On the one hand, children are controlled and protected, and, on the other hand, they are seen as self-managing individuals. According to Gulløv, surveillance and self-management co-exist in preschools, and this is one aspect of the ambiguity of the institution.

The ambiguous character of the preschool can be analysed in terms of negotiations about the use of different spaces, and in terms of children's work in making spaces into important and meaningful places of their own. In using three detailed ethnographies, I have discussed the meaning of the hall, picture books and artwork in relation to the possibility for children to establish their own places. In the preschool, where space is organized in relation to adults' ideas of what places for children should be like, the children form their places. These can be places for peer culture to develop or places for contemplation. Sometimes they are created in opposition to adults, and other times by using the adults' acceptance of individuality and the ideology of a free childhood.

Does placing children in an institution lead to an institutionalized childhood?

If childhood is institutionalized due to the expansion of the preschool system, it has, however, also been characterized as individualized due to changes in the organization and ideology of the institution. Jan Kampmann has written about the two phases in the institutionalization of Nordic childhood: the periods during the 1970s and the 1990s, respectively (Kampmann, 2004). In his analyses he focuses on the discourse in preschool reforms, and the fact that the institution was in the first period described from a developmental perspective and in the latter period from an educational[3] and neoliberal perspective.

This second institutionalization is double-edged, and Kampmann describes it as, on the one hand, new opportunities and freedom for the individual and, on the other hand, new ways of controlling children and making them responsible for choices and their own socialization. There is, within the preschool, a strong rhetoric of taking the individual child as the point of departure, and in this sense we can talk about an *individualization of the institution*. The individual child is a competent child who must have the opportunity to make choices and to learn from individual interests and potentiality. The introduction of a National Curriculum, on the other hand, can be seen as an *institutionalization of the individual*, a way to see the institution as a part of all children's lived childhood. The preschool can be looked upon as an institution that accepts and creates an individualized childhood, and at the same time an institutionalized childhood. The process of individuation emphasizes equal conditions, but, as shown in the empirical examples, also standardization and collectivism.

If we want to focus on how individual children use this social context, we can see how social actions take place and how children form their own individuality as well as peer relations and a child culture. This implies that an acceptance of the idea of an institutionalized childhood does not lead to seeing the individual child as controlled by an institution and, in that sense, as being institutionalized. On the contrary, we can acknowledge children's agency and possibility to establish free zones and use institutional spaces for their own projects. The 'Three Is' are important for an understanding of childhood's position in society. At the same time, we can see how children act and form their places in areas that are arranged for them.

Preschool as an area where children establish relations to places

If we focus on children's practices and adopt a child's perspective on the meaning of listening to children's voices, we can highlight how preschool becomes children's places. I will argue that the three ethnographies discussed here, together with other studies (Gulløv, 2003; Nilsen, 2000; Strandell, 1997), have shown that in their activities children identify places where they can establish a free zone. These places can be so-called forbidden places, such as the hall – a transitional area between the institution and the home. They can be in a remotely situated room where children are not always under the supervision of adults. They can also be in a place without visible borders, such as when involved in an activity with a book that creates an invisible circle around the child and a focal point for contemplation. The three examples used in this chapter show how a place can be created by a peer group or by individual children. This also shows how children, in their meaning-making, cross borders and create places in flexible ways.

It has been argued that the preschool is an ambiguous space that combines control of the child with an ideology of the competent child who is able to control themselves. In this sense, surveillance and self-management co-exist in preschools (Gulløv, 2003). The institution can be analysed in terms of an individualization and institutionalization of childhood (Kampmann, 2004). When focusing on individual children's everyday lives, however, we can see how children use the possibilities inherent in the ambiguity and create places with personal meaning. These places can be shared places where peer culture is developed, and they can be a private place within the collectivism. Taking a child perspective and looking upon children as the users of the institution, we can acknowledge a counter-culture created by the children. The discourse of the competent child that goes along with the individualization and institutionalization of childhood is also an opening for children's free choices.

In this chapter, I have discussed lived childhood by drawing on ethnographies. These practices are modelled in relation to structures established by the welfare state and on discourses about flexibility, individuality and free choice. The emphasis on practices and the importance of children's perspectives has been advocated within childhood studies. It is also argued that these practices and perspectives contribute to an understanding of society. Children are not only objects of care and the projection of adults' ideas and plans for the future, but social beings who act within institutions. In studying these processes of negotiation, we add to an understanding of how a social contract is established as opposed to resisted. Studying children's practices helps to explain the lived childhood, but also reconstructs childhood in society as a result of the double hermeneutic (James and Prout, 1990, p. 9). This means that childhood studies are of great political importance. The application of the concepts of space and place and children's sense of place in analysing preschool practices highlight children as actors in creating the institution.

The preschool is an arrangement in the welfare state aimed at accommodating the dual-earner family and equality policy, and it is a space where private and public meet. As well as being an institution that is part of the public domain, it is also a space where the private life of the family is exposed and where children act in their own interests. This opens up the possibility for us to see the preschool as a children's place, a place packed with events and excitement, and a place carrying memories and symbols. In their daily practices, children become attached to places and develop a sense of places that is personal and sometimes part of their private life.

Notes

1. In Sweden, as many women as men are in higher education or in the paid labour market, and 95 per cent of all one- to five-year-olds attend childcare facilities of different forms, such as preschool and family daycare. A total of 83 per cent of these joined preschool in 2005. This is an increase in the proportion in relation to 1990, when 54 per cent took part, and it shows that the preschool is more accepted now as a place for small children than it was previously.

2. I am following Gulløv (2003) and using 'adult' when referring to professionals. The word 'teacher' was never used by the children, who sometimes used 'Miss' and sometimes 'adults'.

3. The educational aspect means a focus on the individual's free choice in contrast to a focus on developmental psychology.

References

Änggård, E. (2005) *Bildskapande – en del av förskolebarns kamratkulturer* (Making pictures – a part of children's peer cultures) (Linköping: Studies in Arts and Science 315, Linköping University).

Asplund, J. (1983) *Tid, rum, individ och kollektiv* (Time, space, individual and collective) (Stockholm: Liber förlag).

Corsaro, W. (1993) 'Interpretive Reproduction in Children's Role Play', *Childhood*, 1, 64–74.

Corsaro, W. (1997) *The Sociology of Childhood* (Thousand Oaks: Pine Forge Press).

Douglas, M. (1966) *Purity and Danger: An Analysis of Concepts of Pollution and Taboo* (Harmondsworth: Penguin Books).

Gulløv, E. (2003) 'Creating a Natural Place for Children: An Ethnographic Study of Danish Kindergartens' in K. F. Olwig and E. Gulløv (eds) *Children's Places. Cross-Cultural Perspectives* (London: Routledge).

Halldén, G. (2001) *Changing Preschool and a New Meaning of Childhood* (Research project, Swedish Research Council).

Holquist, M. (ed.) (1981) *The Dialogic Imagination. Four Essays by M. M. Bakhtin* (Austin: University of Texas Press).

James, A. and Prout, A. (1990) *Constructing and Reconstructing Childhood* (London: Routledge).

James, A., Jenks, C. and Prout, A. (1998) *Theorizing Childhood* (Cambridge: Polity Press).

Kampmann, J. (2004) 'Socialization of Childhood: New Opportunities? New Demands?' in H. Brembeck, B. Johansson and J. Kampmann (eds) *Beyond the Competent Child. Exploring Contemporary Childhoods in the Nordic Welfare Societies* (Roskilde: Roskilde University Press).

Key, E. (1900) *Barnets århundrade* (The century of the child) (Stockholm: Albert Bonniers förlag).

Kylin, M. (2003) 'Children's Dens', *Children, Youth and Environments*, 11, 1, http://cye.colorado.edu, accessed 15 June 2009.

Markström, A.-M. (2005) *Förskolan som normaliseringspraktik. En etnografisk studie* (Preschool as normalizing practice – An ethnographic study) (Linköping: Linköping University).

Markström, A.-M. and Halldén, G. (2008) 'Children's Strategies for Agency in Preschool', *Children & Society*, DOI:10.1111/j.1099-0860.2008.00161.x.

Mayall, B. (2002) *Towards a Sociology for Childhood. Thinking from Children's Lives* (Buckingham: Open University Press).

Näsman, E. (1994) 'Individualization and Institutionalization of Childhood in Today's Europe' in J. Qvortrup, M. Bardy, G. Sgritta and H. Wintersburger (eds) *Childhood Matters. Social Theory, Practice and Politics* (Aldershot: Avebury).

Nilsen, R. D. (2000) *Livet i barnehagen. En etnografisk studie av sosialiseringsprosessen* (Life in day-care centre. An ethnographic study of the socialization process) (Trondheim: Norwegian University of Science and Technology, Faculty of Social Sciences and Technology Management).

Olwig, K. F. and Gulløv, E. (2003) 'Towards an Anthropology of Children and Place' in K. F. Olwig and E. Gulløv (eds) *Children's Places. Cross-Cultural Perspectives* (London: Routledge).

Qvortrup, J. (1994) 'Childhood Matters: An Introduction' in J. Qvortrup, M. Bardy, G. Sgritta and H. Wintersburger (eds) *Childhood Matters. Social Theory, Practice and Politics* (Aldershot: Avebury).

Rasmussen, K. (2004) 'Places for Children – Children's Places', *Childhood*, 11, 115–173.

Relph, E. (1976) *Place and Placelessness* (London: Pion).

Simonsson, M. (2004) *Bilderboken i förskolan en utgångspunkt för samspel* (Picture books in preschool – an interactional perspective) (Linköping: Studies in Arts and Science 287, Linköping University).

Stafseng, O. (1996) *Barnets århundrade. Omläst hundra år senare med introduction och kommentarer av Ola Stafseng* (The century of the child. Reread one hundred years later with an introduction and comments by Ola Stafseng) (Stockholm: Informationsförlaget).

Strandell, H. (1997) 'Doing Reality with Play. Play as Children's Resources in Organizing Everyday Life in Day-Care Centres', *Childhood*, 4, 445–464.

Tuan, Y.-F. (1974) *Topophilia* (Englewood Cliffs: Prentice Hall).

11
Flexible Spaces – Flexible Subjects in 'Nature'
Transcending the 'Fenced' Childhood in Daycare Centres?

Randi Dyblie Nilsen

In Norway, traditional constructions of a good childhood 'in nature' are repeated in diverse domains, supported by politics, and are in accordance with cultural ideas of a good life for everyone (Gullestad, 1997; Nilsen, 2008). At the same time, childhood today involves an increasing process of institutionalization, which interconnects with the individualization process. Hence the majority of children below six years of age regularly depart from their family and home to attend daycare centres (*barnehager*). In contrast to localization in natural environments, educational institutions may be thought of as providing a specific and 'fenced' childhood space separated from the rest of society. Further, and of relevance in this chapter, such institutions are usually materially fenced-in, adult-organized and structured places of buildings and playgrounds (Nilsen, 2000; Zeiher, 2003). In a Norwegian context, tension may arise between such features of modern childhood and traditional constructions of a 'good' childhood outdoors related to the spatial realm of home and neighbourhood (Kjørholt and Tingstad, 2007), in which playing in non-fenced places and areas of the natural environment are highly valued (Nilsen, 2008).

Although an emphasis on nature and outdoor play is a traditional and common aspect of all Norwegian daycare centres, such features are even more emphasized in nature daycare centres (*naturbarnehager*) (Borge et al., 2003; Nilsen, 2006, 2008, 2009), which are the focus of this chapter. Only 30 nature centres were thought to have existed between the time of their introduction in 1987 and the late 1990s, but subsequently there has been a continued increase. In the absence of national statistics, one estimate has suggested that there were approximately 400 such centres in 2006 (Moen et al., 2008).

This chapter is based on a study of a nature daycare centre, located in one of the larger cities in Norway. Fieldwork, with a particular focus on children's and staff members' practices concerning 'nature' and outdoor life, was carried out from late autumn to early summer.[1] Furthermore, I draw on social studies of childhood (James et al., 1998; Jenks, 1996) and children's geographies, respectively, which offer the insights that constructions of child subjects and space/place are interrelated (Holloway and Valentine, 2000). I will explore how what might be viewed as flexibility regarding places and related practices in nature interconnects with diverse constructions of children. Interestingly, this spatial flexibility is expressed by the staff of the studied nature daycare centre, who use *nomads* as a metaphor for 'us', meaning the centre and its inhabitants. It refers to a core practice that will be elaborated throughout this chapter; namely, during all seasons and weather conditions, the group visits various places in the neighbouring woods and fields. Similar to the majority of children's daycare institutions in Norway, the studied centre is located in a house with a playground. However, and in contrast to ordinary early education and care institutions in Norway and elsewhere, a different kind of childhood space is created when daily life is located in publicly accessible and non-fenced natural environments. This makes certain subject positions available for the children, as will be presented below.

The first section of the analysis explores how a *participant and rational child subject* is constructed in nature and connected to both the rights of the child discourse and features within neoliberal policy. Secondly, I will elaborate on how a flexible alternation between a *playing and learning child subject* is constructed by relating this to practices in and constructions of places in the woods. Thirdly, I illuminate how *flexible borders* are created through particular practices. Lastly, in the final section of the analysis, I highlight two interrelated aspects of the subject position 'nomad' – constructions of a 'true' outdoor life subject and an environmentalist subject – which are actualized through the localization in the public space of nature. This location manifests traditional ideas of a good place for young children to spend their daily lives. However, continuities and changes are often intertwined, and as I will discuss at the end of this chapter, daycare in nature makes an interesting case in that respect. Before presenting the analysis, I will briefly touch on recent neoliberal orientations in daycare policy (see Introduction, Kjørholt and Tingstad, 2007) and other contextual features of early education and care institutions in Norway, and then give an outline of the theoretical approaches used in the analysis of fieldwork data.

The nature daycare centre and national policy

Daycare centres usually comprise a house (including 'living' rooms, a kitchen, toilets, cloakroom, staffroom and office), surrounded by a fenced-in playground with fixed installations, such as climbing bars, swings, slides, play houses, large sand boxes and large wooden tables with benches. Children have 'outdoor' play equipment at their disposal, such as tricycles, balls, buckets and shovels, and toy cars. The landscape of the playgrounds varies, but usually there is some sort of hill and both 'grey' and 'green' areas with grass, bushes and possibly trees. In ordinary centres, everyday life alternates between time spent indoors and outdoors, usually including a minimum period of two hours spent playing outdoors, regardless of the season.

The typical house and playground arrangement described also applies to the studied nature centre. However, on four days each week the two staff members[2] and 13 children, aged three to six years, either walk or ski to different, but regularly visited, places in nature, where they stay for approximately four hours.[3] In this nomadic practice, the children and adults carry what is needed for the day in their backpacks (for example, packed lunch, cups, drinks, extra clothing). No toys are taken since the children (and staff) use whatever is available in nature. They do, however, take various tools and equipment (for example, saws, sheath knives, binoculars, and books about fauna and flora). Thus, nature makes up the core content in terms of learning and as a resource for child-initiated activities such as playing, and is a site for eating and even use as a 'toilet'. Additionally, the staff have chosen to focus on social competence and children's participation.[4] The premises are situated close to a large public area of woods and fields, where narrow paths cut through hilly woodland that is inhabited by birds and animals.

In the late 1980s, idealists working within, or closely related to, professional early childhood education seem to have played a fundamental role in the development of nature centres in Norway (Lysklett, 2005). Even before such centres had been mentioned in central policy documents,[5] and while fewer than 30 were thought to have existed, nature daycare centres were embraced and used in the rhetoric within a turn to a neoliberal orientation in daycare policy, which from the mid-1990s launched concepts such as flexibility, choice and user sovereignty (see Introduction, Kjørholt and Tingstad, 2007). The government argued for 'freedom of choice' for parents (and children), and nature centres were promoted as one among other types of daycare centre with 'various content, pedagogies and ideologies'.[6] Traditionally, early education and care institutions have been rather homogeneous in Norway (Korsvold, 1997), and today all daycare centres are still regulated by public authorities, and are governed by state and local policy. All adhere to the Kindergarten Act and Framework Plan (Ministry of Education and Research, 2006), in which 'nature, environment and technique' constitute one of six subject areas.

Local authorities have been working to rapidly transform the present (and earlier) government's promises of full daycare coverage. Apart from increasing the number of ordinary centres, additional nature centres/groups[7] have been established and are receiving increasing attention. It is interesting to note the changes within a policy context. The following statement by a representative of one large municipality[8] near Oslo illustrates the argument.

> The purpose of the strong bid of making more nature centres/groups in this municipality is to combine the intention of meeting the demands for more places in day-care centres with the need for flexible offers, to stimulate physical activity, provide closeness to Nature, knowledge about the local culture, etcetera. (Christiansen, 2005, p. 82, my translation)

In a Norwegian context, it seems as though we are facing a political vitalization of nature (centres) as a childhood space, which might partly be framed by the present neoliberal orientation.

Theoretical approaches to analysing children in nature

When studying children in natural environments one needs to bear in mind the strong cultural and ideological relationships between children, childhoods and nature. Hence, viewing children and childhoods as socially constructed is a way to abandon naturalization and ideas of children as 'natural' (James et al., 1998; Jenks, 1996). To strengthen this prominent view of the social studies of childhood in my exploration of diverse constructions of children in nature, I lean on post-structuralist approaches that follow on from Michel Foucault in applying the concept 'subject'[9] (Cavallaro, 2006). Subjectivity theory moves away from a fixed concept of identity and opens up to grasping multiple (child) identities.

Being aware that discourses create subject-positions that constitute subjects (Neumann, 2001), I find the underscoring of practice and the following statement by Valerie Walkerdine useful as a departure for my analytical efforts:

> It is necessary to examine what subject-positions are created within specific practices and how actual subjects are both created in and live those diverse positions. . . . [T]he issue becomes how to examine both how social practices work and how they create what it means to be a subject inside those practices. Thus, the understanding of how cultural practices operate and how subjects are created inside them becomes one and the same activity. (Walkerdine, 1998, pp. 223–234)

In the following, I present an analysis of diverse subject-positions, created *for* and *by* the children in the studied nature centre. I also draw upon geographers who have provided the insight that 'identity is spatially as well as socially constructed' (Little, 2002, p. 36). Further, I take account of the idea that the subject is a construction of language, politics and culture (Cavallaro, 2006, p. 86). In working analytically with the fieldwork data, I was inspired by the neoliberal influences discussed briefly above and elsewhere in this book. I have first and foremost used flexibility, but also choice, as a sensitizing notion in the process of analysis. I pay attention to the child–adult[10] relationship, and although intra- and inter-generational interactions have been analysed, staff-initiated practices will also be elaborated. The analysis is presented in the four following sections.

Participant and rational child subject – in nature

The children's rights discourse has been highly visible on the political agenda and in public debate in Norway for several years (Kjørholt, 2004). This obviously influenced everyday life in the studied nature centre, although the fieldwork was carried out a few years before the principle of child participation in planning and evaluating daily life in daycare centres was stated in the revised Kindergarten Act and Framework Plan for the Content and Tasks of Kindergartens (Ministry of Education and Research, 2006). This section of the analysis focuses on how the subject-position 'nomads' involves constructions of a *participant, rational and individual child subject.*

Children's voice and participation in choosing today's place

At ten o'clock all children gather by the gate, properly dressed according to the weather and carrying their backpacks. This is usually the time and place when adults and children decide which place in the woods should be visited today. Besides different affordances and activity possibilities, changing seasons and weather conditions are important factors in the choosing and use of the different places. As revealed in the following example from the field notes, the staff might suggest a limited selection in the choosing routine that incorporates children's voices:

> One of the adults addresses the children by saying that now we have to find out whether we should walk to Spruce Wood or Blackfoot Wood.[11] When saying that those who want to go to Spruce Wood should raise their hand, only three children do so, but when asking who wants to go to the other place, the adult counts seven and concludes that we[12] will then head for Blackfoot Wood.

In the situation described above, the young children are participating in what might be termed a democratic voting procedure that rests on an understanding of an *individual and active rational subject.* Even though adults have 'nominated' certain places, the final decision is made by the majority of the child 'voters'. This practice concurs with the staff's outspoken idea that children shall have a voice in choosing the place and it is in line with what later was formulated in the National Framework Plan and Kindergarten Act: 'children shall regularly be given the opportunity to take active part in planning and assessing the activities of the kindergarten' (Ministry of Education and Research, 2006, p. 8).

In addition to the children's voices, the adults consider the changing weather and wind conditions when selecting today's place. Whether the ground is wet, dry, bare or covered with snow and ice provides diverse opportunities and obstacles for bodily activities (such as walking, running, skiing and playing). To cope with different weather conditions demands some flexibility, and this was illustrated on the same day as that referred to above:

> When the group arrived at Blackfoot Wood, the adult looked around and said that the ground was too icy and since there were many sharp stones they could not stay there. The adult then decided that they had to proceed to Spruce Wood (the place that was voted for by the minority in the voting procedure).

Ultimately, the adult made the final choice of place. One can, however, imagine that the democratic decision of the majority of the children had to be put aside because of safety reasons and the place chosen by the children was considered by the adults as poorly conducive to play. In this respect the required flexibility regarding which place the group should visit applies to children as well as adults. As 'nomads', who carry what they need and use what is at their disposal in the woods, the group can easily move on to a more suitable place. This flexible mobility contrasts with the situation of ordinary daycare centres.

Participating in evaluating the day

In the nature centre, there is a routine practice that anticipates intentions outlined in the aforementioned documents regarding children's participation in assessing daycare centre activities (Ministry of Education and Research, 2006). Given that various members of the group are located in different places of their own choosing in the woods, the group is gathered by the sound of a 'cow-bell' ringing. Thereafter, and before returning to the daycare centre, an assessment practice is then usually carried out as follows:

> One of the adults asks each and every child questions such as: How has this day been? What does she/he think about this day in the woods, and what was good or very good? The children usually answer with reference to the activities they have engaged in and with whom. For example, one day in mid February, one of the girls tells that she has been climbing a tree, some other girls inform that they have been playing together in 'the hut',[13] and one boy has been playing 'ghost' together with a girl. Yet another boy tells that he has been playing with another boy and tells about a boat and a pistol, while a third boy says that he has been strolling around.

Usually the children respond positively, saying that they have had a nice day, and thereby they adapt to adult expectations. The adult in the referred situation asked different follow-up questions of each child, thereby emphasizing *an individual child subject*. For example, when asking *each* child *who* had decided what they had been engaged in, the 'correct' answer seemed to be 'myself'. The expectation of children's individual choice and responsibility was illustrated by the adult's concluding comment on the day in question: 'And you have decided all by yourself what you were going to do? Wow! What a nice daycare centre!' This staff member explained (to the research assistant) that the questioning practice is framed by the centre's focal area of children's voice and participation, and that the staff aim to make the children aware of this.

Through the described evaluation practice, it may be argued that children are positioned as *individual participant child subjects*. The adult's concluding comment emphasizes the importance of the individual child subject having the *freedom to choose* what to engage in and that this is what constitutes a good daycare centre (see Kjørholt, 2005). The matter of individual choice has been selected as something worth pointing out to the children. One might wonder whether current neoliberal trends, including recent daycare policy, are contributing to such an emphasis and thereby (re)producing the importance of individual choice (Kjørholt and Tingstad, 2007).

It is interesting to note that the two procedures that aimed to include the children's voice and participation differ somewhat on the question of individuality. While the individual voice and freedom of choice were emphasized in relation to the evaluation practice, it was the 'collective' voice of the majority of the individual voters that was heard when today's place was to be decided. Constructions of a participant child subject are made available through adult routines, first at the premises and then in the woods prior to returning.

Playing and learning child subjects in nature

Daycare institutions are places created for playing and learning child subjects. In that respect, the studied nature centre confirms widespread constructions of childhoods (see Dahlberg et al., 1999). However, taking account of the fact that *place matters* in several respects (Holloway and Valentine, 2000), certain practices at the nature centre created a particular flavour to such subject positions. I will elaborate on what seems to be a flexible alternation between constructing playing and learning child subjects and places in nature.

The account from field notes on a day in October continues. When arriving at Spruce Wood, the children are told that they can play before lunch, and the following extract illustrates that children are adapting to the expectations of a playing subject in nature, which they also construct themselves:

> Four boys start to build a hut with large and small branches from piles by the path. They help each other in carrying the branches to lean against a tree so that a hut is formed. While doing this, they also explore and discuss whether the branches are likely to break. One of

them thinks one branch is too hard, but it breaks and then they all find branches that they bend until they break. One boy also starts to use a long branch to hit the biggest branch on the ground, and the others follow in this activity. One of the adults approaches them and gives a caution, saying: 'Can the lumberjack with the biggest "axe" be a bit careful? It may happen that someone is behind you, Bastian.' The boy looks behind himself, sees one of the other boys and responds with a 'Yes'. The boys carry on with these activities until lunchtime.

A clear acknowledgement of the play activity can be observed in this example. Even when giving a warning about security, the adult is constructing a playing subject. The caution is framed in a language of play; as if the boy has taken on a play role as a 'lumberjack', and the adult 'transforms' the big branch to an 'axe', a tool that the children know one should be careful with. A playing subject in nature is supposed to use whatever can be found in the environment, and the boys are acting out such a playing subject. That they initiate building a hut is further adding to meanings of the playing child subject in nature and (re)producing traditional constructions of a good childhood in Norway (see Kjørholt, 2003).

During the course of the days, there is a shift between constructing a playing subject/place and a learning subject/place. This flexible alternation is connected to being situated outdoors and the choosing and use of flexible places in nature. For example, on the same day as referred to above, meal time and informal chatting are disrupted and a *learning child subject* is constructed when the following happens:

Suddenly one of the staff members jumps up, bursting out: 'There's our squirrel!'[14] He points towards a tall tree and several children jump up too, and the adult starts to ask questions: 'Does anyone know which colour the squirrel has at present?' One of the children answers: 'Grey-brown?' 'Yes, that is correct', the adult confirms, and asks more about which colour the squirrel has during the summer. While addressing Eric the adult comments: 'You have drawn the squirrel as it looks during the summer.' Eric suggests: 'Red-brown?' And the adult confirms that it is red-brown.

Following the discovery of the squirrel, the staff member is spontaneously initiating a sequence of 'school questions' that individual children answer correctly. This is a well-known pedagogical method, which is more associated with a learning subject in formal teaching situations in school or in the circle-time in a daycare context (Dahlberg et al., 1999; Rismark, 1994). At the places the children and adults visit in the woods there are different points that they term the 'eating places', at which children and adults sit on their sitting mats to eat their packed lunch. During the event referred to, the eating place suddenly takes on the meaning of a place for learning, like a classroom, and the children are positioned as learning subjects. The staff are recurrently using such unforeseen events, and a learning child subject and place can be spontaneously constructed at any time or place (Nilsen, 2006).

Flexible places and borders in nature

The adult generation is viewed as powerful in relation to structuring and using space in educational institutions (James et al., 1998). Although the staff still play an important role, a different childhood space is created for and by children when everyday life is spent in the woods, in non-fenced places without any built space. Places in nature can be viewed as flexible with several possible choices of shifting between different activities, initiated by children or adults. In an interview with a staff member at and about one of the winter places, he elaborates on the flexible possibilities of the place: various types of skiing (such as ski-jumping, cross-country skiing and downhill skiing) with different levels of skills according to age, climbing trees, social role play and traces of animals, together with the likelihood of seeing some (such as moose, deer, hares, squirrels, foxes). The shifting meanings of places and subjects can be constructed from such a variety of possibilities. While learning is related to animals and playing to social role play and climbing trees, skiing blurs the boundaries between learning and playing as it is an activity to be learned as well as integrated into playful activities. Skiing is necessarily a way to move about, and an emphasized activity at the studied nature centre (Nilsen, 2009).

The nomadic practice at the nature centre is characterized by a high degree of *movability*. In order to allow each child to move at their own pace, the adults had created a particular practice of using *waiting places* by specific *landmarks* along the routes (for example, a rock, tree, fence or crossroad in the woods). Likewise, the borders of the non-fenced and rather large places in the woods were agreed upon with reference to elements in the landscape. In an interview at one of the winter places, the staff member points out and explains the borders to Line (the research assistant):

In that direction the border is where the ski slope curves. In the opposite direction the children should ask. They [the children] know themselves when they are going too far. They [the borders] are not precisely defined; it is hopeless to do this when snow covers the ground, because there are no distinct markers. But they [the children] know that they should not go further. If the children want to go further, for example out of sight down to a steep hill that is great for sledging, they have to ask. Then we [the staff] decide whether it is suitable or not. And it looks as if that's OK [for the children]; sometimes it is suitable, sometimes *not*.

In other words, some sort of *flexibility and choice* is practised with regard to borders in the woods. Borders are objects for negotiated agreements that might become even more negotiable when the landscape is covered in snow. Landmarks only provide points and contrast with fixed fences, such as those found in playgrounds that may effectively stop crossing of the boundary lines. It might be said that the practice of landmarks provides possibilities for children's agency. They are trusted in knowing and negotiating a certain freedom of where to go. It is within such flexible borderlines that children themselves participate in drawing them up so that they can run about and choose where to be.

Additionally, the staff have left an opening in the fence around the nature centre premises to make it possible for the children to situate themselves outside the playground, although they have to ask permission first. As one of the staff members states, this is also a way to teach the children 'freedom with responsibility' (*frihet under ansvar*). In the woods, such a freedom is acted out on a larger scale and the adults said that there were almost no violations of the agreed and flexible borders.

Nomads in nature: 'true' outdoor life subject and environmentalist subject

The localization of daily life in natural environments conditions a flexible practice of transcending a fenced childhood in the material sense. In this final section of the analysis I will look at the ingrained social aspects of daily life in the nature centre: the 'nomads' moving about in *public* recreational environments.

In Norway there is a discourse on outdoor life (*friluftsliv*) in nature as a (leisure) activity that manifests cultural ideas of a good life for everyone. This is pertinent in the studied nature centre (Nilsen, 2009). The nomadic practice resembles a traditional cultural practice of Sunday trips when families, friends or individual persons, with a backpack, walk or ski in nature to different but regularly visited places and hence experience the Norwegian version of 'a love of nature' in more or less unspoiled natural environments (Gullestad, 1997).

Constructing a *'true' outdoor life (child) subject* is interwoven with the nomadic practices described above and this relates to how 'a robust, rational and independent child subject' is constructed in the studied nature centre, which I have elaborated on in a previous analysis (Nilsen, 2008). Children experience cold and wet weather and it is expected that they should verbalize (not whine about) their needs and *do* something to prevent from freezing (for example, being bodily active through rough, self-governed play). Coping in nature requires knowledge and skills concerning outdoor life (Nilsen, 2009) that have been touched upon above; for example, how to walk, stay and eat meals, and how to use natural environments as a resource for diverse activities.

As mentioned above, being skilled at skiing is important in the nature centre. Acting properly with regard to ski tracks when cross-country skiing is a type of outdoor knowledge relating to cultural (traffic) rules, and which the staff in the nature centre made explicit to the children. Such rules point at how skiing should be performed to constitute a 'true' outdoor life subject: ski in the right-hand set of tracks, those who ski down a hill have the right-of-way, if one stops while skiing then step out of the track (which is particularly important in connection with hills). The proper use of a (ski) slope and the rule of never walking in ski tracks were brought to the fore one day when a group from an ordinary centre had camped at one of the places frequented by those from the nature centre:

> One of the boys, Oliver, approached this group alone and when returned he reported that he had told those from the other centre not to sledge down the ski slope. This message was repeated a little later by one of the staff members who also approached 'the others'. In reporting back to his colleague, the staff member told that the woman did not look as if she agreed when he told her that it was not too wise to sledge down the 'ski hill', and then the two colleagues laughed a little.

This example illustrates that both children and adults at the nature centre might position themselves as 'true' outdoor life subjects who protect the prepared public ski tracks from being 'ruined' by sledging activity and walking. Generally speaking, sledging is actually a very common and popular use of snow-covered slopes by children (and adults).

In recent years the national discourse on outdoor life in nature has been closely connected to the (global) discourse on environmental protection. The interconnectedness of these two discourses is clearly visible in the studied nature centre (Nilsen, 2009). Diverse practices deal with the protection of nature and help to construct an *environmentalist subject* that applies to both children and adults (Nilsen, 2007).

The staff said that with regard to the relationship between the centre and nature, they considered themselves to be *guests in Nature*. Ideally, there should be no signs of their visits to the places in question. With recurrent or incorrect us, there is a danger that the natural environment will be ruined. The 'nomads' face this dilemma by shifting within a rather large selection of places in an effort to prevent these from being worn down. Further, the staff conscientiously take the litter they produce back to the centre. The rule of not dropping any litter is also stated in child–child interactions and the children also witness that staff members pick up litter that other people have left behind. In the event referred to above, where Oliver confronted the group from the ordinary daycare centre, the boy also reported that he had asked them if they had dropped any litter, which they had not. Thereby the boy positioned himself as an environmentalist subject.

The adults in the nature centre do not correct Oliver for his policing actions; rather they seem to approve. Through his direct questioning, the boy indicates a morality of right and wrong in preserving nature, and he also points out such a morality in protecting the ski tracks in relation to a 'true' outdoor life subject. The boy is positioning himself as powerful in relation to adults (from another centre), whom he presumably does not know. In a way, the ordinary daycare centre might represent the unknown public from which the children (and staff) have experienced traces in the form of litter.

Constructing an environmentalist child subject is clearly stated as an aim in the educational documents of the nature centre. Within an environmental protection discourse, children are positioned as core agents in both national and international politics (Kjørholt, 2002). This is clearly of relevance when studying daily life in a nature daycare centre (Nilsen, 2007). Both adults and children might share an environmentalist subject position, contributing to constructing an inter-generational *political subject*. Oliver can be seen as acting out a political subject when, as a kind of political environmental activist, he confronts 'the others', who he suspects might not act in accordance with keeping the environment clean.

Transcending the 'fenced' childhood in daycare centres?

In this final section I will address some pertinent issues that arise from the presented analysis. Compatible with traditional constructions of a good childhood in Nordic countries, the playing child subject described in this chapter is expected to be competent as an *active, independent* and *social* child (see Brembeck et al., 2004). Such expectations of active children in 'free play', choosing what to do, where and with whom, have been a cornerstone within the child-centredness in early education institutions in Norway (and Nordic countries) (Korsvold, 1997). For the 'nomads' at the studied nature centre, such playful activities benefit from the existence of large, non-fenced outdoor spaces offering diverse possibilities for activities.

Activities such as climbing trees and hut building, and the absence of commercial toys, forge traditional ideas of a good childhood in nature, which might be viewed as concurrent with nostalgic and/or romantic images and constructions of a 'natural child' in nature (Gulløv, 2003; Kjørholt, 2002). In the staff members' language, the children at the nature centre are granted 'freedom with responsibility', moving between different places, within flexible and negotiable borders. Children who actively and independently play together in nature are partly breaking a 'fenced' childhood. The nature centre might be seen as (re)producing traditional constructions of a good childhood in Norway in several ways, and possible tensions in relation to increasing institutionalization might be eased. However, from looking more closely at practices, subjects and space/place, it is also evident that what is associated with 'a modern' childhood is integrated into daily life at the nature centre.

Along with a playing and learning child, a participant and rational child subject is constructed in the studied nature centre. In addition to the children's rights discourse, one may ask whether this participant child subject is also signified by neoliberal ideas; for example, in stressing an individual subject-position (see Kjørholt and Tingstad, 2007). Adult-initiated routines created to construct the participant child subject were carried out at the beginning and end of the day in the woods by choosing the day's place and in evaluating the day in the woods. The terms of *giving* children a voice were made by adults at the studied daycare centre and in 'child politics' beyond this local context. It is interesting to note that children's agency in this kind of participation is granted first and foremost on adult terms. We might speculate whether the participant child, framed that is by an increased impact from children's rights discourses and changes in daycare policies, has become 'a token of modern childhood'. This in turn may contrast with the playing child, whose agency is acted out as a more fluid part of daily life, which is facilitated by the staff and the localization in nature.

Flexible spaces – flexible subjects?

Owen Jones (2000, pp. 40–41) points out that:

> Boundaries are critical in the structuring of children's lives. These can come in both physical and symbolic forms and often are constructions combining both to varying degrees.... The more rigid this structuring is, the more it will constrain children's worlds within it, and the degree of rigidity of such structures is determined in part by the extent to which the boundaries within it are permeable or impermeable.

Constructions of a 'true' outdoor life and an environmentalist child subject were facilitated by the nomadic practice outside a fenced childhood space in the studied centre. Undoubtedly, protecting the environment is high on today's political agenda, both nationally and internationally. As such, and in the material sense, boundaries at the nature centre can be seen as permeable and open. However, in a symbolic sense there is a certain kind of rigidity in the choice of emphasizing nature and outdoor life that can be viewed as limiting in the sense that the tight knot between children/childhood and nature is (re)produced.

In contrast to ordinary daycare centres, the material borders at the nature centre were flexible, with negotiable and multiple landmarks. This raises the question of whether coping with a flexible and changing spatiality is part of the implicit 'curriculum' in the nomadic practice at nature daycare centres such as the one described in this chapter. The spatial aspects of the nomadic practice contribute to a different version of an institutionalized childhood from that experienced in ordinary daycare centres (see Kjørholt and Seland, Chapter 9; Kjørholt and Tingstad, 2007; Nilsen, 2000). The analysis has illustrated that multiple meanings of child subjects and places are intertwined and shifting (Valentine, 1997, p. 147). In addition to constructions of a participant rational and individual child and playing child discussed above, I have pointed out the alternation between the latter and a learning subject, where different places in nature are constructed accordingly, as spaces for play, learning and eating. Further, 'the nomads' applied inter-generationally constructions of a 'true' outdoor life subject intertwined with an environmentalist subject, which involved a political subject in a non-fenced public space. In short, through child- and adult-initiated practices, multiple and shifting child subject-positions seemed to be constructed for and by the children. The question is, then, whether this multiplicity, the discussed flexibility and moving spatiality are helping to produce flexible subjects? Perhaps such subjects, who are framed by traditional constructions of a good childhood 'in nature', might meet the demands of neoliberal ideas in a (post)modern society? Lynn Fendler draws attention to how:

> ...current social circumstances call for 'flexible' and 'fluid' ways of being. These terms rightly pertain to a shift away from the rigidly defined social roles characteristic of modernity, such as the assembly-line position in a Fordist factory or the efficiency models in a Taylorist school. The conception of a fixed role or position has now shifted to a more multifaceted and response-ready capacity. (Fendler, 2001, p. 119)

Viewing different available subject positions for children that are dis-cussed, we might ask whether a readiness to shift and flexibility are at stake here. Is the availability of multiple and shifting child subject positions compatible with or forging what Fendler regards as a more multifaceted and response-ready capacity? It appears as though daycare in nature can provide a space for shifting and flexible constructions of places and multiple subject positions. However, this depends upon the adult and child practices.

Notes

1. I was the research coordinator of the project 'Natural childhoods in Norwegian daycare centres?' The fieldwork was carried out by assistant Line Hellem, to whom I am very grateful. Field experiences were documented as notes and video recordings. Participant observation was complemented by guided interviews conducted with members of staff at particular places in the woods. All names have been changed. I also draw slightly on an earlier ethnographic study (Nilsen, 2000) as well as fieldwork data relating to an ordinary daycare centre, within the current project.
2. The group was staffed by one preschool teacher and one assistant.
3. Opening hours were from 07.45 to 16.30 hours.

4. In Norwegian this is expressed as *medbestemmelse og medvirkning som satsingsområde.*
5. Nature centres were first mentioned in a White Paper (St. meld. nr. 27 (1999–2000)), in which it was assumed that fewer than 30 existed.
6. As, for example, stated in the Minister of Family and Children's Affairs, Grete Berget's (Labour Party) speech, in Sunndal, 24 September 1996, http://odin. dep.no/odinarkiv. Accessed 9 January 2006.
7. Apart from separate nature daycare centres, nature groups within ordinary daycare centres have been established in recent years.
8. In 2004 the municipality established 241 places in 20 nature centre/groups (Christiansen, 2005).
9. Several authors who cite Foucault and his followers are still using and intertwining the use of notions such as (social) identity and/or identities (see Davies, 2003, p. 8 for elaboration).
10. In Norwegian daycare centres, 'adult' is an actor category that both children and staff members use when talking about someone who is a member of staff. I follow this practice in my written account, although children and staff members also use the adults' first name.
11. These are names of places that the children and adults at the nature centre have given as the places they use regularly.
12. A total of 11 children participated in this instance, but one child did not raise a hand to express a preference for either of the places.
13. The meaning here is framed by play and 'the hut' does not refer to a built house.
14. Different Norwegian animals are chosen as 'the animal of the month' and a focused object for learning at the centre (drawing, singing, reading stories and so on). The squirrel is included in this selection and is therefore referred to as 'our'.

References

Berget, G. (1996) Speech held at Sunndal municipality, 24 September, http://odin. dep.no/odinarkiv. Accessed 9 January 2006.

Borge, A. I. H., Nordhagen, R. and Lie, K. K. (2003) 'Children in the Environment: Forest Day-Care Centres. Modern Day Care with Historical Antecedents', *History of the Family*, 8, 605–618.

Brembeck, H., Johansson, B. and Kampmann, J. (eds) (2004) *Beyond the Competent Child. Exploring Contemporary Childhoods in the Nordic Welfare Societies* (Roskilde: Roskilde University Press).

Cavallaro, D. (2006) *Critical and Cultural Theory. Thematic Variations* (London: The Athlone Press).

Christiansen, T. (2005) 'Ett skritt på veien mot full barnehagedekning i en naturskjønn kommune' (One step towards complete day-care coverage for children in a municipality with beautiful nature) in O. B. Lysklett (ed.) *Ute hele dagen!* (Outdoors all day!) DMMH's publication series no. 1 (Trondheim: Queen Maud University College of Early Childhood Education).

Dahlberg, G., Moss, P. and Pence, A. (1999) *Beyond Quality in Early Childhood Education and Care: Postmodern Perspectives* (London: Falmer Press).

Davies, B. (2003, revised edition) *Shards of Glass. Children Reading and Writing Beyond Gender Identities* (Cresskill, NJ: Hampton Press).

Fendler, L. (2001) 'Educating Flexible Souls. The Construction of Subjectivity Through Developmentality and Interaction' in K. Hultqvist and G. Dahlberg (eds) *Governing the Child in the New Millennium* (New York: RoutledgeFalmer).

Gullestad, M. (1997) 'A Passion for Boundaries', *Childhood*, 4, 1, 19–42.

Gulløv, E. (2003) 'Creating a Natural Place for Children. An Ethnographic Study of Danish Kindergartens' in K. F. Olwig and E. Gulløv (eds) *Children's Places. Cross-Cultural Perspectives* (New York: Routledge).

Holloway, S. and Valentine, G. (2000) 'Spatiality and the New Social Studies of Childhood', *Sociology*, 34, 4, 763–783.

James, A., Jenks, C. and Prout, A. (1998) *Theorizing Childhood* (London: Polity Press).

Jenks, C. (1996) *Childhoods* (London: Routledge).

Jones, O. (2000) 'Melting Geography: Purity, Disorder, Childhood and Space' in S. Holloway and G. Valentine (eds) *Children's Geographies. Playing, Living and Learning* (London: Routledge).

Kjørholt, A. T. (2002) 'Small is Powerful. Discourses on "Children and Participation" in Norway', *Childhood*, 9, 1, 63–82.

Kjørholt, A. T. (2003) 'Creating a Place to Belong: Girls' and Boys' Hut-Building as a Site for Understanding Discourses on Childhood and Generational Relations in a Norwegian Community', *Children's Geographies*, 1, 1, 261–279.

Kjørholt, A. T. (2004) *Childhood as a Social and Symbolic Space: Discourses on Children as Social Participants in Society* (Doctoral Thesis) (Trondheim: Norwegian University of Science and Technology, Faculty of Social Sciences and Technology Management).

Kjørholt, A. T. (2005) 'The Competent Child and the Right "to be Oneself": Reflections on Children as Fellow Citizens in an Early Childhood Centre' in A. Clark, A. T. Kjørholt and P. Moss (eds) *Beyond Listening. Children's Perspectives on Early Childhood Services* (Bristol: Policy Press).

Kjørholt, A. T. and Tingstad, V. (2007) 'Flexible Places for Flexible Children? Discourses on New Kindergarten Architecture' in H. Zeiher, D. Devine, A. T. Kjørholt and H. Strandell (eds) *Flexible Childhood? Exploring Children's Welfare in Time and Space. Vol. 2 of COST A19: Children's Welfare* (Odense: University Press of Southern Denmark).

Korsvold, T. (1997) *Profesjonalisert barndom. Statlige intensjoner og kvinnelig praksis på barnehagens arena 1945–1990* (Professionalized childhood: State intentions and women's praxis in the day-care arena 1945–1990) (Doctoral Thesis) (Trondheim: Norwegian University of Science and Technology).

Little, J. (2002) *Gender and Rural Geography. Identity, Sexuality and Power in the Countryside* (Harlow: Prentice Hall).

Lysklett, O. B. (2005) 'Uteleik året rundt i kjente omgivelser' (Playing in familiar environments outdoors during all seasons) in O. B. Lysklett (ed.) *Ute hele dagen!* Outdoors all day! DMMH's publication series no. 1 (Trondheim: Queen Maud's College of Early Childhood Education).

Ministry of Education and Research (2006) Framework Plan for the Content and Tasks of Kindergartens, http://www.regjeringen.no/en/dep/ kd/selected-topics/ kindergarten.html?id=1029. Accessed date 25 March 2011.

Moen, K. H., Blekesaune, A. and Bakke, H. K. (2008) 'Hvem bruker natur- og friluftsbarnehager?' (Who uses nature day-care centres?), *Barn*, 26, 3, 37–56.

Neumann, I. B. (2001) *Mening, materialitet, makt: En innføring i diskursanalyse* (Meaning, materiality, power: An introduction to discourse analysis) (Bergen: Fagbokforlaget).

Nilsen, R. D. (2000) *Livet i barnehagen. En etnografisk studie av sosialiseringsprosessen* (Life in the day-care centre: An ethnographic study of the socialization process) (Doctoral Thesis) (Trondheim: Norwegian University of Science and Technology, Faculty of Social Sciences and Technology Management).

Nilsen, R. D. (2006) 'Dyrene i skogen. Om kunnskap, barn og voksne i naturbarnehagen' (Animals in the woods. About knowledge, children and adults in a nature day-care centre), *Barn*, 24, 3, 61–81.

Nilsen, R. D. (2007) 'Good Citizens Within an Environmental Discourse. Exploring Young Children as Political and Learning Subjects in the Post Modern Consumer Society', Unpublished paper, Presented at 3rd seminar in the NordForsk Network Children as Consumers, Citizens and Learning Subjects, 19 September.

Nilsen, R. D. (2008) 'Children in Nature: Cultural Ideas and Social Practices in Norway' in A. James and A. L. James (eds) *European Childhoods. Culture, Politics and Participation* (London: Palgrave Macmillan).

Nilsen, R. D. (2009) 'Friluftsliv i naturbarnehagen – et norsk eksempel' (Outdoor life in the nature day-care centre – a Norwegian example) in G. Halldén (ed.) *Naturen som symbol för den goda barndomen* (Nature as a symbol for the good childhood) (Stockholm: Carlssons Bokförlag).

Rismark, M. (1994) *Classroom Participation: Roads to Success and Roads to Failure* (Doctoral Thesis) (Trondheim: Norwegian University of Science and Technology, Faculty of Social Sciences and Technology Management).

St. meld. nr. 27 (1999–2000) Barnehage til beste for barn og foreldre (Norwegian White Paper: Day-Care centres for the good of children and parents) (Oslo: Barne- og familiedepartementet).

Valentine, G. (1997) 'A Safe Place to Grow Up? Parenting, Perceptions of Children's Safety and the Rural Idyll', *Journal of Rural Studies*, 13, 2, 137–148.

Walkerdine, V. (1998) 'Children in Cyberspace: A New Frontier?' in K. Lesnik-Oberstein (ed.) *Children in Culture* (London: Macmillan Press).

Zeiher, H. (2003) 'Shaping Daily Life in Urban Environments' in P. Christensen and M. O'Brian (eds) *Children in the City. Home, Neighborhood and Community* (London: RoutledgeFalmer).

12
Policies of Early Childhood Education and Care

Partnership and Individualization

Harriet Strandell

Introduction

The beginning of the 1990s brought with it crucial shifts in the relations between children and the state in Finnish society. A child policy expressing a political will to shift the national child welfare agenda from a set of limited measures concerning specific groups of children into a full-blown policy pertaining to the child population as a whole first appeared on the state-level policy agenda in 1995. The background for such shifts can be found in the opening up of the Finnish economy and society to international influences and global competition in the aftermath of the deep economic recession at the beginning of the 1990s. Welfare services were reorientated towards improving the national economy, especially in relation to employment. In both public discourse and welfare policy making, more emphasis was placed on economic factors, such as efficiency and competitiveness. Policy measures pertain to all areas of society, embracing children and childhood as well. Finland's ratification of the United Nations Convention on the Rights of the Child in 1991 and its membership in the European Union (EU) in 1995 have both had a great impact on putting children and childhood on the political agenda and giving them a central place in the nation's concerns about its future (Alanen et al., 2004).

One area in which changes in child policies have been deep is early childhood education and care (ECEC). A shift from more prescriptive and rigid regulation towards knowledge-based educational policies is discussed in this chapter. Changes and continuities in the area of early education and care are approached from three different angles. The issue and its theoretical dimensions are introduced by discussing two different models of steering and regulating *children's everyday lives* and activities in daycare centres, on the basis of an ethnographic study in Finnish daycare centres in the 1990s (Strandell, 1994, 1997). From children's everyday lives the focus shifts to recent *reforms* in early childhood education and care, and to discourses and models of steering and regulating children in the Finnish public daycare system, as they are represented in *national steering documents in the daycare sector* from the 1980s and the 2000s. Questions of control and regulation, flexibility and choice, participation and autonomy, social inclusion and exclusion are vital dimensions, both in children's everyday lives and in administrative discourses.

Towards self-organization in everyday life

Ethnographic study reveals considerable differences between daycare centres when it comes to how the flow of everyday life activities and the temporal and spatial organization are managed. A comparison between the models then helps to introduce the theoretical approach of this chapter.

One of the models relies heavily on teachers' explicit steering and organizing of activities in time and space. Efforts made by the staff in order to make the day 'move forward' and to pass the whole group of children through curriculum activities are explicit. When the children arrive at the daycare centre in the morning, the staff suggest a pre-organized and pre-structured activity for them. The children glide into the activity and follow the given instructions. Reluctant children are enticed or mildly persuaded to participate in the activity. Children are kept in their place, and initiatives from the children to initiate something else are deterred. The spatial and temporal order is largely predefined for the children. The teachers provide help and step-by-step instruction in how to perform the task, and encourage and correct them if needed. Children ask the staff if they do not know how to proceed. The communication goes typically in one direction, from teachers to children, and communication between the children is scarce. In this teacher-dominated model, the explicit guiding and planning done by the teachers seems to be what makes the children act and what creates social order and social inclusion. The sphere of activity appears as a vacant space, and it is the teachers' task to fill that space with pre-planned activities. Children's own ideas, initiatives and resources remain largely hidden (Strandell, 1994, pp. 149–151).

Another steering model identified in the study relies to a greater extent on children's participation in the organizing of the everyday life of the institution. Children's ideas and initiatives are used as a resource, and are allowed to influence the course of action. In this model we can find episodes in which the staff have partly withdrawn from explicitly guiding and controlling the children's actions. Children are invited to participate in the arranging of events and in creating social inclusion. Instead of being directed and instructed in concrete situations, children are taught how to be more self-organized and how to manage social relations. The object of the children's self-organization is the seemingly trivial everyday routines, which, however, form the core of the spatial and temporal organizing of everyday life: choices regarding whether to stay indoors or to go outside, how to use indoor space and how to deal with rules for using this space, where to sit, what to do next and in what order to do things. Everyday routines also include situational groupings of children according to age, gender, competencies and preferences, and the solving of conflicts among the children. The teachers may 'delegate' some decision making, control functions and solving of (minor) conflicts to the children and also expect them to take responsibility for their actions and decisions. There is room left for children's own initiatives and suggestions, which are utilized in the organizing of everyday life (Strandell, 1994, pp. 159–166).

The latter model introduces elements of flexibility and choice into everyday routines and builds upon a more active and interactive view of the child than what was the case in the more teacher-foregrounded model. It is important, however, to note that children's self-organization is not simply a result of a release from regulation and the increased influence left to the children over the course of action; self-organization is produced by deliberate pedagogical and institutional techniques that operate with different conceptions of what a child is (active participant) and of how social inclusion can best be obtained (by inviting the child to participate in the organization and administration of everyday activities). The control of the child is more indirect and implicit. In this model, inclusion and participation are also more up to the individual child and his/her competencies to manage, while the teacher-organized model relies to a greater extent on collective group control.

Instead of just celebrating children's increased participation and competence as an emancipatory outcome of changes in late modern society and childhood, elements of freedom and self-organization have increasingly been regarded as ingredients in new ways of governing and controlling children. Demands for fluidity, flexibility, choice and individuality influence organizational structures and everyday life in contemporary society, and they also reach children (Zeiher et al., 2007). The 'participating child' has become a dominant discourse in thinking about childhood in a global context (Kjørholt and Lidén, 2004), and references to the United Nations Convention on the Rights of the Child have become almost routine in administrative steering. These kinds of expected competencies increasingly become the new norm in guiding children (Kampmann, 2004, p. 147). However contradictory it may seem, children's autonomy and self-governance is produced by increased intervention and intrusion into the child's life, which builds upon detailed knowledge about the child (Fendler, 1998).

The social investment state and new forms of governance

In many respects, then, the self-organized model presented above seems to echo new demands on flexibility and self-regulation. It seems to be an early representative of a shift in regulatory practices that has become more rooted in Finnish preschool discourses in the 1990s and the 2000s. One context in which such shifts can be studied is national steering documents worked out in the 2000s for early childhood education and care (ECEC), as well as specific guidelines for the preschool class[1] aimed at six-year-old children[2] and guidelines for school children's morning and after-school care.[3]

The teacher-organized model above, on the other hand, largely parallels the guiding principles referred to in pedagogical and administrative documents of the 1980s, steering the development of public daycare in its early period. The first national plans for public daycare institutions in Finland were drawn up in the early 1980s. The two models discussed above show that there is some correspondence between policy documents and social practices (see also Välimäki and Rauhala, 2000, pp. 397–398), even though policy and curriculum writers only to a limited extent may control the meanings and implementations of their texts. All texts are 'leaky' documents, which are subject to re-contextualization at every stage of the process (Apple, 2006, p. 479).

The aim of the remainder of this chapter is to study the policies of ECEC in Finland as they appear in (1) recent administrative reforms and (2) the formulation of national educational goals for ECEC. Changes and continuities in the *relations between the child and forms of state governing* will be in focus.

Among the steering documents of the 2000s, two administrative papers are of special interest. The *Government Resolution Concerning the National Policy Definition on Early Childhood Education and Care* (GR), drawn up by the Ministry of Social Affairs and Health, was launched in

2002. The document gathers together the main principles and focuses of development of Finnish ECEC. It aims to promote an equal implementation of ECEC across the country as an integrated whole. The second document is the *National Curriculum Guidelines on Early Childhood Education and Care in Finland* (NCG), drawn up by the National Research and Development Centre for Welfare and Health in 2003. The document is based on the GR and provides nationwide guidelines for implementing the content of ECEC to local municipalities, which are responsible for organizing and financing public daycare.

The documents of the 1980s will be used as a background and for analyses of changes and continuities. The first is entitled *Curriculum Guidelines for Six Year Olds* (my translation), launched in 1984. The second document is from 1988 and is entitled *Action Plan for Three- to Five-Year-Old Children in Daycare* (my translation). Both are drawn up by the former National Board on Health and Welfare and are aimed at developing age-specific educational goals for public daycare.

The documents will be read and discussed through two theoretical discussions pointing to important changes in steering and regulating in contemporary Western societies. The first discussion refers to changes in the *welfare state* and its *child politics*. From the earlier, more structurally operating welfare policy, a subtle shift has been observed to be taking place towards a policy that increasingly defines childhood in terms of social investments, on the one hand, and risks, on the other (Esping-Andersen, 2002; Harrikari, 2004; James and James, 2005). Understanding childhood in terms of risk, which children should be protected against, functions as a mighty legitimation for increased control and discipline of children, and for adult society's support of this control, spreading control and regulation out across all sectors of children's lives (James and James, 2005). A fear of cultural disorder accompanying rapid social change is easily projected onto children and childhood.

The term 'social investment state' indicates changes in the direction taken by the welfare state.[4] According to Anthony Giddens (2007), the 'European Social Model' is, for a range of different reasons, currently under great strain. Worries about the EU's capacity to compete on a global market push national economies and social policies closer to questions of economic growth, productivity rates, efficiency and redistribution, and, in this 'race', the Nordic countries seem to be the top performers in the EU (ibid., pp. 11–15). A guideline for the social investment state is investment in human capital, whenever possible, rather than direct provision of economic maintenance (Lister, 2003, p. 429), pushing welfare policies towards empowerment of its (future) citizens. In sketching the 'new economy', Esping-Andersen (2002) claims that life chances and social inclusion depend increasingly on the cultural, social and cognitive capital that citizens can amass.

Social investment made in children is in this new situation regarded as a main policy focus. 'A concerted child-focus is ... sine qua non for a sustainable, efficient and competitive knowledge-based production system' (Esping-Andersen, 2002, p. 28). Ruth Lister (2003) notes that children in this 'child-centred social investment strategy' become constructed as 'citizen-workers of the future', a construction that overshadows the present wellbeing of children *as children*. Although there is no necessary conflict between the two temporal perspectives on childhood, according to Lister the child takes on an iconic status in the social investment state, and 'the quality of children's childhood risks being overshadowed by a preoccupation with their development as future citizen-workers' (Lister, 2003, p. 437).

Changes within a longer historical perspective are discussed in the second theoretical tradition, which will be drawn upon in this chapter. The concept of *governmentality* – with reference to Michel Foucault – points to questions of power and how power works. Governmentality operates with a productive notion of power, pointing to a move from who has and exerts the power to the system of ideas that circulates through institutional practices, and in this circulation normalizes and constructs the rules through which intent and purpose in the world are organized (Fendler, 1998, p. 59; Popkewitz and Brennan, 1998, pp. 18–19).

Governmentality refers to the power-knowledge regimes and institutional technologies used to construct modes of subjectification and practices of normalization (Fendler, 1998; Popkewitz and Brennan, 1998). It refers to a specific combination of freedom and control, in which control becomes internalized and operates in and through freedom and autonomy. Freedom here refers in the first place to the freedom to choose what society values as the right thing to do, to want what is necessary (Kryger, 2004). Of particular interest are institutional technologies that join together adult surveillance and control, and the mobilization of children's own agency, their autonomy, self-regulation and self-evaluation in the production of the modern individual (Hultqvist and Dahlberg, 2001).

In the following section, changes and continuities in the relations between the child and forms of state governing will be discussed, first through recent administrative reforms. What educational goals reveal about the production of the modern individual will be discussed in the section thereafter.

From a focus on parents' need for daycare to a more direct interest in children and their futures

The public daycare system has been one of the cornerstones of the welfare system in Finland. Public daycare has even been regarded as a flagship for new, social thinking, which emphasizes society's responsibility for increasing equality and the distribution of resources (Välimäki and Rauhala, 2000).

The passing of the Act on Children's Day Care in 1973, and the political process underlying it, was an answer to the need for full-time daycare for children while their parents are working.[5] Daycare gradually became regarded as a normal social service for all families, regardless of socio-economic status, and was clearly connected to mothers' increasing participation in working life. The demands for the development of daycare were directed towards the state; state intervention was seen as natural (Välimäki and Rauhala, 2000, p. 396). To begin with, the emphasis was on quantitative expansion, increasing the supply of full-time daycare. Daycare centres and family daycare expanded from 30,000 to over 200,000 places at the beginning of the 1990s.

However, the 'progress' from home care to public daycare has not been linear; on this point Finland differs from, for example, Sweden and Denmark. Since 1985 the mother or the father of a child under three years of age has had the option to take unpaid leave from their work and receive a child home care allowance paid by the local authority for the period of leave (ECEC in Finland, 2000, p. 16). With the introduction of the private childcare allowance in 1997, the possibilities of caring for the child in their own home increased.[6] Together the home care allowance and the private care allowance mean that the child's parents, as well as private daycare centres, are now defined as a publicly supported care arrangement (Välimäki and Rauhala, 2000).

The support of publicly subsidized home care is the outcome of a political controversy that accompanied the passing of the Act on Children's Day Care (Välimäki and Rauhala, 2000, p. 396). It reflects the ambivalence concerning the 'proper place' for children – home or daycare – which has been a continuous theme through the history of public daycare. Such a heavy reliance on home care is gradually becoming a paradox in a system that in other respects is giving increasing weight to expert knowledge and increased professional intervention in childhood, as will be shown below.

Studies (Alanen et al., 2004; Lister, 2003) have pointed to considerable changes in the way of thinking about children and childhood in relation to the economy and the state in the 1990s. In Finland, the 1990s have been defined as a period of rupture and crisis of the economy and the welfare state. The national economy fell in the first years of the 1990s into its deepest recession in the country's post-war history. Unemployment increased rapidly and was in 1994 close to 20 per cent. Because of unemployment, the demand for daycare decreased, and the available places for children were reduced. Towards the end of the 1990s and beyond, a new economic recovery slowly began (Alanen et al., 2004).

Staying home for shorter or longer periods with children under three years, made possible by the home care allowance, has been an answer to the high unemployment in the 1990s and has also otherwise become a 'flexible' strategy for dealing with a labour market characterized by instability and an increasing proportion of short-term jobs. This is true in particular in the public sector in branches employing women in the first place. Only 37 per cent of one- to two-year-old children and 58 per cent of all children aged from one to six were in daycare outside their home in 2005 (Suomalainen lapsi, 2007, p. 180). Most children under three, then, were actually cared for at home.

In the recovery period, two important reforms of the daycare system were implemented. The unconditional or *subjective right* to a daycare place was extended to all children under school age in 1996. Children under three years had received the right already in 1990. The reform providing *preschool education* for six-year-olds was implemented in 2000. The subjective right reform signals a weakened link between parents' work and the need for daycare for the child. The child has the right to a daycare place even if parents are, for example, unemployed or stay at home for other reasons. The preschool reform, on the other hand, draws daycare more in the direction of school education and the child's identity towards being a 'learning subject' (Kryger, 2004). This connection is strengthened by the fact that preschool education for six-year-olds is administered by the Ministry of Education, while daycare for one- to five-year-olds is still under the Ministry of Health and Social Affairs.

The reforms indicate a growing interest on the part of society to intervene more directly in childhood and also to invest in childhood. As long as public daycare was seen primarily as a supplement to children's upbringing in their homes by their parents – which was largely the case during the 'first institutionalization' in the 1970s and 1980s (see Kampmann, 2004, pp. 132–137) – the comparison with care at home by the mother was the important one to make when discussing the pros and cons of public daycare. Home care by mothers was regarded as the ideal that daycare should try to emulate. The Act on Day Care includes a frequently quoted paragraph stating that daycare should support the care of children at home by their parents.

The reforms suggest an emerging shift towards regarding daycare in more educational terms. Another sign of such a shift is the change in terminology that took place in the early 2000s: 'daycare' was supplemented by 'early childhood education and care' (ECEC), a term used in the Organization for Economic Co-operation and Development (OECD) evaluations of European daycare systems (ECEC in Finland, 2000). The change in terminology indicates the opening of the Finnish daycare system to more direct international comparison and evaluation, of the widening of perspectives beyond national horizons. Comparisons with home care become less relevant as home care can less and less function as a model for daycare.

When looking at the development of the Finnish public daycare system in its first two decades, it becomes clear that there has been considerable quantitative expansion, reflecting mothers' increased working outside the home. The need for daycare and the supply of it has thus been mediated by parents' participation in working life. The reforms discussed above already indicate a more direct and unmediated relationship between the child and state governance.

From prescriptive goals to knowledge-based educational policies

The pedagogical-administrative reforms of the 2000s and the change in terminology can be seen as forerunners to what has been discussed as 'the second institutionalization' (Kampmann, 2004, pp. 137–142), implying among other things a shift from an emphasis on quantitative expansion towards more qualitative goals and rationales connected to transformations of the welfare state. A new type of normalization sees an institutional upbringing as necessary for the child's basic individuation process – a process becoming increasingly complex and dependent on special expert knowledge.

The drawing up of pedagogical goals for ECEC is a step in this direction: goals are drawn up on a national level, defining the standards and the contents of upbringing as a national interest and defining the knowledge needed in order to accomplish the project. Demands for special forms of expert knowledge suggest that public daycare is more than a mere supplement to home care.

The preparing of educational goals started in 1983 when the Act on Children's Day Care was amended with the inclusion of educational goals (Early Childhood Education and Care in Finland, 2000, p. 28). For the first time in the history of daycare, national pedagogical goals were formulated, the aim of which was to promote the child's physical, social and emotional development and to support their aesthetic, mental, ethical and religious education, with due consideration shown to Finnish cultural legacy. The paragraph on educational goals prompted the preparation of a series of national curricula in which very detailed pedagogical *content areas* and sub-areas for different age stages as well as instructions for implementation were drawn up. The core of these programmes from the 1980s (Kuusivuotiaiden lasten esiopetussuunnitelma, 1984; Salminen, 1988) consists of detailed concretizations of the content areas. All activities to be planned should be motivated by the child's developmental stage. To support parents in the fostering of their children is the starting point for all activity.

The 1980s have been characterized by Välimäki and Rauhala (2000, p. 397) as a period of centralized governing of daycare by the state. The national curricula of this decade have an explicitly *prescriptive approach* to early childhood education, meaning that strict rules and standards for steering daycare activity are worked out. Normal developmental stages are expressed in objectivistic and universalistic terms and in great detail: a six-year-old child, for example, 'has a strong need to stretch himself. He likes to lie on the floor on his stomach and hang on the wall bars' (Kuusivuotiaiden lasten esiopetussuunnitelma, 1984, p. 7, my translation), or 'a five year old has confidence in himself but also trusts other people ... emotionally he is more balanced than before' (Salminen, 1988, p. 18, my translation). Social, emotional, physical, aesthetic, ethical and religious themes that are to be put to practice in different kinds of pre-planned and controlled activities constitute the core of the programmes (ibid., p. 31). According to Vähämäki and Rauhala (2000, pp. 397–398), the process of putting activities into practice in daycare was in the 1980s so strongly guided by centralized norms concerning administration, education of staff and the daycare activity itself that an orthodoxy and a fear of doing things wrong were brought into the daycare culture.

With the economic, social and cultural turbulence of the 1990s, these kinds of prescriptive and rigid instruction expressed in an absolute and universal way quickly became obsolete. Today they are primarily of historical interest, and there is a clear discontinuity in relation to the ECEC documents worked out in the 2000s. In the administering of the daycare system, the period from the early 1990s up to the present day has been characterized by *de-regulation* and a call for more flexible solutions that pay attention to both local and individual variations. The responsibility for both organizing and financing the services has been delegated to the municipalities, giving these 'freedom and responsibility' as well. Välimäki and Rauhala (2000, p. 399) have characterized the 1990s as a period of transition and decentralization. The state withdrew its responsibility for governing and financing social services in detail, and delegated the responsibility to local governments. In the GR from 2002, this change was formulated as follows:

> From the perspective of organizing services an important change took place in the early 1990s when the reform of the system of central government grants gave the municipalities greater freedom and responsibility for service development. This strengthening of municipal self-government brought a reduction in normative steering by central government, with the emphasis shifting more towards steering by the provision of information. (GR, pp. 4–5)

Increased flexibility and the opening up to local and individual variations can be interpreted as an adaptation to major changes in the *operating environment* of ECEC: a globalized economy with open competition, an information-based society and a transformation of vital functions of the welfare state in a direction that, in Finland, has been called a *competitive state* (Sipilä, 2006). Echoing the goals of a social investment state, a competitive state is characterized rather by investment in human capital that promises demonstrable payoffs in the future than by favouring economic transfers to poor and vulnerable groups in society. Education policies and family policies provide the main targets for a competitive state (ibid.) – with childhood located in the intersection between the two policy fields. Sipilä finds the competitive state in particular in Great Britain and the Nordic countries, among them Finland.

When the first NCG were worked out at the beginning of the 2000s, the process took place in an operating environment very different from that of the 1980s. Content areas are included in the NCG, as they were in the steering documents of the 1980s. However, they have lost their strongly prescriptive status. They are now called content *orientations* and are given a more 'loose' formulation allowing for more flexibility 'depending on environment and situation' (NCG, 2003, p. 24), and depending also on 'children's own interests and needs' (ibid.). The six orientations included in the document are mathematical, natural sciences, historical-societal, aesthetic, ethical and religious-philosophical. They are motivated by their continuity with the subjects of preschool education for six-year-olds. In the context of the entire document, the content orientations do not occupy a significant position; the important accentuations are to be found elsewhere in the document.

Apparently the implementation and monitoring of the programme also take place in a changed operating environment that values flexibility rather than strict directives: implementation is understood as part of a process of continuous quality improvement in which the guidelines should be adapted to local circumstances and take into account plans and policy definitions at different local levels. The guidelines should further be converted into individual ECEC plans for each child (NCG, 2003, pp. 29, 37–39). One forum for these 'ECEC processes' is the internet, where special sites for networking and the exchange of experiences have been created (http://varttua.stakes.fi).

Partnership bridging the private–public divide

According to Esping-Andersen, the crucial issue in promoting children's life chances and the amassment of cultural, social and cognitive capital lies in 'the interplay between parental and societal investments in children's development' (2002, p. 26). This interplay is a main focus in the NCG and is called 'ECEC partnership'. The partnership idea contains more than mere cooperation between home and daycare. Partnerships represent a policy initiative for coping with a less stable and less secure world; partnership links the state to civil society and is a policy for bringing 'government, business, the voluntary sector and citizens together around issues of public policy' (Franklin et al., 2003, pp. 3, 6–7). The ECEC partnership is in the GR expressed in the following way:

> Parents should work in partnership with early childhood education staff to support the growth, development and learning of their children. Interacting on a basis of equality, the two parties to this educational partnership can bring together the different expertise and knowledge they both possess. Parents should be allowed to participate in the early childhood education of their own children outside the home, and in planning and assessing it. (GR, 2002, p. 8; see also NCG, 2003, p. 28)

An important quality of the partnership model when compared with earlier thinking about daycare as a supplement to home care is the vanished, or at least blurred, boundary and distinction between *public* and *private* (Franklin et al., 2003, p. 3). Education is pictured as a common effort with a common goal, into which all available resources and knowledge about the child must be activated. The greater engagement of parents is underlined.

It is, however, difficult to clarify the meaning of the formulations stressing 'cooperation on equal terms' in the programme: on the one hand, parents are invited and given the status of experts in the joint venture. They are confined to an educational task, aimed at the realization of children's best interests and rights, but their role in defining what the project should be about is at best marginal. Formulations in the document suggest that the parents' role is reduced to some influence on the implementation and assessment of early childhood education and cooperation in drawing up the child's individual ECEC plan. Cooperation also seems to mean that parents themselves become targets of education and assessment in order to take in the *right attitudes* towards the common education task: 'ECEC partnership addresses first and foremost the attitudes of parents and staff members towards their common education task' (NCG, 2003, p. 28). The professional expertise seems to have the primary responsibility of employing the partnership approach and of defining what partnership should be about: 'Staff have the primary responsibility for employing the partnership approach...' (NCG, 2003, p. 28). Educational partnership resembles a 'so-called social contract' (Krejsler, 2006, p. 200), which makes the partners believe that they are engaged in a symmetric dialogue, where the professionals as masters of 'the better argument' settle what the social contract should consist of. Partners have to realize the inevitability of the goals to which they are bound and want to commit themselves (Krejsler, 2006, pp. 200–201; Franklin et al., 2003, p. 11).

Another dimension of partnership given much weight in the documents is the need for new approaches and working methods in the *cooperation between different administrative bodies*, such as social welfare, health care and schools (GR, 2002, p. 14; NCG, 2003, p. 33). The flexibilization of administrative rules and practices enables networking and an intensified exchange of knowledge, and thus an all-embracing knowledge-based governing and control of the child:

A move has been made towards encouraging cooperation between different administrative bodies by proposing a relaxation in the regulations governing the administrative arrangements for daycare at municipal level. (GR, 2002, p. 5)

Partnership has, then, become another political and administrative *steering instrument* through which expectations and demands can be communicated to parents in order to engage them in the 'joint venture'. Partnership is another expression of society's interest in how childhood is governed. The new discourse underlines both parental authority and responsibility for children's welfare and, on the other hand, the necessity of increasing professional involvement and intervention in children's lives.

Individualized childhoods

Already in the definition of ECEC in the National Curriculum, as well as in the GR underlying it, children's *growth, development and learning* form the guiding principle for all activities to be planned and carried out with the children: 'ECEC is educational interaction aimed at promoting children's balanced growth, development and learning' (NCG, 2003, p. 12). The focus on development and learning is repeated and underlined all through the documents. A developmental approach was already strong in the documents from the 1980s. In this respect little has changed, although it seems that adulthood as the goal of a successful development has faded and been replaced by never-ending change and improvement.

However, the understanding of development in the new documents differs substantially from the older documents. Though acknowledging individual variations in developmental levels, the documents from the 1980s define in universalistic terms and in great detail developmental age stages in different areas of development, such as motor activity, and emotional, cognitive and social development. In the documents of the 2000s the universalism has been replaced by a more *individualized* view of development: 'The educator should be aware of the stage of each child's growth and development' (NCG, 2003, p. 24). Teachers should 'continuously observe the child's development and take account of their observations when planning activities' (NCG, 2003, p. 29). Growth and development have been individualized; individuality and the child's own unique personality have become crucial values in ECEC. A manifest expression of a more individualistic approach is the stress put upon drawing up an *individual* ECEC plan for every child. Both the child's parents and to a certain extent also the child themselves should be involved in this process and 'the implementation of the plan should be monitored and assessed regularly' (GR, 2002, p. 11; NCG, 2003, p. 29).

The child's individual ECEC plan should tackle many different aspects of the child's life: their personality, experiences, current needs and future perspectives, interests and strengths, individual needs for support and guidance, ways of communicating and learning, family culture and the circumstances that they live in (NCG, 2003, pp. 15, 18, 29). Gaining such a deep knowledge of the child apparently presupposes the close monitoring of the individual child and knowledge of the child's inner thoughts and feelings, exceeding by far the familiarity with developmental stages in childhood that informed the teacher of the 1980s. Empowering the child and producing 'normal' development then entails intrusion into the 'inner child' through control and regulation of them:

> Educators need to be committed, sensitive and able to react to the child's feelings and needs.... they enable a good atmosphere, where children have a feeling of togetherness and inclusion. (NCG, 2003, p. 16)

> The educator's commitment to the education and learning situation manifests itself as sensitivity to children's feelings and emotional well-being. (NCG, 2003, p. 17)

Children's developmental and other 'needs' have been replaced by 'the child's way of acting' (NCG, 2003, pp. 19–23) as a guiding principle in all interaction with the children and in the planning of activities. While the needs of children used to be derived from developmental psychology, 'the child's way of acting' entails careful monitoring of and interaction with the child. Certain ways of acting are understood as 'peculiar to children'. These consist of play and a playful disposition, playing with words and making up stories, children's play culture, fantasy and creativity, the importance of the peer group and so on. Such an understanding of the child can be traced back to both a romantic discourse of play, to innocence and purity, and to the developmental discourse of play, in which it serves important functions in children's physical, emotional and social development (Ailwood, 2003, pp. 288–290).

In order to answer to 'the child's way of acting', a more sensitive and *reflexive* orientation of the teacher is asked for. Sensitivity and reflexivity have largely replaced the strong prescriptive character of the older documents. Good teachers recognize children's verbal and non-verbal initiatives and intentions, and they respond to them. However, the response should be made in certain directions: when carefully observing children's imaginary play, educators should analyse play situations *in terms of learning* (NCG, 2003, p. 12). There is an interesting doubleness, then, in the ways children should be met: certain ways of acting are understood as 'natural' but have to be firmly guided in order to succeed. Educators should:

> …allow freedom to children who are engaged in play, but to be successful, children's play also often needs to be guided directly or indirectly. (NCG, 2003, p. 20)

An instrumental attitude towards 'children's ways of acting' is displayed. Although play is regarded as natural for children, it does not have an intrinsic value; its importance comes from its capacity to promote development and learning – for the future (Ailwood, 2003, p. 290).

Sensitivity and reflection, then, have become vital steering concepts in ECEC. Close monitoring and interaction are the means by which teachers gain knowledge of the individual child. Sensitivity is a way of getting access to the children's inner feelings and moods, the 'inner child'. Children are no more 'empty bottles' to be filled with knowledge and wisdom; they are allowed, and they need, to express their thoughts and feelings, reflect on their own performances and achievements, and communicate their reflections to their teachers. 'No aspects of the child must be left uneducated; education touches the spirit, soul, motivation, wishes, desires, dispositions, and attitudes of the child to be educated' (Fendler, 2001, p. 121).

Discussion

Characteristic of the changes in discourses and models of steering and regulation in ECEC has been a move from an 'either-or' way of thinking towards a 'both-and' way of thinking, which is, in itself, characteristic of the blurring of boundaries in late modern society (Zeiher et al., 2007). From preferring either home care or public daycare, attention has shifted towards laying stress upon ECEC as a joint endeavour involving parents and daycare staff, both of which are attributed expertise. Partnership represents the boundary-crossing idea, which blurs the public–private divide and facilitates flexible solutions.

The relationship between the child and the interests of the state has become more direct and less mediated by family concerns in the time period discussed in this chapter. This more direct relationship both presupposes and builds on the individualization of children, on recognizing children as individual right holders and to some extent participants. There is an interesting ambivalence built into the concept 'the child's way of acting', in relation to the stress on children's individuality: by depicting a specific children's culture, differences between individual children are downplayed. On the other hand, a picture of separation and difference between children and adults is being generated (Kjørholt and Lidén, 2004), making children 'the Others'.

The new terminology of investment, capital and productivity has made its entry into policy concerns about children and child institutions, reflecting a growing interest in discussing childhood in connection with economic and social success. The language of investments in children is, however, confusing. It can imply that the same or even a better output or quality should be reached with smaller inputs of money – a trend well recognized throughout the public sector of Finnish society today. It can mean the closing of smaller daycare centres in favour of big institutions, an ongoing development that is reinforced by a diminishing child population. Or it can mean demands to do more or do better.

Investing in children can, however, be discussed without reference to economic terminology. Discussions about governmentality stress the historical continuity of recently recognized trends: 'investing' in children is rooted far back in the history of the modern and should be thought of rather as a change in mentality and competencies than as a matter of recent changes in the economy and the welfare state.

Notes

1. Core Curriculum for Pre-School Education in Finland, National Board of Education 2000.
2. Preschool education refers to education for six-year-olds. Children start primary school at the age of seven.
3. The act on school children's morning and after school care (L1136-1138/2003) came into force on 1 August 2004; Guidelines for school children's morning and after school care, The Finnish National Board of Education, 2004.
4. 'The social investment state' is a term coined by Anthony Giddens (1998) in his discussions about the 'third way' in Britain.
5. A characteristic trait of Finnish working life has long been its inflexibility when it comes to working hours. Reducing daily or weekly working hours

has never been regarded as a strong alternative for parents of small children (Alanen et al., 2004).
6. The private childcare allowance can be paid to a private childcare minder who cares for the child in the child's home or to a private daycare centre of the parents' choice (Early Childhood Education and Care, 2000, p. 17).

References

Ailwood, J. (2003) 'Governing Early Childhood Education through Play', *Contemporary Issues in Early Childhood*, 4, 286–299.

Alanen, L., Sauli, H. and Strandell, H. (2004) 'Children and Childhood in a Welfare State. The Case of Finland' in A.-M. Jensen, A. Ben-Arieh, C. Conti, D. Kutsar, M. Phádraig and H. W. Nielsen (eds) *Children's Welfare in Ageing Europe Vol. 1* (Trondheim: Norwegian Centre for Child Research, Norwegian University of Science and Technology).

Apple, M. (2006) 'Producing Inequalities: Neo-Liberalism, Neo-Conservatism, and the Politics of Educational Reform' in H. Lauder, P. Brown, J.-A. Dillabough and A. H. Halsey (eds) *Education, Globalization, and Social Change* (Oxford: Oxford University Press).

Early Childhood Education and Care Policy in Finland (2000) Ministry of Social Affairs and Health, Publications 2000:21.

Esping-Andersen, G., Gallie, D., Hemerijck, A. and Myles, J. (2002) *Why We Need a New Welfare State* (Oxford: Oxford University Press).

Fendler, L. (1998) 'What Is It Impossible to Think? A Genealogy of the Educated Subject' in T. Popkewitz and M. Brennan (eds) *Foucault's Challenge. Discourse, Knowledge, and Power in Education* (New York: Teachers College Press).

Fendler, L. (2001) 'Educating Flexible Souls. The Construction of Subjectivity Through Developmentality and Interaction' in K. Hultqvist and G. Dahlberg (eds) *Governing the Child in the New Millennium* (New York: RoutledgeFalmer).

Franklin, B., Bloch, M. and Popkewitz, T. (2003) (eds) *Educational Partnerships and the State. The Paradoxes of Governing Schools, Children and Families* (New York: Palgrave Macmillan).

Giddens, A. (1998) *The Third Way* (Cambridge: Polity Press).

Giddens, A. (2007) *Europe in the Global Age* (Cambridge: Polity Press).

GR (2002) *Government Resolution Concerning the National Policy Definition on Early Childhood Education and Care* Ministry of Social Affairs and Health, Publications 2002:9.

Harrikari, T. (2004) 'From Welfare Policy Towards Risk Politics?' in H. Brembeck, B. Johansson and J. Kampmann (eds) *Beyond the Competent Child. Exploring Contemporary Childhoods in the Nordic Welfare States* (Roskilde: Roskilde University Press).

Hultqvist, K. and Dahlberg, G. (eds) (2001) *Governing the Child in the New Millennium* (New York: RoutledgeFalmer).

James, A. and James, A. (2005) 'Changing Perspectives, Changing Childhoods? Theorising the Role of Law in Mediating the Policy and Practices of Children's Welfare'. Paper presented at the international conference Childhoods 2005, Oslo 29 June–3 July 2005.

Kampmann, J. (2004) 'Societalization of Childhood: New Opportunities? New Demands?' in H. Brembeck, B. Johansson and J. Kampmann (eds) *Beyond the Competent Child. Exploring Contemporary Childhoods in the Nordic Welfare States* (Roskilde: Roskilde University Press).

Kjørholt, A. T. and Lidén, H. (2004) 'Symbolic Participants or Political Actors?' in H. Brembeck, B. Johansson and J. Kampmann (eds) *Beyond the Competent Child. Exploring Contemporary Childhoods in the Nordic Welfare States* (Roskilde: Roskilde University Press).

Krejsler, J. (2006) 'Education as Individualizing Technology: Exploring New Conditions for Producing Individuality' in T. Popkewitz and K. Hultqvist (eds) *'The Future Is Not What It Appears To Be', Pedagogy, Genealogy and Political Epistemology* (Stockholm: HLS Förlag).

Kryger, N. (2004) 'Childhood and "New Learning" in a Nordic Context' in H. Brembeck, B. Johansson and J. Kampmann (eds) *Beyond the Competent Child. Exploring Contemporary Childhoods in the Nordic Welfare States* (Roskilde: Roskilde University Press).

Kuusivuotiaiden lasten esiopetussuunnitelma (Education plan for six year olds) (1984) (Helsinki: Sosiaalihallituksen julkaisuja 1/1984).

Lister, R. (2003) 'Investing in the Citizen-Workers of the Future: Transformations in Citizenship and the State under New Labour', *Social Policy & Administration*, 37, 427–443.

NCG (2003) *National Curriculum Guidelines on Early Childhood Education and Care in Finland* (Helsinki: Stakes).

Popkewitz, T. and Brennan, M. (1998) 'Restructuring of Social and Political Theory in Education: Foucault and a Social Epistemology of School Practices' in T. Popkewitz and M. Brennan (eds) *Foucault's Challenge. Discourse, Knowledge, and Power in Education* (New York: Teachers College Press).

Salminen, H. (1988) Kolme – viisivuotiaiden lasten päivähoidon toimintasuunnitelma (Activity plan for three to five year old children in day care) (Sosiaalihallituksen julkaisuja 2/1988).

Sipilä, J. (2006) 'Äiti, koti ja isänmaa kilpailuvaltiossa' (Mother, home and native country in the competitive state), *Yhteiskuntapolitiikka*, 71, 411–415.

Strandell, H. (1994) *Sociala mötesplatser för barn. Aktivitetsprofiler och förhandlingskulturer på daghem* (Day care centres as social meeting places for children) (Helsinki: Gaudeamus).

Strandell, H. (1997) 'Doing Reality with Play. Play as a Children's Resource in Organizing Everyday Life in Day-Care Centres', *Childhood*, 4, 445–464.

Suomalainen lapsi (Children in Finland) (2007) Statistics Finland, Population 2007 (Helsinki).

Välimäki, A.-L. and Rauhala, P.-L. (2000) 'Lasten päivähoidon taipuminen yhteiskunnallisiin murroksiin Suomessa', *Yhteiskuntapolitiikka*, 65, 387–405.

Zeiher, H., Devine, D., Kjørholt, A. T. and Strandell, H. (eds) (2007) *Flexible Childhood. Exploring Children's Welfare in Time and Space Vol. 2 of Cost A19: Children's Welfare* (Odense: University Press of Southern Denmark).

Part III
Concluding Thoughts

13

Users and Interested Parties

A Concluding Essay on Children's Institutionalization

Jens Qvortrup

Introduction

Who are the users of institutions for children like schools and daycare centres? The notion 'institutions for children' is not unequivocal: it could mean institutions built to house and/or to serve children in the interest of people other than children, or it could mean institutions that are established in the best interests of children without any hidden agenda. Since I do not belong to what one might call 'institutional Luddites', who would rather see daycare centres disappear from the surface of the earth, I believe that we cannot do better than to make them desirable places for children; at the same time we should not make ourselves victims of a vain illusion about daycare centres and schools as the unconditional and categorical fulfilment of children's dreams. Perhaps we simply know too little about them from the children's point of view. The following story from real life is most likely not representative of children's feelings about daycare centres but I cannot resist the temptation to share it with readers since it is both thought provoking and comical:

> Four four-year old boys had disappeared from their daycare centre. Well hidden behind some bushes they had been digging a tunnel under the fence around the daycare centre. Luckily, they were soon found and brought back without retribution while rules were firmly reiterated to the effect that skipping out and running away from daycare centres was strictly forbidden. Parents were shocked. The daycare centre leader promised that it would not happen again. (Read in the Danish daily *Politiken* on 1 February 2007; my translation and adaptation)

Unfortunately, the four boys' version was not told. Perhaps they simply had great fun without knowing exactly where the tunnel would take them; perhaps it *was* an act of liberation from their status as being locked up, confined or imprisoned. Indeed, the association that immediately comes to my mind is the prison, for you have the confinement; the alluring territories just beyond the fences; the drive towards freedom; and the astuteness and inventiveness. To make the case worse, the freedom-seeking inmates were not guilty in the first place of any offence that qualified for negative sanctions, such as being detained behind fences.

There are hardly any good reasons to draw too far-reaching conclusions from this story; symbolically, however, it should attract our attention to the feelings some children may have as a reaction to their free movement being hampered. For other children, daycare centres are simply joyful and fun.

In this chapter I shall seek an answer questions about who the users of child institutions are and why we have them. My main answer is that they hardly would have been established if they were merely there for the sake of children, let alone just for children's fun. This thesis can be formulated in a different way: only because daycare centres and schools serve some interest of adult society are they delivered, traded and maintained; and institutionalization of children is variable and changing, but always in response to a prevailing society's dominant interests. Currently, these interests may be couched in terms of neoliberal economy and politics; at other times they have assumed other forms and contents.

It remains to be seen what changes will occur in the wake of the current crisis; since the 1970s, neoliberal economy has clearly left its imprint on all areas of society, including the whole span of educational institutions, from crèches to universities (Giroux and Giroux, 2008). There has been an increasing emphasis on standardization, tests, individualization, competition, accountability and user adaptation, as it is called. Models and formats from corporate society have come to penetrate and influence the pedagogical world without much proof of their justification.

In general terms, the idea is neither new nor surprising that any purposeful institutionalization has always been impacted by, or largely adapted to, the dominant economy and polity – a proof of its importance, one might argue. Its uses have always been measured in terms of its attractiveness as an investment object with an eye to the labour market and the future of the economy and society (see Brandth and Kvande, Chapter 3). The question is to what extent it is possible to make a direct connection between the world of small children and economic trends at the societal level.

Institutionalization

Institutionalization is more and more a common condition for children in modern society. The process of institutionalization is a relatively new historical trend that encompasses others than just children – not least the elderly. No other age group, however, is forced to spend such a huge part of their time in institutions than children. How do we justify this? Is it primarily for children's sake? This chapter will address such questions, while having in mind the crucial one: Would we – society, adults, parents – have gone that far in institutionalizing children if it did not benefit, first and foremost, exactly society, adults and parents? In other words, had institutionalization merely benefited children while they were still children, it would probably have been dispensed with a long time ago. This chapter will consequently discuss who the primary users of institutions are.

Institutions are often referred to as something negative and frightening in terms of incarceration and control of adults, in more or less total institutions of the type analysed by Goffman (1961) and Foucault (1979), even if also children and youth may be considered, for instance, in juvenile justice (see Platt, 1977). Institutionalization, as it is used here, stands for a secular trend (see Zeiher, 2009), which is characteristic of the historical development towards modernity, and which befalls or includes persons who are not necessarily deviant, unruly or intractable. Even in the latter institutions (the 'non-total' ones), institutionalization presupposes a particular material or physical framework in terms of formal organization and buildings, and not seldom a disciplinary regime. This is a type that includes hospitals and old peoples' homes, and, more importantly for our purpose, schools and centres for early childhood education and care (ECEC). In addition, there is a wide variety of voluntary organizations that include children after ordinary school hours, such as sports clubs, music schools and so on.

In comparison to pre-modernity, children's everyday lives are now to a large extent institutionalized in the sense that they are subjected to, and have become objects of, organized forms of protection and control, which are directed towards knowledge requirement and socialization, including proper upbringing – whatever that may mean. Both in quantity and intensity, this has entailed a massive and dramatic change to children's everyday lives, indeed of childhood as an institution.

From a tiny start in the nineteenth century, children are now, and eventually will be on a massive scale, spending more and more of their time in institutions. It is therefore an obvious reflection that there must be a correspondence between the forms and contents of child institutions, indeed their very occurrence, and the prevailing interests of prevailing dominant groups in the prevailing mode of production. The pertinent questions are, therefore: Under what conditions did they take off, under what conditions did they persist and under what conditions did they change?

This book focuses especially on institutions for small children; yet, this formulation is already going too far in suggesting an answer to the questions raised. We cannot take for granted that the institutions are *for* children in the sense that they are unequivocally there to serve children or are for the sake of children. At the same time, we cannot conclude that children not like to be in institutions even if one were to conclude that they are not basically meant for children but rather for some adult segments.

Neither schools nor daycare centres have been asked for by children (which is far from proving that they would not have approved, had they been asked). They have come about because of requirements of current economy. More specifically, (1) schooling became a mass phenomenon because our industries could not do without a literate workforce, and (2) daycare became widespread because the trades and corporate culture (in conjunction with the family economy) needed the participation of both men and women in the labour market. These basic theses are immediately challenged by the complexity of the world; for if they are true, why is it that the prevalence of institutions varies between different countries?

The main issue in this chapter is, as already mentioned, daycare or ECEC. Nevertheless, it might be instructive to begin with schools and their historical development since this story suggests an answer to questions of 'prime movers' (Anderson, 1995). Was mass scholarization a result of child savers' efforts, of dominant political forces' legislation, of, as Ariès would have it, a cultural rearmament in the name of clergy and nobility (Ariès, 1982),[1] or demands from the 'economy'? A likely but unhelpful answer to the effect that it was a combination only begs the question about whether one of the forces was stronger than the others?

The discussion about schooling along these lines is meant to be helpful in addressing related questions about ECEC and, by comparison, in highlighting differences and similarities.

Schools: users and their interested parties

The history of schools, and how they became an established and accepted institution in Western Europe, is the history of a struggle over children's time and labour; it is the history of a phenomenon that changed from being a highly contested one to one that everybody demanded. The pupils were arguably the immediate users of schools, but the struggles behind their establishment suggest a tug-of-war between other and more significant parties, which all claimed to serve the interest and futurity of pupils. These struggles obscured the question of who really were the users of schools in the sense of who exerted major influence on it, when and how. What were, in other words, the prime movers behind schools and mass scholarization?

The observation that schooling in Western Europe and North America became a mass phenomenon – for example, that the enrolment of children converged towards 100 per cent at more or less the same historical juncture in the late nineteenth and early twentieth centuries – suggests that there were plain and determined political and economic interests behind it. I think it is possible to substantiate this suggestion without completely denying the credibility of idealistic forces' assistance. I will do this by making a brief comparison between Denmark and Great Britain, where – as in all other countries – a change took place from children's manual labour to schooling.

In Great Britain, bills were issued against child labour as early as the beginning of the nineteenth century, and were accompanied by huge protests from the big owners of factories and coal mines. The most significant legislation to oblige children's schooling came in Britain only towards the end of the nineteenth century. In Denmark, the order of things was reversed. The bill obliging children to attend school until the age of confirmation was issued as early as 1814, whereas the bill against child labour was issued as late as 1872 – partly under the influence and fear of the 'social democrat Carl [*sic!*] Marx' (Hornemann, 1872). It was remarkable that the initiative came from the employers' organization.

In both countries we saw child savers movements, which interestingly enough did not have much influence on implementing legislation. British children continued to work despite legislation against it, while children in Denmark failed to attend school if more important work in the community was demanded. Even with legislation made to either effect, the significant fact was – and this is the point

I want to make – that throughout Western Europe *mass scholarization was realized* about the same time; that is, almost all children in relevant ages attended school between, say, 1890 and 1910, and all parties had eventually come to be supportive of this solution.

One corollary of these historical occurrences is, it seems to me, that only when necessary material conditions are available are people ready to follow suit, and this is, of course, an answer to the question of prime movers. Another one is that, at the end of the day and when it favours them, people deliberately choose to adapt to the new dominant ways of production[2] – in this case to the industrial economy. Thirdly, it was very significant that the dominant advocates of the new ways of production, including the state, with determination stimulated an interest in schooling, which most parents only reluctantly embarked on. The state, for instance, was in the lead of investing in school buildings that, at the time, often were remarkably monumental compared with the modest lives children came from (de Coninck-Smith, 2000).[3] Fourthly, although children became the users, or at least the inmates and arguably actors, within the new premises, it is hard to submit to the idea that children themselves should have been noticeably influencing ensuing changes to their daily lives. They were fully, and without reservations, objects of societal changes upon which they had no influence; schools were, as we have seen, the results of a tug-of-war between societal forces; that is, representatives of various adult interests.

This clarification is, I believe, important also for addressing the question of users: Who are the users of institutions and, to begin with, who are the users of the institution we call school? Of course, in a sense, children – or pupils – are the users of schools, and obviously schools are unimaginable without pupils, exactly as hospitals must have patients and factories raw material and a labour force. It is interesting in this context that according to the law – including the United Nation Convention on the Rights of the Child (UNCRC) – children not only have a right to attend school but they are also obliged to attend, and the latter claim clearly suggests that there are other interests in play than simply a generous and universal offer to children. As a matter of fact, we will not, as polity, as economy, as parents, and probably as several other parties, allow that children are not scholarized.

Schools represent the most significant institutionalization of childhood – in terms of the amount of time spent in them by children, in terms of universality of schooling and in terms of their existence being generally accepted (non-contested). Schools are here to stay as a requirement of prevailing political economy, for which they are indispensable; without schools, modern society would not be able to function in the long run.

Daycare centres: users and their interested parties

To some degree it is possible to extend the arguments about schooling to preschool children's institutionalization in modern society. The expansion of daycare centres is grossly impacted by the development in and of society. It is unlikely that they would have been here to any noteworthy extent had it not been for adult employers' and employees' mutual interest in buying and selling labour force, but even so it is to be doubted that daycare centres will ever become obligatory for all preschool children. We may eventually, in a number of states, see a convergence towards universal coverage, but hardly more than that, even if it is already a normatively accepted offer and option in most modern countries.[4]

Institutionalization of preschool children was originally not predicated on a labour market argument (Allen, 1986; see also Gulløv, Chapter 5). You had the significant pedagogical argument with Fröbel as a major inspiration, underlining daycare centres' importance for children's wellbeing and development; it was in other words an argument that focused on children and was launched in the best interests of the child – without a hidden agenda to advance ulterior and/or external motives. Simultaneously, we saw institutions that opened up for orphans and other underprivileged children without proper guardianship.[5] In quantitative terms relative to all children, their institutionalization had a very limited coverage.

Although pedagogical reasons for enrolling children into daycare centres are still with us, they are hardly the most important ones.[6] It is now in principle an institution for all children in relevant ages (see Korsvold, 2005). As already pointed out, the strongest demand factor seems to be parents' employment. For this to be efficient, it requires that it is met by an adequate supply, which is not always the case – for economic, political ideological and religious reasons – and therefore the parental employment thesis is contested. The next issue, then, is whether we will be able to find out which factor is the strongest.

1. Strong evidence for the labour force thesis is found when society is under pressure in the sense of being forced to make choices. Historically, the most convincing examples are from countries during the Second World War. In many of these, and very notably so in the

Netherlands, the USA, the UK and Japan, large numbers of women entered the labour market, while their husbands were involved in the war in one way or another (Summerfield, 1989). Interestingly, as the war came to an end, many women returned to their homes – to give the jobs back to their husbands and/or to have children; it was the period of the baby boom. Although this greater labour market involvement of women was not accompanied sufficiently by institutionalized childcare, it did set significant priorities. Patriotic reasons came before classical ideological, religious or pedagogical reasons about the upbringing of children and seemed to inhere with economic arguments. Under these circumstances, nothing was more important than survival of the country or nation.

2. In the rare cases where there are both popular and political demands for full inhere centre coverage, we can assume that pedagogical arguments for children's attendance may loom large. Not least, the Nordic countries aspire to reach this situation. Yet, whenever the demand is greater than the supply, some prioritizing is required, and experience tells us that children who are in inhere mainly for pedagogical reasons will typically have to give way to others with more convincing grounds. There were, for instance, some years ago discussions in Denmark about whether it was right that children of an involuntarily unemployed parent take up places that children of working parents desperately need. In such a case the lines are clearly drawn: the importance of employment (to the benefit of women and the family, including, of course, children, the economy and society) or the importance of a pedagogical off to a child who is already disadvantaged by belonging to a family hit by unemployment. The dilemma fell, in this case, to the advantage of the child of the redundant parent; however, this is likely to be a question of numbers. If too many children of jobless persons are preventing parents from working, a more 'realistic' position will soon come about in public opinion and among politicians (see Strandell, Chapter 12).

3. The argument launched here as the strongest, namely, the positive correlation between female employment rates and inhere centre coverage, is ambiguous.

   (a) On the one hand, it seems likely that no country exhibits wide inhere centre coverage without high female employment rates (see below on nursery schools). The reason is that low female employment is tantamount to a weak demand for inhere centre places, although it may be difficult to know for sure what is cause and what is effect: one could imagine, for instance, that low coverage is causing low female employment.

(b) However, on the other hand, we cannot be sure that high female/parental employment is followed by broad coverage of inhere centre places. This may not be the case if parental demands for inhere clash with competing goals that are, at least, momentarily strong enough to prevent a supply that matches these demands. This was, for instance, likely to be the case in post-war Norway (see Korsvold, Chapter 1); only half a century later, Norway is now catching up with Sweden and Denmark in this respect. The reasons could be (i) failures in turning childcare centres into small homes as the ideal in Norway was said to be (see Korsvold and Kjørholt and Seland, Chapters 1 and 9); or (ii) to do with a very strong self-understanding as a 'nature-loving-people' (see Nilsen, Chapters 11), which could suggest a preference for having children outside the fences of inhere centres (that is to say, 'inhere centre' and 'nature' being kind of antonyms); or (iii) interpreted as the failure of politicians to fol-low the wishes of parents, as seen perhaps in the fact that in no other Scandinavian country do we find so many private inhere centres as in Norway.

Other examples are found both in more traditional and Catholic countries on the European continent and in liberal regimes as in the UK and the USA, and thus seem to reflect ideological positions – be they cultural, religious, economic (neoliberal) or a combination of these. These modern countries, with a well-educated female workforce, can increasingly be seen as paradoxical as long as it is made difficult for them to have both children and employment. Perhaps this is the reason why at least some of them have found a kind of compromise in terms of nursery schools (see below).

Of irrefutable weight in the argument for establishing childcare centres are, it seems to me, arguments external to children as such. If one would insist on the pedagogical argument, it might suggest that chil-dren were the real users of the daycare centres – together with their parents who would see them as promoting children's development. The latter argument might imply a parental instrumentalization of children, who would then no longer be primary users.

By and large, inhere centres seem to be ever more widespread because they have become indispensable, in general terms, the economy, parents and mothers. They have become indispensable mothers in the sense, of course, that without daycare centres, it would have been impossible for them to enter the labour market to the extent that we have experienced. It is, admittedly, too narrow to talk merely of an advantage to mothers. It is true that women, as they are ever better educated, are looking for work outside the home. It is however also true that it is eventually becoming a necessity for family prosperity and affluence to have an additional income, as statistics on family income and child poverty show (Bradshaw, 2007; Johansen, 2009).

Women's entrance into the labour market obviously presumes a demand from employers – private and/or public; it also presupposes a women's labour force that is not only large enough but also sufficiently broad in scope to meet a demand for varied qualifications. The development has worked away from the classical family wage, which took for granted that one salary (historically that of the husband) would suffice (Fraser, 1994). Eventually, expectations of a higher standard of living as well as a more unfavourable balance between income and cost of living, or a relative deterioration in the family's income purchasing power, have forced the family to seek two incomes in the labour market.

We are thus allowed to infer that family-external pressures have emerged to make it more and more difficult for parents to resist placing their children in daycare centres even if they want to. The pressure has come from the economy, understood in a broad sense (or from the market, as some would say). In this sense, the expansion of the daycare 'market' is not necessarily to be seen as a deliberate attack on the idea of bringing children up in the family; it could just as well be interpreted as a result of increasing competition for labour power, which eventually left parents with a fait accompli, or at least a dilemma, that for many would be highly undesirable: either you bring your children to daycare centres or you increase their risk of living in relative material hardship.

It is, nevertheless, interesting that this development – purposeful or not – brings a liberal market economy into collision with ideological ideas of politically Conservative or Christian Democratic provenance. The latter is at least traditionally much more in favour of the family as the proper place for the upbringing of children.

In other words, we may as potential *users* of daycare centres propose one or more of the following:

- *children*, in a pedagogical argument (despite their risk of being instrumentalized for various ideological, religious and other adult interests and goals);
- *parents*, since mothers now want to be on a par with fathers in the labour market, the result being a larger demand for daycare places as well as an increase in the living standard of the family;
- *corporate society*, which interestingly enough is sharing interests with parents in a desire to make daycare centre places available, while shoving expenses onto parents and the public purse;
- *the market* itself as the embodiment of various parties' interests in and/or demand for additional labour;
- *the state* as the common will that is there to support a favourable economic climate and therefore able to influence the daycare market with regard to the supply side in terms of producing concrete, physical daycare centres – buildings, and also supplying staff, not least sufficient teachers or pedagogues.

In the first place we might suggest that external factors are becoming more and more influential; it is increasingly unlikely that we will have institutions that are merely pedagogically motivated without pressure from the economy.[7] This is what we may call *the political economy of daycare*. At the end of the day, there would not be such a thing as daycare centres without a demand for additional labour in the economy (inclusive, ironically, of additional (female) labour to staff the daycare centres), or there would merely be tiny, probably privately financed institutions, counting as persevering idealistic, pedagogical experiments, or finally a number of daycare centres run by corporate society – firms, companies and so on. By the same token, daycare centres are much more vulnerable than schools. Schools remain an indisputable and unanimously politically supported and popular requirement in and for any modern society, and therefore the claims for their universality are omnipresent.[8] The same cannot be said about daycare centres. They will at best be dependent on prevailing economic conditions, and therefore, for instance, in danger of being cut back in the case of recessions and unemployment (see Strandell, Chapter 12). This again shows their precariousness.

The fact that schooling is a universal claim means that it is an offer, a right, that no child (or parent on its behalf) can decline since it is, at the same time, an obligation.[9] Daycare attendance is not a requirement from the state; it may be difficult, as we saw, to do without it for economic reasons, but no one will force children directly (or parents on their behalf).[10] In some countries, winds are blowing in the direction of providing a real choice; that is, it is becoming a politically induced demand to make daycare places available for all children. In other words, if there is a demand from parents, this demand must be met.

In comparison to the development of schooling, we do not find the same historical simultaneity among countries in terms of massive attendance. As we saw, a 100 per cent school attendance was more or less the case around the turn of the twentieth century. In fact, daycare centre attendance exhibits dramatic differences between countries, which demonstrate that there are other significant factors in play than the economy. Unlike to schools, daycare centres are subject to considerable ideological controversy,[11] which is likely to have added to the difference in popularity and demand. In order to make an explanation of the variance, one would probably be well advised to consult typologies like Esping-Andersen's. As we see, the prevalence of daycare centres is much greater in the Nordic welfare states than in conservative or liberal countries – for various reasons (see Esping-Andersen, 1990, for a detailed account of the typology). I think it is perhaps particularly worthwhile to underline also a religious factor, which is especially relevant in the conservative welfare state type; yet, as we shall see in the next and last section, the picture is not that neat.

Care and/or education – who is paying for what?

This chapter has so far made a distinction between school and daycare centres as representing two different forms of institutionalization. Faced with the realities in European countries, it is difficult to sustain such a distinction. The two forms have experienced different attraction and attention, as we have seen, and continue to some extent to do so. What happens if they more and more merge due to pressure from parents, state and corporate society? We will, I will argue, probably see not only a blurring of the traditional division between private and public interests and responsibilities, but also a convergence between European regimes as far as ingrained practices of care and education are concerned.

The very notion of ECEC points to both care and education as elements of its institutionalization, and it is admittedly difficult to keep the two apart both theoretically and practically. Until recently, one could observe a north–south divide in Europe in the sense that the southern countries were underlining education and training (and still are), while Scandinavian countries insisted on giving preference to development, care and a social aspect for children under six or seven years. Also in

England a division between care and education was drawn (see James, Chapter 6). This distinction is becoming more and more obscured as also northern countries have begun to measure much more the importance of the educational aspect in daycare centres, without going so far as to calling it school, let alone making attendance obligatory. What conclusions can we draw from that in terms of trends towards institutionalization of 'early childhood'?

The new trend in the Nordic countries brings them closer to their southern neighbours and signifies a more outspoken and self-conscious tendency towards adapting to economic requirements than has so far been the case. To the extent that education and training are more and more explicitly underlined as an integrated part of daycare centres, corporate society and the state are better served and can therefore, only at great pains, circumvent the consequences of being counted as users proper. Can the state in this situation, for instance, defend the position not to fully finance ECEC centres?

The main arguments launched in this chapter are that the scope or the extent of school and daycare supply must ultimately be explained in terms of political economy. This is in line with the political strands that seek to introduce a new balance in the contents or curriculum of the daycare centres – from one that traditionally underlines the playful elements to one that more and more turns institutional surroundings into sites for learning. The change is more or less explicitly advocating the view that children are too priceless not to be priced, to paraphrase a famous book title (Zelizer, 1985). Institutionalized children are more and more perceived as raw material to be processed for future use. Given this highly realistic view, it is no wonder that ever less is left to contingencies, including parents who, in this process, could easily be seen as a risk factor.

On the one hand, one might argue that this reasoning is hard to recognize in Central and Southern Europe where 'private virtues' reign over 'public virtues' and where schools are rather seen as a subsidiary to the family (see Dahrendorf, 1967) – which is the case also for (rare) daycare centres. On the other hand, one might counter that the Nordic model is an already for decades hopelessly backward one compared with the conservative model in Southern Europe. I have in mind here nursery schools (the French *écoles maternelles* and the Italian *scuolo per l'infanzia comunale*), where children typically get their institutional debut at the age of three on an all-day basis. Since this offering is not only a legal right for young children between three and six years of age but also free of charge, it has a striking similarity with schools (see Chamboredon and Prévot, 1975a, 1975b). Do we therefore, as the conventional pedagogical position, take our point of departure in the age of children and thus conclude from a developmental point of view that they are too young to attend a school and infer that they basically remain a private matter? Or do we take our point of departure in the kind of institutional arrangement represented by nursery schools, and thus seem to be deducing that children are taken seriously enough to be found competent to receive teaching and consequently are required to be enrolled free of charge, as in schools?

It is interesting to see that countries in Southern Europe, thought of in terms of family values, principles of subsidiary and low welfare expenses, are more likely to leave children from an early age to institutional care that is paid by the public purse and includes an educational aim. Countries with greater trust in the welfare state are much more reluctant to leave their young children to an educational regime, while accepting parents pay (at least partly) for children's daycare attendance. In other words, in the southern family-oriented countries, children are left free of charge in public care, while in the Nordic welfare societies parents continue to pay for daycare as if children were merely a private good.

In the Nordic countries the development of childcare rather threatens to end up between two chairs. On the one hand, it seems to be drifting towards a curriculum-based institution, that is, one that becomes more and more difficult to distinguish from a school, or at least one that anticipates schooling while preparing children for it. On the other hand, it remains a non-obligatory offer and thus lacks one of the clearest signs of being universal. One is therefore creating an illusion of voluntariness, since even if nobody is legally forced to accept the offer it is one that cannot be declined by parents without fearing that their children will be failing to obtain something important and/or risking that they will be losing in competition with other children (see James, Chapter 6).

This illusion of voluntariness, of having a free choice, may then serve as a justification to continue forcing parents to pay for services that more and more look like those provided by nursery schools. The 'famous' Nordic model therefore seems to offer its citizens the worse of alternatives, namely, to pay for something that parents in the less celebrated conservative model in France and Italy actually get free of charge.

The payment issue is interesting as an indication of the meaning of institutionalization and of who its users are. There are probably no rules without exceptions about the relationship between kind of institution and payment. In all European countries, schooling is free of charge, while expenses for daycare practically everywhere are shared between parents and the public purse.[12]

One would expect, according to the rules of reciprocity, or the market, that the family will be paying for goods or services that are privately desired and thought of as beneficial primarily for the family. If this is not the case, one is not going to buy them. If, on the other hand, goods or services are imposed on us in the sense that we are obliged to receive them – perhaps even against our will – we must surmise that they are highly significant and indispensable for other interested parties, and hence they should be gratis.

According to this logic, schooling should be without charge. Children (and their parents) have no choice and, as we saw, historically it was imposed on many people from the lower classes. For them it would have been even more difficult to accept schooling if they also had to take expenses for it into account (as is currently the case in many developing countries). The fact that schools were, and remain, available at no cost is an indication of their indispensability in the eyes of the political authorities and the dominant economy.

It is different with daycare centres, which are typically partly paid for by parents. It is not uncommon that some children attend daycare centres free of charge for social reasons, but otherwise expenses are shared between parents and the public. This solution suggests that daycare centres are not, like schools, considered indispensable for society. Attendance is, in the end, left to parents to decide and remains therefore as a quid pro quo: we leave our children in your hands and we pay for this service. This position has not been changed, even when the dual income model has become a requirement, for three reasons: (i) obtaining a decent level of living for the family; (ii) meeting both parents' desire to work outside the home; and (iii) making a broader and more qualified workforce available to the public and to the economy. It is, however, a position that is squarely based on the standpoint that children are private goods (see James, Chapter 6), and thus a position that will be ever more difficult to retain when daycare centres become sites of learning and quasi-obligatory.

As mentioned, some countries in the southern part of Europe have solved this problem by lowering the school age to three years or, as in Britain by making children start school at the age of five. Even if nursery schools are not strictly speaking obligatory for children, it is an obligation for the public authorities to guarantee the supply side; that is, make them available for children who – or rather whose parents – want to make use of the offer. Attendance by all children thus seems to be taken for granted and is thought to be of benefit to children; the fact is in any case that they are attended by practically 100 per cent of children at the relevant ages. Contrary to that, offers to children below three years of age are few and far between. In this sense the logic remains intact: the more attendance in an institution is legally or normatively a must, the more likely it is to be available free of charge.

At the same time, as more preparations for future schooling become an integral part of the curriculum in daycare centres, the more parents seem willy-nilly forced to accept it. It is therefore a dilemma for parents whose preference is the pedagogical style, since it is not only, as hinted at, that parents will do everything not to see their children fall behind other children; it is also an issue that neighbourhoods will eventually be evacuated for the same reasons, and hence children will hardly find any playmates in the vicinity of their home.

In the long run, scholarization of daycare centres will be a reality; the users remain to be, in a sense, children and their parents, but more and more on terms set by the prevailing economy and long-term needs of the society. We will most likely see a growing convergence between the European countries: children three years and over will experience more and more scholarized institutions with nursery schools as a model, while daycare centres for the younger children will have to be accepted by the southern European countries, the UK and Ireland. It remains to be seen if Nordic parents will succeed in having the quasi-obligatory scholarization paid for by the public. It would be ironic if the self-complacent Nordic welfare states were the last ones to offer their children and parents this privilege.

What I am arguing is, in other words, that there is a qualitative difference between, on the one hand, care that includes merely pedagogical offerings in terms of mainly play and, on the other hand, public programmes that include education and training. One of the clearest signs of the qualitative difference is whether parents are asked to pay for the institutionalization in question. Whether one, by the same token, should make a distinction between the private child and the public child or, even better, between children as private or public goods is another matter. Personally, I would argue that already the inclusion of children into daycare centres without any educational curriculum should count as being a public interest, and thus an offer free of charge for parents; that is, an offer that is paid for by the public purse and thus by all taxpayers. A detailed argument to that effect will, however, lead too far at this place and time.

Notes

1. This Danish edition of Ariès' famous opus is referred to because it includes a translation of the author's new preface to the new French edition (Ariès, 1973). To the best of my knowledge, this preface does not exist in English.
2. I hesitate to use the notion 'modes of production' because this has to do with changing ownership of means of production, which is not really the case here. Rather it was a change of dominant means of production – from hand to machine, as we may now be talking about a change from machine to information technology and knowledge. Whether the latter is a pertinent way of portraying current shifts is, of course, another and controversial issue.
3. Many would argue that schools and other institutions have eventually lost their imposing look as the need to motivate parents to bring their children to schools has disappeared. Already in the 1960s the Canadian economist Harry Johnson talked about 'the schools look like factories used to look and factories like schools ought to look' (1962, p. 190); that is, that children's work places deteriorate compared with those of adults.
4. This view depends though on our definition of ECEC; the situation in France and Italy may be interpreted as full coverage, but is nursery school a school or a preschool? (see further below).
5. To the extent that these children were 'saved', the institution in question would rather not comply with the definition of daycare centres as used in this chapter or book, but be a full-time, permanent institution – an orphanage or a correctional institution.
6. This statement does not contradict the reality of a pedagogical programme for children's stay *in* the daycare centres.
7. But also the other way round: no daycare centres are merely economically motivated, cf. *Bewahranstalten* (storage place) (see Allen, 1986).
8. This is the case in all affluent societies but does not tell us about the level or variance in generosity – in terms of up-to-date buildings and support of amenities, like school utensils, meals, outings and so on.
9. The fact that in some countries it is education, and not schooling, that is a right and a duty is in principle not uninteresting for our discussion; although the choice of one or the other of these two options would hardly impact the degree of institutionalization. Since so few parents choose to teach their own children at home, the discussion becomes an academic one.
10. See though, perhaps, experiences from former socialist countries and maybe also children of immigrants.
11. We are here talking merely about their presence, or existence, and not about the contents or possible curriculum; as to the latter, ideological discussions are also found in a school context.
12. How it is shared is another matter, which differs considerably between countries either in terms of fractions of expenses, as tax deductions, a free place or in monetary terms. The point here is merely to illustrate the principle.

References

Allen, A. T. (1986) 'Gardens of Children, Gardens of God: Day-Care Centers in Nineteenth-Century Germany', *Journal of Social History*, Spring, 20, 1, 433–450.

Anderson, M. (1995) *Approaches to the History of the Western Family 1500–1914* (Cambridge: Cambridge University Press).

Ariès, P. (1973) *L'enfant et la vie familiale sous l'Ancien Régime* (Paris: Editions du Seuil).

Ariès, P. (1982) 'Forord' (Preface) in P. Ariès *Barndommens historie* (The History of Childhood) (Copenhagen: Nyt Nordisk Forlag Arnold Busck).

Bradshaw, J. (2007) 'Some Problems in the International Comparison of Child Income Poverty' in H. Wintersberger, L. Alanen, T. Olk and J. Qvortrup (eds) *Childhood, Generational Order and the Welfare State: Exploring Children's Social and Economic Welfare. Vol. 1 of COST A19: Children's Welfare* (Odense: University Press of Southern Denmark).

Chamboredon, J. C. and Prévot, J. (1975a) *Infancy as an Occupation: Towards a Sociology of Spontaneous Behaviour* (Paris: Studies in the Learning Sciences 3, OECD).

Chamboredon, J. C. and Prévot, J. (1975b) 'Changes in the Social Definition of Early Childhood and the New Forms of Symbolic Violence', *Theory and Society* 2, 3, 331–350.

Dahrendorf, R. (1967) *Society and Democracy in Germany* (New York: Doubleday).

de Coninck-Smith, N. (2000) *For barnets skyld. Byen, skolen og barndommen 1880–1914* (For the child's sake. The town, the school and the childhood) (Copenhagen: Gyldendal).

Esping-Andersen, G. (1990) *Three Worlds of Welfare Capitalism* (Cambridge: Polity Press).

Foucault, M. (1979) *Discipline and Punish: The Birth of the Prison* (New York: Vintage).

Fraser, N. (1994) 'After the Family Wage: Gender Equity and the Welfare State', *Political Theory* 22, 4, 591–618.

Garbarino, J. (1986) 'Can American Families Afford the Luxury of Childhood?', *Child Welfare* 65, 2, 119–140 .

Giroux, H. A. and Giroux, S. S. (2008) 'Beyond Bailouts: On the Politics of Education After Neoliberalism', *Truthout*, 31 December, http://www.truthout.org/123108A (accessed 15 January 2009).

Goffman, E. (1961) *Asylums: Essays on the Social Situation of Mental Patients and Other Inmates* (New York: Doubleday).

Hornemann, E. (1872) 'Om Børns Anvendelse i Fabriker, særlig med Hensyn til vore Forhold' (On the application of children in factories with particular regard to our conditions), *Hygieiniske Meddelelser og Betragtninger* (Hygienic messages and considerations), 7, 3, 151–194.

Johansen, V. (2009) *Children and Distributive Justice between Generations. A Comparison of 16 European Countries* (Doctoral Thesis) (Trondheim: Norwegian University of Science and Technology).

Johnson, H. G. (1962) *Money, Trade and Economic Growth* (Cambridge, MA: Harvard University Press).

Korsvold, T. (2005) *For alle barn. Barnehagens framvekst i velferdsstaten* (For all children. The evolution of childcare centres in the welfare state) (Oslo: Abstraktforlag).

Platt, A. M. (1977) *The Child Savers. The Invention of Delinquency* 2nd edn. (Chicago, IL: University of Chicago Press).

Summerfield, P. (1989) *Women Workers in the Second World War: Production and Patriarchy in Conflict* (London: Routledge).

Zeiher, H. (2009) 'Institutionalization as a Secular Trend' in J. Qvortrup, W. A. Corsaro and M.-S. Honig (eds) *The Palgrave Handbook of Childhood Studies* (Basingstoke: Palgrave Macmillan).

Zelizer, V. A. (1985) *Pricing the Priceless Child: The Changing Social Value of Children* (New York: Basic Books).

14

Childhood and Social Investments

Concluding Thoughts

Anne Trine Kjørholt and Jens Qvortrup

Introduction

There is, and has always been, a correspondence between the prevailing economy and the way people think – perhaps most tersely expressed by Marx in *The German Ideology*: 'The ideas of the ruling class are in every epoch the ruling ideas, i.e. the class which is the ruling material force of society, is at the same time its ruling intellectual force.' This is a remarkable fact, but it is not a new one. Nevertheless it remains a controversial insight, which is likely to arouse debate and conflict, not least during periods of economic transition.

We currently live in a capitalist economy *and* in a democratic society. This means that there will continuously be a struggle between 'the primacy of economics' and the 'primacy of politics' – or, in more common parlance, between market and state. Even if this description has been valid for more than a century, there are constantly changes and fluctuations within any mode of production. During recent decades the label – or epithet – has been a *neo-liberal economy* or simply *neo-liberalism*, indicating a shift in the power balance in the direction of the market or 'primacy of economics'.

This is supposed to mean also that a change in the economy will leave its imprint on other sectors of society – the family and its children are no exception. The market has been demanding an increasing involvement of women – mothers – in the labour market, which in turn requires means for taking care of children, in particular young children not yet in school. Making public childcare available is not, one might argue, exactly an expression of the 'will' of the market. However, faced with the alternative of underemployment and thus pressures on wages, it seems increasingly to be the preferable option to establish childcare centres, even for state and corporate society. Subsequently, they become a battlefield for economy and polity, whether in terms of attempts to make them into direct market objects (privatization) or in terms of efforts to conquer children's minds.

It belongs to the lead ideas of the project, of which this book is the last explicit result, that dominant ideas from the economy make inroads into what so far has been seen as the sanctity of childhood. Although approached with some delicacy as far as childcare institutions are concerned, the introduction of a discourse and practice compatible with neoliberal ideas and mentality cannot remain a clandestine endeavour. Notions of flexibility, innovation, monitoring and the like are met with increasing frequency but are couched in compassionate discourses (see Brandt and Kvande; Rantalaiho; Gulløv; Strandell, Chapters 3, 4, 5, 12, this volume).

Daycare centres are no longer a site merely for blissful play; they have, for better or worse, become a place where play is increasingly purposeful and combined with education and training. They are locations for development, yes, but more and more for development of human capital, of the refinement of precious resources, more so than simply the development of the child. This is not in itself wrong, but one has to be aware that the price for having such places for children may be that traditional development in pedagogical terms is combined with well-intended aims to produce useful adults.

The cultural versus the economic man

A long time before the notion of 'the economic man' (homo economicus) became en vogue, Max Weber formulated strong criticisms and warnings against trends towards secularization and demystification (*die Entzauberung der Welt*), phenomena that allegedly were following the advancement of 'the first modernity' (as Beck, 1992, would have put it).

In a context dealing with 'rationalization of education and training', Weber was in a sense setting up culture and economy against each other:

> Behind all the present discussions of the foundations of the educational system, the struggle of the 'specialist type of man' against the older type of 'cultivated man' is hidden at some decisive point. This fight is determined by the irresistibly expanding bureaucratization of all public and private relations of authority and by the ever-increasing importance of expert and specialized knowledge. This fight intrudes all intimate cultural questions. (Weber in Gerth and Mills, 1958, p. 243)

This statement, written early in the twentieth century, confirms to us the lasting topicality of Weber's writings. We are currently, 100 years later, observing an accentuation of this movement from culture to rationalization – in mentality and political reality. Apparently it is encompassing the whole range of our educational system from universities to preschools and daycare centres.[1] Bologna,[2] Lisbon and Pisa have become catch words for processes aimed at standardization, harmonization and monitoring. They are associated with notions of efficiency, innovation, flexibility, rationality, flow rates of candidates, testing, and result- and outcome-orientation at all levels, including daycare centres where the new trends are recognizable in terms of learning as an ever-stronger rival of classical pedagogical ideas that gave primacy to playing and other spontaneous expressions.

The lead ideas behind the reforms are economical – a fact that is hardly hidden. They are intended to make our countries more efficient and competitive. At the same time they are supposed to benefit the citizens of the countries in the long run through economic growth. It is hardly a surprise, therefore, that the reforms have been welcomed in neoliberal regimes while benevolently couched in terms of 'investment strategies' and, where labour politicians are concerned, preferably 'social investment strategies'.

At economic-political levels, therefore we have perceived the changes manifestly in terms of a transition from (in Britain) 'old' Labour to New Labour with its so-called *Third Way* and the *social investment state* (both concepts coined by sociologist Anthony Giddens) – which are, of course, changes that have been embraced widely by not only Britons themselves (notably their chief instigators, former Prime and Finance Ministers Tony Blair and Gordon Brown).[3] Closely connected are initiatives within the European Union (EU), not least in the more or less programmatic writings by Gøsta Esping-Andersen (2002, 2009), who was invited to Lisbon to launch a 'new social investment strategy' for the EU.

Although the changes are arguably compatible with current neoliberal orientations in the sense of more deliberate openings to market thinking (see Moss, Chapter 7), it is an interesting fact that their strongest proponents are rather of social-democratic provenance. It will not only motivate and oblige its citizens to increased responsibility but also ensure more monitoring and control through the state (see James; Strandell, Chapters 6 and 12). The emergent social investment state can, as Lister says, be characterized as 'the enabling, managerial, partnership state' (Lister, 2003, p. 437).

Children in the social investment state

The confrontation between the cultural and the economic man is one that has followed us over centuries. It does, however, potentially take a new turn when we are dealing with children. If the match between culture and economy is controversial, the correspondence between children and the economic world is for many disturbing. We could hold Garbarino's position that in our modern era to be a child is:

> ... to be shielded from the direct demands of economic, political and sexual forces. ... childhood is a time to maximize the particularistic and to minimize the universalistic, a definition that should be heeded by educators, politicians, and parents alike. (Garbarino, 1986, p. 120)

Or are we permitted to appreciate children as genuine participants in society at large?

Viviana Zelizer, not least known for her seminal book *Pricing the Priceless Child* (1985), has recently addressed this issue in terms of what she calls:

> the widespread, potent idea of *hostile worlds* which imagines social existence as falling into two distinct spheres, one of rationality and self-interest, the other of sentiment and solidarity. Let them mix, goes the argument, and two forms of corruption result: the entry of sentiment and solidarity into the rational arena causes cronyism and inefficiency, while the entry of self-interest into the sentimental arena weakens solidarity, empathy and mutual respect. In a children's version, many observers fear that exposing tender youth to market-place logic destroys virtuous childhood while introducing unreliable economic actors into the world of serious business. According to this logic, erecting a staunch boundary between childhood and adulthood defends against corruption in both directions. (Zelizer, 2005a, p. 186, her italics; see also Zelizer, 2005b)

Defenders of the hostile world's doctrines run the risk of overprotecting children, of being accused of moralization and locking children up on the one side of the 'staunch boundary' – a critique that Ariès (1982) and Benedict (1938) have been strongly airing. But where do investment theorists and strategists stand in this discussion? In a sense they appear not to accept the hostile world's idea in as much as they do consider economics as significant in connection with children.

However, far from acknowledging children as agents, contributors, claims makers and rights holders, they rather uphold ideas of childhood as 'virtuous' and children as 'unreliable economic actors', while instrumentalizing them in a vision of 'citizen-workers of the future' (Lister, 2003) – but definitely not of the present. This is a crucial point.

The underlying vision of 'citizen-workers of the future' is doubtless a legitimate one. It can be expanded to include other worthy visions for children's futurity – to become a good and loving partner and parent, to become a reliable and efficient worker – in other words, to become a contributing and trustworthy member of society. These perspectives are worth fighting for in general, and for politicians in particular they are goals the fulfilment of which deserves *investment*. Politicians and others are hardly to blame for being future oriented and for making prudent plans for a good life in the future. The problem that if there is a price to be paid for this future orientation, how high is it and who is to pay for it?

It has been an important concern of social studies of childhood to critique a thoughtless future orientation – often under the banner of claiming priority to children's 'being' rather than their 'becoming'. Is there a contradiction between being and becoming? Not necessarily, but we cannot be sure that they are always compatible or overlapping. What will 'we' be doing if they are not? And who are these 'we'? Will children have a say in solving the issue?

Before discussing this issue in the light of investment strategies, let us briefly use another example that everybody knows about: corporal punishment of children. It has for centuries been not only parents' (and teachers') right, but more or less their duty, to punish children corporally – according to conventional normative standards and, not least, with an eye to children's future as adults. In most countries of the world it is still a parent's right to choose the appropriate form of punishment, and more often than not it is physical punishment. 'Spare the rod and spoil the child', the old biblical proverb goes. In so-called progressive countries, this parental right has been abolished for two reasons: because we want to protect our children and/or because we think it will produce better adults. In a sense it does not matter as long as the two reasons coincide – in that case we have a win–win-situation (Table 14.1). It is only when we have a situation of no coincidence that we will have to opt for one of them – for children's being or their becoming. The lose–lose option is easy to discard.

What are we doing if we have to choose between lose–win and win–lose? An apparent wise way of untying the Gordian knot was to

Table 14.1 From favourable to unfavourable options following degrees and/or types of social investments (or corporal punishment of children)

	Childhood/Children	Adulthood/Society
Option 1	Win	Win
Option 2	Lose	Win
Option 3	Win	Lose
Option 4	Lose	Lose

argue that it is in the best interests of children to become a good adult (in the meanings mentioned above); this answer is, however, tautological in the sense that children's best interests are made contingent on a positive adult outcome. Even if a positive adult outcome is presupposing a poor child life, the latter must be understood as being in the child's best interests. In fact, this proposal would be nothing but an argument for lose–win (option 2 in the table).

The social investment strategy represents in its generational perspective a clear analogy to corporal punishment. Exactly as corporal punishment is seen as a positive means of socialization, the social investment strategy strongly underlines the importance of human capital building in children. This is so if we look at the British case in terms of the Third Way and the social investment state; it is true also for a group of economists with Nobel Prize laureate James Heckman in the lead; and it is very explicit also for Gøsta Esping-Andersen in a number of publications.[4] There are no, or should not be, good reasons as such to object to making investments in children since positive effects are typically presumed, which is exacerbated by foreseeing, if not predicting, them to last over the life cycle.

> If poverty harms children's life chances [, he says,] *and* if it also creates negative externalities, we see the contours of a positive-sum strategy: minimizing child poverty now will yield an individual and social dividend in the future. And in the far-off future, it should diminish the risks of old age poverty (and possibly also the need for early retirement). (Esping-Andersen, 2002, p. 55, his italics)

This is thus a clear win–win situation and, as with any win–win situation, there appears not to be any good reason to avoid them, exactly as we have hardly any good arguments for accepting lose–lose situations.

The problem is, again, that we cannot always be sure that a win–win situation will result. As both Heckman (2009) and Esping-Andersen

(2009) argue, there are many reasons to believe that reduction of poverty among children will have a positive pay-off in the long run, but they also know for sure that many countries or regimes are not prepared to invest this money in children – in terms of combating poverty, improving health and education, housing and so on. In these countries we are dealing with a lose–win prospect because the priorities are not with children and the advocates for prioritizing children are not strong enough.

What, then, about a win–lose situation? In principle, if we are to believe the proponents of the investment strategy, it is an option that should not arise because – as they claim – clever investments in children will be to the benefit of the society in the long run. And yet, there are cases that do suggest that if the choice is forced upon regimes, then adulthood/society is prioritized.

One case is given by the Australian demographer John C. Caldwell (1982), whose so-called wealth flow theory suggests that as long as the wealth flow between generations is positively benefiting generations older than children, then fertility will stay high and thus children will remain a preferred public good. On the other hand, as the demographic transition proves, when the wealth flow changes direction, that is, when costs of children are higher than gains, investments will decrease and children will become fewer.

In another case, the so-called structural adjustment policies imposed on quite a number of Majority World countries, and some East European countries, typically force the poor countries to weaken investments and even cut public expenditure (education, health, sanitation, families and so on) – exactly the resources required to obtain a win–win situation, but given the lack of resources this is turned into a lose–win option.

In a third case, even within the arguments launched by Esping-Andersen as well as Heckman and colleagues, there are reasons to suspect that choices could be made. In the first place, the wording is without exception that investments in children are made *because* they are supposed to have a long-term positive effect and not because they, as such, favouring children's current life worlds. Also the policy is selective among age groups of children. Evidence seems to prove – and there is no reason to doubt that this is true – that investments in very young, disadvantaged children are much more efficient in terms of long-term pay-off than investments in older children, especially boys (Cunha and Heckman, 2006; Esping-Andersen, 2009). Are we on this basis allowed to conclude that policy makers will be tempted to (over)invest in these young children and (under)invest in older ones? If this is the reality, will older children come to suffer relative deprivation to the advantage of younger children?

In general terms the question that must be raised is if investments that favour adulthood (whether done in childhood or not) have preference over investments that benefit children here and now, because the long-term positive effects of the latter are uncertain. An argument to the effect that they in any case may sweeten current children's life worlds does not necessarily count if the likelihood is great that the investments will not carry long-term profitability. A good guess would be that politicians will only reluctantly embark on such an investment course.

Early childhood education and care services

Different early childhood education and care (ECEC) services, such as daycare centres or kindergartens, definitely belong to the part of childhood that has optimal potentials as an investment object. There seems to be unanimity between possible investors – the parents, the public, and sometimes corporate society or the business world. The three parties have at least to some extent different motivations to enter into an investment. Parents are forced to find a solution if both want to have a job; state and municipality, as servants of the common interests, are willing to support daycare arrangements both to secure a sufficient labour market supply and to keep to some control of forming young children's minds. Corporate society should have an interest as well but is reluctant to get directly involved unless its profit is safeguarded, which does not prevent its lobbying for investment strategies for childcare with a long-term outlook. The question is how this will be impacting the daily pedagogical practice in daycare centres.

This key question can be addressed from a variety of different perspectives. It relates to overall questions pertaining to the relationship between policy and practice, or the relationship between the political and educational ideas and plans, on the one hand, and the pedagogical practices with children on the other. There are three levels to consider: political discourses; educational aims and curricula, as these are made by the teachers; and pedagogy, as this is practised in daily life within the daycare centres.

Educational research based on observation of daily practices in kindergartens in Norway reveals that there is a discrepancy between what members of the staff plan, intend and think they do, and what they actually do. In other words, their intended priorities and educational plans are not necessarily realized through their pedagogical practices with children (Haug, 1992). This suggests that as human beings we not only act on the basis of intended thinking but do so spontaneously and unintentionally. The implication of this is that there is no simple and straightforward relationship between political discourses on social investment, educational plans and curricula, and educational practices in daycare centres. An informed position on social investment thinking's impact on pedagogical practice requires empirical research in different countries.

However, as revealed in several chapters of this book, changes regarding pedagogical practices within ECEC institutions seem to be a shared experience in many countries. In the following section we will briefly highlight some of these changes and discuss their likely implications for children and staff working in ECEC services.

Play or learning?

As pointed out in Kjørholt's introduction to this volume, recent trends emphasizing early childhood as an object of investment are pertinent in all the countries included in this anthology. This emphasis implies a growing focus on knowledge, skills and learning. The pedagogical practices within ECEC services has 'traditionally' been characterized by the term 'educare', indicating a particular pedagogy where education is merged with caring practices from the teachers. A child-centred pedagogy, emphasizing play and children's opportunities to engage in a variety of different creative activities with their peers, is highlighted. Furthermore, this pedagogy implies creating a 'child-friendly' environment with space for children's own initiatives, exploration and self-governed activities. The importance of creating an inspiring environment for children also reflects a focus on childhood 'here and now', connected to qualities such as emotional wellbeing joy, self-esteem and children's social connectedness to others in a caring environment. Cognitive learning is thus seen as closely interconnected with social learning, social inclusion, care and opportunities for children to explore on their own. Across countries, this particular pedagogical thinking related to ECEC has been characterized by similarities, differing from a school-oriented curriculum, which relates learning to subjects such as maths, science and language. The particular child-centred pedagogy within ECEC can historically be traced back to ideas from Friedrich Fröbel, and to some extent also to philosophers like Jean-Jacques Rousseau.

Recent trends in early childhood as an object for investment imply, as we have seen, a move towards a school-oriented curriculum, putting play and practices related to 'educare' under threat. In his chapter, Peter Moss describes two different approaches to ECEC practices: one approach emphasizing cognitive development and the acquisition of skills and knowledge seen in France and the UK, and a social pedagogy tradition (Nordic and Central European countries) seeing kindergarten in a perspective of lifelong learning development and a play-oriented curriculum (Moss, Chapter 7; OECD, 2006). However, as Gulløv (Chapter 5) and Kjørholt and Seland (Chapter 9) clearly demonstrate, there is currently an increasing emphasis on cognitive skills and a school-oriented curriculum by policy makers in Denmark and Norway as well.

Assessment and documentation

What does this trend imply for children and for pedagogical practices? One impact of emphasizing cognitive skills and learning is an increased requirement for documentation and assessment of skills and outcome. Teachers and other staff members invest more time in writing reports and other forms for recording practices and results, both for individual children and for groups of children. This demand on the staff, of new ways of allocating time, will be at the cost of spending time with children, participating in social interaction, care, play and other activities in direct interaction with children. We may ask if this also implies a trend towards creating a greater distance than before between the teachers and the children (cf. above on the historical increasing distance between generations). The particular child-centred pedagogy in daycare centres has historically been characterized by a close social relationship between children and their caregivers. The new school-oriented curriculum, which requires more time allocation for teachers doing administrative work, may then have unforeseen consequences. There is a need for empirical research related to this particular issue.

Closely intertwined with this is the shift identified in the ECEC sector towards 'new public management' thinking. Recent research conducted in Norway documents that this trend has implications for the ways in which the daycare centres are led and organized, moving towards increased centralization, bureaucracy and larger administrative units, organizing children in larger and more flexible groups (Seland, 2009). However, the consequences for children's wellbeing and learning are still to be seen.

Besides time allocation, an increasing emphasis on assessment and evaluation also implies a risk of moving the focus from social processes and 'here and now thinking' to the outcome and assessment of aspects that are possible to measure. As documented by Eva Gulløv (Chapter 5), this has happened in Danish daycare centres, now putting more emphasis on measurable cognitive skills at the cost of social processes among children. The latter, related to joy, emotional excitement, play, creativity and feelings of connectedness, are more difficult to assess than, for instance, skills in literacy and maths. However, this depends on the further development of these practices. In Denmark, national and standardized tests related to the assessment of individual language skills for children in daycare centres have already been introduced, whereas in Norway we currently witness a debate following the initiative from the Ministry of Education to implement practices regarding the documentation of children's literacy skills. It has been argued that national standardized testing is just one out of a variety of different ways of documenting children's literacy skills. Observation of how children communicate and use their language skills in everyday life in kindergarten is another way of gaining knowledge about children's skills in literacy. It remains to be seen which practices will be chosen in Norway.

Being or becoming?

As mentioned previously in this and in Kjørholt's introductory chapter, the current trends in early childhood as an object for investment also implies a shift towards a greater emphasis on children as human becomings rather than as current beings. A central question to be addressed is, however, whether an emphasis on children as coming adults or human becomings is irreconcilable with a recognition of children as competent human beings 'here and now'. In the OECD report *Starting Strong*, it is argued that:

> Many countries are seeking to balance views of childhood in the 'here and now' with views of childhood as an investment with the future adult in mind. These diverse views have important implications for the organisation of policy and provision in different countries. (OECD, 2001, p. 2)

As the different chapters in this book reveal, the solution between these two different discourses seems to go in one direction, representing a threat to the recognition of children as competent human beings here and now and early childhood as a period for play, care and learning connected to social processes and a child-centred curriculum. However, it remains to be seen how the different political discourses are balanced in different countries, and if the two competing discourses are impacting practices in new and creative ways. Public debates related to policy and practice in ECEC services are much needed, as are discussions of children's place in society as well as critical reflections on spaces made available to children. Early childhood in modern societies is to an increasing degree constituted and practised within ECEC settings. This requires a public awareness and responsibility for a critical gaze and an unremitting assessment of the quality of life that is offered to children within these settings. Current changes regarding notions of childhood, pedagogical thinking and practices related to ECEC represent a challenge also for future research. Critical investigation into how the changes affect children's wellbeing and daily lives is exceedingly significant.

Notes

1. Weber might, perhaps, have used the terms *Bildung* for the cultural man and *Ausbildung* for the economic man. These terms, which are notoriously difficult to translate, in a sense capture the difference: the latter is more or less synonymous with schooling and training in a more instrumental understanding, while the former has many similarities with Bourdieu's notion of cultural capital, which is acquired partly independent of schools (although not in contradiction to them, of course).
2. Bologna has the oldest university in the world and the celebration of its 900-year anniversary was used as an opportunity to launch these major changes. This is ironic, one must say, given that the traditional orientation at the classical Bologna University clearly satisfied the cultural (and clerical) rather than the economic man.
3. Also former US President Bill Clinton and former Federal Chancellor of Germany, Gerhard Schröder, Prime Minister Jens Stoltenberg of Norway and many others have eagerly supported the changes.
4. Heckman and colleagues, and Esping-Andersen have in common that they are strongly inspired by developmental psychology and its anticipatory perspectives, which have been an object of criticism by social studies of childhood.

References

Ariès, P. (1982) *Barndommens historie* (abridged Danish edition of Centuries of Childhood with Ariès' preface to new French edition from 1973) (Copenhagen: NNF Arnold Busck).

Beck, U. (1992) *Risk Society: Towards a New Modernity.* (London: SAGE Publications).

Benedict, R. (1938) 'Continuities and Discontinuities in Cultural Conditioning', *Psychiatry*, 1, 2, 161–167.

Caldwell, J. C. (1982) *Theory of Fertility Decline* (London: Academic Press).

Cunha, F. and Heckman, J. J. (2006) 'Investing in Our Young People'. Manuscript.

Esping-Andersen, G. (2002) 'A Child-Centred Social Investment Strategy' in G. Esping-Andersen, D. Gallie, A. Hemerijck and J. Myles (eds) *Why We Need a New Welfare State* (Oxford: Oxford University Press).

Esping-Andersen, G. (2009) *The Incomplete Revolution. Adapting to Women's New Roles* (Cambridge: Polity Press).

Garbarino, J. (1986) 'Can American Families Afford the Luxury of Childhood?', *Child Welfare*, 65, 2, 119–128.

Gerth, H. H. and Wright Mills, C. (edited and translated, 1958) *From Max Weber: Essays in Sociology* (New York: Oxford University Press).

Haug, P. (1992) *Educational Reform by Experiment: The Norwegian Experimental Educational Programme for 6-year-olds (1986–1990) and the Subsequent Reform.* Doctoral Thesis Stockholm University (Stockholm: HLS Publishing).

Heckman, J. J. (2009) 'Investing in Our Young People: Lessons from Economics and Psychology', *Revista Internazionale di Scienza Sociali*, CXVII, 3-4, 365–386.

Lister, R. (2003) 'Investing in the Citizen-Workers of the Future: Transformations in Citizenship and the State Under New Labour', *Social Policy & Administration*, 37, 5, 427–443.

OECD (2001) *Starting Strong. Early Childhood Education and Care* (Paris: OECD).

OECD (2006) *Starting Strong II. Early Childhood Education and Care* (Paris: OECD).

Seland, M. (2009) *Det moderne barn og den fleksible barnehagen. En etnografisk studie av barnehagens hverdagsliv i lys av nyere diskurser og kommunal virkelighet* (The modern child and the flexible labour market. An ethnographic study of day-care's everyday life in light of new discourses and municipal reality) PhD Thesis (Trondheim: Norwegian Centre for Child Research, NTNU).

Zelizer, V. A. (1985) *Pricing the Priceless Child: The Changing Social Value of Children* (Princeton: Princeton University Press).

Zelizer, V. A. (2005a) 'The Priceless Child Revisited' in J. Qvortrup (ed.) *Studies in Modern Childhood. Society, Culture, Agency* (Basingstoke: Palgrave Macmillan).

Zelizer, V. A. (2005b) *The Purchase of Intimacy* (Princeton: Princeton University Press).

Index

Note: The letter 't' following the locators refer to tables in the text